YELLOW POWER YELLOW SOUL

I0895385

STONE S.F.
MONKEY
RHYTHM
STONE S.F.
Giles College
WRITING & PUBLISHING
SEMINARS IN SAN FRANCISCO
ULTERIOR
MOTIVES
HOROSCOPE
MOTIVITY
FISHBONE
FISHBONE FRI SEPT. 6
STONE S.F.
A Soldier's Story
ROXIE CINEMA

THE ASIAN AMERICAN EXPERIENCE

Series Editors
Eiichiro Azuma
Jigna Desai
Martin F. Manalansan IV
Lisa Sun-Hee Park
David K. Yoo
Roger Daniels, Founding Series Editor

A list of books in the series appears at the end of this book.

YELLOW POWER YELLOW SOUL

THE RADICAL ART OF FRED HO

Edited by
Roger N. Buckley
and Tamara Roberts

UNIVERSITY OF ILLINOIS PRESS
Urbana, Chicago, and Springfield

Frontispiece: Fred Ho. Credit: Unknown

© 2013 by the Board of Trustees
of the University of Illinois
All rights reserved
Manufactured in the United States of America
1 2 3 4 5 C P 5 4 3 2 1
∞ This book is printed on acid-free paper.

Library of Congress Cataloging-in-Publication Data
Yellow power, yellow soul : the radical art of Fred Ho /
edited by Roger N. Buckley and Tamara Roberts.
p. cm. — (The Asian American experience)
Includes index.
ISBN 978-0-252-03750-4 (cloth : alk. paper)
ISBN 978-0-252-07899-6 (pbk. : alk. paper)
ISBN 978-0-252-09470-5 (e-book)
1. Ho, Fred Wei-han—Criticism and interpretation.
2. Asian Americans—Politics and government—20th century.
3. Asian American musicians.
I. Buckley, Roger Norman, 1937– II. Roberts, Tamara.
ML419.H6Y45 2013
781.65092—dc23 2012040025

Contents

Foreword

It is often said that music has the power to engage all senses. Its discourse has a sensory dimension that transcends well beyond hearing, to feelings, spiritual meditation, intellectual stimulation, even social action. Why then has it become an esoteric game? The work of Fred Ho helps to provide an answer to this timely question.

Fred Ho is an artist, an unashamedly revolutionary Asian American artist, who offers up music—broadly defined—that is illuminating, daring, informative, scholarly, ambitious, brashly confident and vigorous, meticulous, extravagant, and emotionally sweeping. It is also rightfully polemical and angry—without being bitter. So utterly original, Ho's work, which takes the listener into the jaws of life, makes most of everything previously created by artists and their work seem outdated and pedestrian. Needless to say, Ho's work is pioneering, which led music critic Larry Birnbaum of *DownBeat* to pen that his oeuvre was a "fusion of free-jazz and traditional Chinese music that manages to combine truculence and delicacy with such natural ease that it sounds positively organic" ("Fred Ho," November 1994, 57). In accomplishing all these things he shakes up the Puritan in us.

Here is an artist who—over the years—has unswervingly worn a path through the thick hedge of convention, the money men and commercialism, to an open, unfettered, fresh space where music can take an almost infinite variety of forms while being viewed in all its natural political, historical, and multicultural complexities. If Ho's work does not adjust to contemporary dictates of musical canons, as some would like, so be it. His music has the virtue of combining profound intellectual honesty with a tenacious and unmuddled ideological commitment. How is this possible? Ho possesses a stunning grasp of historical complexities, the courage and vision of an explorer, receptivity to different art forms, and a musical methodology that bridges the realms of music, history, politics, musical instruments, and performance.

The essays in this book speak to these truths. They provide for the first time a comprehensive look at Fred Ho that is at once panoramic in scope and artistic and scholarly in depth. Typically, it is keeping with who Ho is. Nothing is left out: the ups and down of life—all of which gives this work its profoundly human quality along with a visceral understanding of an artist and his music. This highly original and intimate book offers a fascinating portrait of an activist artist and his work. It bears witness, in straightforward language, to Ho's formidable musical abilities, his intelligence, and prodigious and varied cultural productions. Here is an artist, a creator of artistic earthquakes, who was determined from the very beginning of his creative journey never to go quietly into the stygian night of crass commercialism, and it is to our immense benefit that he avoided those seductive and destructive shadows. For his enormous achievement, Ho was awarded the Harvard Arts Medal in 2009, one of many awards and citations garnered over the years. Other illustrious recipients include Yo-Yo Ma, Mira Nair, John Updike, and Pete Seeger. These recognitions point to Fred Ho as an artist of constant creative surprises and as someone on fire creatively and artistically and wanting very much to set others on fire too.

It was that creative fire that led to this critical anthology and probing analysis by scholars and artists who illuminate the extraordinary life and pioneering work of Ho. When the idea for the book was born, like most creations it began with a mere spark, undoubtedly inspired by Fred's great talent that hit this editor like a warm sirocco. Fred had been the subject of several major studies, but none, including editor Diane C. Fujino's magisterial *Wicked Theory—Naked Practice: A Fred Ho Reader,* provided what was missing: a complex and credible portrait of the saxophonist-activist. To accomplish that, the editors, with Fred's help, sought out contributors who knew Fred and his art and could speak to the natural tension between conception and expression and the pace and urgency in Fred's work through different strategies of writing. The result is a kaleidoscope of viewpoints on a variety of themes and a rich array of styles ranging from the lyrical to the academic, to stories, accounts, poems and essays. In accomplishing these things, the book seeks to illuminate the life of an important artist, an aggressive, energetic and creative master, who long ago came to the realization that he must never become a slave of caution or convention.

Roger N. Buckley

Acknowledgments

This anthology is a team effort that has extended over years and would have been impossible without the contributions of many beyond those featured in the following pages. We would like to thank Kristin Eshelman and the staff of the Thomas J. Dodd Research Center at the University of Connecticut for their assistance in our use of the Fred Ho Papers archive and help with obtaining photo permissions. Angela Rola, director of the UConn Asian American Cultural Center, assisted us with compiling the images as well, for which we are grateful. Thanks to Cathy Schlund-Vials, Fe Delos-Santos, and Maxine Haines, of the UConn Asian American Studies Institute, for their comments on and structural support for the project. For assistance in crafting the manuscript, we would like to thank Pattie Hsu, Nicole Fabricant, Melissa Reyes, Daisy Simmons, and the two blind reviewers for their insightful suggestions. We would like to acknowledge Vijay Shah from University of Illinois Press, who believed in this work from the beginning and has offered incomparable guidance. Finally, a hearty thank-you goes to Fred Ho for his continued enthusiasm for this project, his intense organizational support, and, of course, for creating the art that inspired the whole endeavor.

FRED HO'S DEMON BARITONE SAXOPHONE AND HIS GREEN MONSTER BAND BLOWING THE DEMONS DOWN

Fred Ho
imbued with strength of 10,000 warriors
roars in agony

but even in weakness
Fred Ho's demon baritone saxophone
blows the demons down

His hurricane wind
speaks wisdom:

Do not become complacent,
we must never be complacent;
since everything
has been done
we must always try
to do the impossible.

Fred Ho's Sun Ra mantra
his serpentine golden horn
raises gale-force winds

as clouds billow
gather and swell

Fred Ho's Green Monster Band
exhales fire
of reeds and thunder:
hydration, nutrition, oxygenation and love
chasing the demons down

unequivocal
unrelenting
inexhaustible

Fred Ho's
demon baritone saxophone
his monster sound

unmistakable tone
his tunes
of attitude and, oh, such amplitude

Brother Fred Ho
blowing the demons down.

—Richard Hamasaki

Introduction

TAMARA ROBERTS

A Part and Apart

Artist. Intellectual. Activist. Chinese. Chinese American. Asian American. American. Saxophonist. Composer. Arranger. Bandleader. Writer. Producer. Luddite. Revolutionary Marxist. Bolshevik. Matriarchal socialist. Communist. Farmer.

Fred Ho has a penchant for labeling himself and his work, brandishing these monikers as emblems of his political, cultural, and aesthetic fabric. He wears these epithets on his sleeve, making a loud and proud call of who he is and what he believes to all who will listen—and even those who will not. Words are important to Ho. In "What Makes 'Jazz' the Revolutionary Music of the Twentieth Century, and Will It Be Revolutionary for the Twenty-first Century?" he states:

> Oppressed peoples suffer when their history, identity, and culture are defined, (mis)represented, and explicated by our oppressors. The struggle to redefine and reimage our existence involves the struggle to reject the stereotyping, distortions, and devaluation embodied in the classifications of conquerors and racists. The struggle over how to describe past and present reality is the struggle to change reality [. . .] It took a movement of oppressed peoples to adopt new terms and meanings for self-determination and to replace reactionary and oppressive ones.[1]

Ho critiques the continued use of the word *jazz*, believing it springs from a racist etymology and paints the music as a marginal form. As a remedy, he proposes *Afro Asian new American multicultural music*, believing this more accurately reflects the hybrid roots and revolutionary spirit at the historical heart of jazz.[2] Ho trades heavily in these labels, using them as shorthand that can indicate identity, philosophy, and ideology.

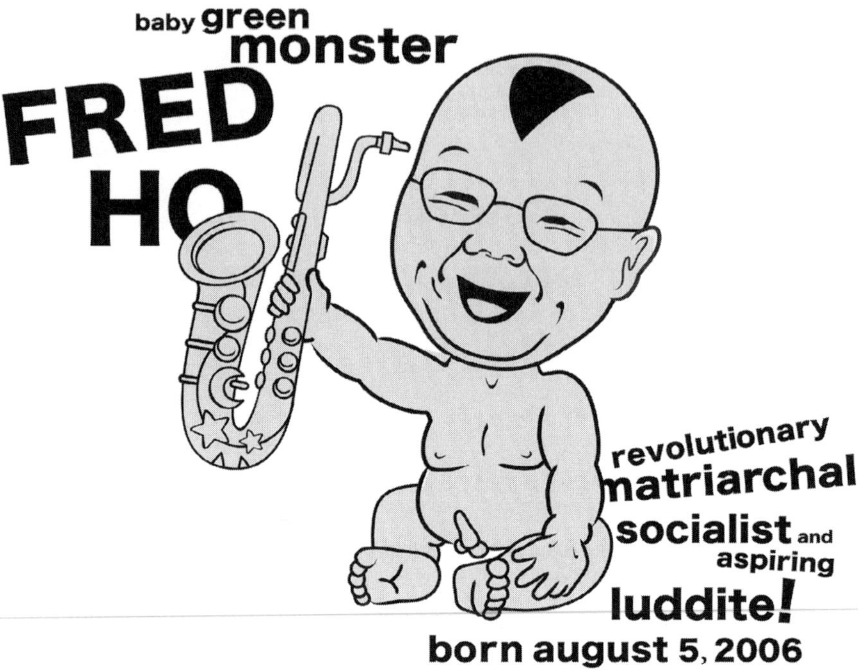

Figure 2. Green Baby Fred. Credit: Chanel Matsunami Govreau

More than static names, Ho weaves these words into a complex of signifiers that, in conjunction, point toward his multivalent artistic and political practices and place him squarely within an array of radical discourses. And he constantly revises and adds to these markers, exposing himself as an ever-unfolding work in progress; a conglomeration of concepts donned, rearranged, and, if necessary, discarded. In a 2010 email blast, he even proclaimed: "After a more than 3 year war against advanced colo-rectal cancer, which included 3 tumors, 7 surgeries, and using all chemo-radiation drugs and treatments devised by Western allopathic medicine, the old Fred Ho died."[3] This announcement of his rebirth—and upcoming performance dates—included a cartoon portrait of the New Fred Ho, aka Baby Green Monster: chubby toddler body, saxophone and genitalia flying, green skin, and his signature glasses and triangle haircut.[4] In a discursive flourish, Ho annihilated his old persona and began the naming anew in an attempt to gain a fresh start.

Yet alongside this constant marking of who he is, Ho also defines his life and career by who and what he is not, often presenting his story as one of exclusions. When I was preparing to write this introduction, he urged me to discuss how his name is rarely mentioned in narratives of Asian American activism, even though he founded or played a large role in numerous organizations, including the Asian American Arts Alliance, Boston's Asian American Resource Workshop, and the New York Asian American Jazz Festival.[5] Ho also constructs himself as an outlier. After disagreements with those in the West Coast Asian American jazz scene, for example, he declared himself as having progressed "beyond Asian American jazz." Similarly, after being "ejected" from the League of Revolutionary Struggle (which shared overlapping membership with the Asian American jazz movement), he has taken a do-it-yourself approach to activism, choosing only rarely to become part of radical organizations.[6] Ho also views himself as situated outside of the broader jazz world and even experimental avant-garde music scenes, railing against the conservatism of Jazz at Lincoln Center and refusing to associate with granting organizations and venues he feels will fail to support his work as new "American" culture. In all of these cases, Ho has played an active role but was painted—or painted himself—an outsider.

This anthology examines the ways in which Ho has been a part of or sat apart from some of the key cultural and political movements since the 1970s. His career is an experiential window onto the challenges artists face in trying to create politically meaningful work in the post–civil rights era. In particular, Ho's struggles indicate a central quandary: how do radical artists work to change the very system in which they must function in order to survive? Ho's perpetual process of self-reinvention reveals a telling contradiction in his desire to be recognized by existing institutions while also operating outside them. As critical as he can be about mainstream arts organizations, for example, he will celebrate widely a premiere of his work at Carnegie Hall, the Brooklyn Academy of Music, or the Guggenheim. And despite his staunch anticapitalist stance, he boasts about his success within the system, such as the benefits of running a for-profit company or having paid off his mortgage by age 35. These unresolved tensions are not unique to Ho; in fact they are key to understanding the broader struggle of contemporary artists to support the current moment emotionally, culturally, and politically while simultaneously forging a new future.

The writers in *Yellow Power, Yellow Soul* offer their takes on these issues through analyses of Ho's musical and dramatic works, dissections of his political pursuits, and personal stories. While Ho has garnered the interest of a fair number of writers, he has never moved squarely into a broader public eye or scholarly discussion, a dialogue we hope this book will stimulate. The extant works on his life and career appear across a number of publications, making this anthology a comprehensive central resource and compendium of new studies. *Wicked Theory, Naked Practice: A Fred Ho Reader* was pioneering in publishing for the first time in one place a variety of his personal writings on music, politics, and identity. Our book takes this same inspiration to conduct an extended conversation on Ho. Yet it departs from *Wicked Theory* by opening the conversation for scholars, artists, and activists to engage with and critique Ho's varied output. Ultimately, we desire this close study of Ho's career to reveal the various strategies he has honed over decades in order to grapple with the aesthetic, political, and economic challenges posed to contemporary cultural and political workers.

Ho's forward-thinking praxis is specifically a result of the gains and unrealized hopes of the civil rights era. He was born in 1957, the same year that Governor Orville Faubus called in the National Guard to prevent the first Arkansas high school from desegregating.[7] He grew up during the spirited hope of the civil rights movement and came of age as it dissolved into riots and despair in the 1970s. As the United States emerged from the Cold War as the leading world superpower, the gains of the civil rights movement were slowly unwound by several presidential administrations, the middle class began to dissolve into heavier poles of rich and poor, and the government launched into an intensive campaign for political and economic domination of the Middle East. Perhaps more than any other time in its history, the second half of the 20th century revealed the nation's longstanding imperialist underpinnings in unabashed relief, but to a population either confounded as to how to bring about greater egalitarianism or too indoctrinated into the religion of consumerism to care.

This transition from the mass—and successful—social and labor organizing of the early 20th century into multiculturalism and neoliberalism raises questions about the role of artists in envisioning and helping to create a new society. A vast network of musicians supported the union struggles of the 1930s and 1940s, with songs that told stories of workers' hardships and provided emotional sustenance for picket lines. Similarly, the 1960s social movements brought a proliferation of African American freedom songs, Black Arts Movement (BAM) free jazz, Chicano farmworkers' *huelga* songs, and new popular songs that denounced the Vietnam War. But with the dissolution of the Left as an artistic platform, increased social conservatism, and the consolidation of the music industry into a few corporate hands by the 1990s, the room for performers to speak out and the infrastructure to allow them to reach audiences was dramatically altered.

Each of Ho's musical works, theatrical pieces, and essays is a proposition for how an artist might contribute to creating tangible change in the world in our current political moment. A foremost voice in the history of West Coast Asian American jazz, the East Coast avant-garde, and numerous antioppression movements, Ho has spent his life redefining the relationship between art and politics. Citing the dual failure of the radical Left and contemporary popular music to serve as an effective political mouthpiece, his work offers a critique of the long unraveling fervor of 1960s radicalism and the Third World movement into Che T-shirts and talking points. His long-term exploration of the confluence of African, African American, Asian, and Asian American people, cultural formations, and political unions promotes a return to Afro Asian internationalism as an antidote to state-proffered multiculturalism and politics-as-style. This attempt to keep alive the spirit of Third World solidarity and political fervor is rendered not only in Ho's compositions, but also in new artistic, economic, and social relationships fostered through their performance. Even his self-naming probes this same relationship between the aesthetic and the political.

Ho's work is an ongoing experiment in how to use sound to illuminate race and class dynamics and how to participate in changing them. His creative philosophy is one in which art and politics do not merely reflect but constitute one another. As Diana C. Fujino describes in chapter 4, Ho creates work based on the belief that aesthetics have the power to decolonize the minds and bodies of oppressed peoples. In his view, art should not just express political sentiments—what Fujino calls "agitprop"—but produce political change at the level of the individual or community through the production or consumption of certain sounds. This work is not simply, as Paul Gilroy says about black music, "a succession of literary tropes and genres but [. . .] a philosophical discourse which refuses the modern, occidental separation of ethics and aesthetics, culture and politics."[8] For Ho, music and performance assert an ideological point of view and have the ability to alter discourse dominated by colonial forces.

In the remainder of this introduction, I orient the reader to three specific aesthetic-political strategies that have been key to Ho's artistic production and that appear frequently in the following essays. First, I discuss how Ho employs African American and Asian American traditions as the foundation of his work in order to promote anti-imperialist interracial and intercultural solidarities. Next, I examine his use of popular culture idioms and media as anticapitalist critique. Finally, I illustrate how he actively cultivates an artistic and political community to extend his work, training musicians, challenging audiences, and using music making as a model for social justice work. Ho is, of course, not the only artist to use these techniques. I hope his case can serve as a pedagogical model for other contemporary artists and activists. To aid this purpose, I also critically engage the ways in which his praxis at times contradicts his ideals and raise questions about its limitations.

Musical Decolonization

A common thread running through many of the twentieth-century cultural nationalist and Marxist-socialist movements was the recovery and embrace of non-Western/white/dominant culture as central to combating imperialism. Max Roach claims that "culture is the final nail in the casket of exploitation. After you bring the army in and you conquer a place, it's too expensive to hold that with an army. So the next step would be to take the culture of the oppressors and impose that on to the mentality of the people who've been conquered physically."[9] Ho fills his works with a variety of Third World musical traditions in order to create sonic space in which this form of domination is contested (see the appendices for a complete record of Ho's recordings, productions, and ensembles).[10] By focusing on these forms, particularly in elite art spaces, racially and culturally marginalized sounds and stories are able to be heard and experienced by the dominant population and people of color who, in some cases, may not have ever heard or seen the culture of their heritage. Music, thus, functions as a tool for education and instilling pride in oppressed peoples' histories.

Riffing on the notion of the Third Stream—the mid-20th-century merger of jazz and experimental classical music—Ho refers to his work as a "Third World Ocean" and places these forms central in his canon.[11] The repertoire of his Afro Asian Music Ensemble (AAME) and other projects features a cornucopia of U.S. and world ethnic styles, including jazz/African American creative music; Chinese, Japanese, Korean, and Filipino folk and classical genres such as Beijing opera, *pansori*, and *kulintang*; West African drumming; and Asian American traditions such as Cantonese opera and woodfish head chants. These musics appear as entire songs, melodies or rhythms, instrumentation, and the use of non-English languages. The AAME's *The Underground Railroad to My Heart* (1994), for example, includes arrangements of Filipino folksong "An Bayan Ko (For My Country)," Tibetan "Kang Ding Love Song," and Chinese "Lan Hua Hua (Blue Flower)." The album also includes "Bambaya," based on a talking drum piece of the West African Dagomba people, and "Joys and Solos," an original piece that features the Chinese *sona* in a free jazz context. Instead of moving to the margins to explore "new" and "exotic" styles, Ho seeks to make the music of marginalized people central to his cultural production in the west.

The influence of the Black Arts Movement and cultural nationalism on Ho is clear in his use of African, Asian, and ethnic American traditions as political discourse. His first radical education came through Black nationalism; he often cites reading *The Autobiography of Malcolm X* as a teenager as the genesis of his racial consciousness and even joined the Nation of Islam for a brief time. And his aesthetic orientation was greatly marked by studying jazz and working with BAM figures such as Archie Shepp and Amiri Baraka. In fact, Ho began his musical life playing African American music and only later came to learn about Asian traditions as a young adult. After graduating from Harvard in 1979, he helped found the Asian American Resource Workshop in Boston. While working there he was first exposed to an Asian musical culture, forming a Chinese folk singing group comprised primarily of immigrant workers. Through the ensemble—as well as old world music and ethnographic recordings—he learned traditional techniques, songs, and notation, which formed the basis for his future experimentation and incorporation of other Asian and Asian American musical elements into his work. Through the late 1980s, Ho also actively participated in the West Coast Asian American jazz scene, recording for Asian Improv Records, and worked with several of the label's artists, especially Jon Jang. Alongside artists such as Mark Izu, Glenn Horiuchi, Francis Wong, and Jang, he actively worked to produce an "Asian American" sound by infusing a jazz/creative music base with Asian instruments and idioms.

As Arthur J. Sabatini explores in his essay, Ho's work is unique in that it expands beyond a single cultural orientation and incorporates multiple Afro Asian traditions into the same piece. In 1989, Ho sharply divided with his Asian American jazz comrades over political differences, including what he terms "a political directive that required music and art to be 'accessible' (which became a codeword for culturally mainstream and politically reformist)."[12] In that period he began to plumb the depths of juxtaposing Third World traditions for the expression of interracial and intercultural political solidarities and shared radical histories. His work presents an Afro Asian smorgasbord in which multiple cultural roots are showcased and placed in dialogue, creating a cultural internationalist aesthetic that ignores national boundaries and honors a history of joint struggle, shared social spaces, and cultural similarities and dialogue.

This aesthetic choice reflects Ho's belief in the value of building interminority coalitions as an antiracist tool. As a number of scholars have documented, manufacturing conflict between nonwhite populations has been a tool used by whites to maintain power through a strategy of "divide and conquer."[13] Vijay Prashad describes how, in multiple historical moments in the United States, the seemingly benevolent image of Asians and Asian Americans as a "model minority" has been used as a discursive "weapon" against other minorities, particularly blacks.[14] The notion that simple bootstrap pulling can right the economic ramifications of racial disparity makes it easier to vilify blacks as lazy or dysfunctional and, thus, the cause of their own disenfranchisement. Not only does Ho's choice of a career in arts and politics negate the "model" image of science or math wizardry and political docility, he promotes the importance of people of color (and whites concerned with injustice) to look beyond their limited definitions of self and singular struggles in order to draw links to other oppressed people. Ho's biography reflects a similar path led by other radical Asian Americans, Latinos, and Native Americans who looked to the struggles of blacks to understand their own. The original Afro Asian spirit—inspired by the 1955 Afro-Asian Solidarity Conference in Bandung—is the model of unity in diversity: oppressed people rallying around interconnected yet differently realized experiences of injustice. And it is this template that fuels Ho's aesthetic.

The result of Ho's foregrounding of world music traditions is the decentering of the Western classical and popular musical canon, the two placed on the margins of the nondominant forms or left out entirely. In more mainstream "world beat" or "fusion" styles, non-Western sounds are fit into a dominant form or merely painted onto the surface to add a bit of "spice." In Ho's work, these traditions become the central reference for form, meter, melody, or harmony, often challenging normative Western musical perceptions. By employing diverse instruments such as *erhu*, *pipa*, *kulintang*, and a variety of world percussion, Ho presents sonorities not generally reflected in the Western tradition. And his incorporation of melodies, rhythms, and languages from other traditions gives credence to non-Western aesthetics, positioning them not only on par with Western musical ideals but also of potentially greater cultural, emotional, and political value to people of color in the West. His *A Chinaman's Chance*, for example, was written in Mandarin, Cantonese, and English, displacing European languages as the lingua francas of the genre. Through these gestures Ho also claims a space for nonnormative Asians and Asian Americans in the popular sphere. Those rendered in television or film are often of a limited palette, generally reinforcing the model minority myth or typified as foreign and exotic. And one is hard-pressed to find specifically Asian American musicians (outside of the realm of Western classical music) or styles not rendered as antithetical to U.S. culture. By contrast, Ho's theatrical works feature a diversity of characters that express a range of Asian and Asian American experiences and behaviors. Making Asians and Asian Americans and their cultural contributions visible and audible, he proclaims them as integral to the fabric of the nation.

Ho's heavy reliance on Afro Asian forms, especially in dominant cultural spaces, however, opens up the possibility for misinterpretations. Reviews of his work often highlight his or the music's Asianness with titles such as "East Meets West," "East Wind Blowing," and "East Winds."[15] These statements paint Ho and his work as Other to the United States and simplify and conflate traditions with vastly different national origins and cultural contexts into a singular performed Orient. Further, these critics make assumptions about Ho himself by drawing links between his Asian visage and the sounds of his ensemble. Not only is Ho squarely located within the U.S. sociopolitical realm but also, as I show above, only came to knowledge of Asian musical traditions as an adult. The Orientalist dynamic expressed in these titles, however, marks him as a perpetual foreigner, a stereotype often placed on Asian Americans whose families may have been in the United States for generations. Even more, his work is not just a fusion of East and West but a combination of multiple Eastern, Western, and other styles—an amalgamation meant to trouble these very binaries. Yet the sounds Ho chooses—in some cases specifically because of their "unusual" sonorities—are overwrought with racial connotations that Ho, despite his desires, carries into his own works.[16]

And why is Ho's use of these forms not Orientalist in their own right? Reading the following essays on Ho's life and aesthetic in tandem, this volume raises the question of his relationship to and ownership of the forms he uses. In many cases, Ho has no personal connection to the people or cultures he uses, drawing them into his projects but not necessarily forging broader or bidirectional conversation. What gives him the right to these traditions and a say over how they are reformulated within his pieces? While the white appropriation of marginalized cultures has been treated in numerous studies, this same gesture done by other people of color is much less explored. Ho gets around this critique by positioning himself as connecting to the political and emotional intent of the traditions. As Elaine Song writes, his "music is heavily influenced by Japanese and Chinese folk music, which he describes as 'closest to the people.' Though he said he cannot replicate that tradition since his background is rooted in America, his music 'pays respect to those roots,' he said. 'I take from that sentiment and spirit.'"[17] But despite his distancing of himself from the culture of Third World styles, Ho's voice and interpretation of them stands in for those from within the tradition. Despite his anti-imperialist goals, it is his privileged position in the West that allows him access to the myriad styles and the power to render them at will.

The prominence of Third World traditions in Ho's work, as well as connecting them to radical black jazz, is a decisive gesture meant to promote Afro Asian cultural politics as an alternative to Western domination. But some of the traditions Ho employs actually reflect elite institutions and imperialist histories in the Afro Asian world. The erhu, for example, was a Chinese folk instrument that was embraced in the early twentieth century as a classical instrument, its practice codified into conservatory training. And Japan and Japanese popular culture have long been a colonial presence in a number of East and Southeast Asian countries. An all-encompassing embrace of the "Third World Ocean" can miss some of these subtleties. Rather than place a value judgment on this dynamic, however, I encourage readers of this book to use Ho's identity and work as a way to examine these inevitable questions of cultural ownership and representation. These issues become even more pertinent when thinking beyond an individual artist to the larger culture industry.

Playing High and Low

Ho believes that culture, politics, and economics must be confronted together, and he looks to popular culture as fodder for unsettling class bias in the culture industry of the late 20th and early 21st centuries. This industry—including popular music, television, and film; city arts and tourism programs; and granting agencies such as foundations and corporations—operates according to the principals of multiculturalism. The predominant racial system in the United States from the 1990s onward, multiculturalism is the social arm of neoliberalism. Initially a progressive movement that brought more attention to people of color and their associated cultures, it solidified into government policy that merged with neoliberal practices. Neoliberalism is based on the tenet that the market will right all social ills and, similarly, multicultural policy manifests in ways to suggest the representation of racial difference within the market or civic sphere is evidence of more substantive social or political inclusion.[18] The merger of these two ideologies has meant that minority groups often vie for visibility and audibility over economic redress or the dissolution of the racial system. Thus, as Jason Stanyek points out, "the multicultural and cross-cultural [. . .] cloaks the persistence for racial and ethnic violence and hierarchy in a gauzy, celebratory scrim."[19]

Ho's split from the Asian American jazz scene can be understood, in part, as a conflict over the effect of multiculturalism on arts practice. He links the deradicalizing of LRS—particularly what he describes as a rejection of "socialism, Marxism, and Revolution"—to the selling-out of artists who make their work more palatable to mainstream institutions for funding.[20] "As revolutionaries," he says, "the goal of our work must be the raising of both consciousness and cultural and artistic levels and standards, as well as the popularization of innovative, oppositional, transgressive, radical work."[21] And this work cannot be done, he believes, if artists are catering to granting institutions and playing it safe in order to gain access to public arts venues and funding. In multicultural arts programming, surface representations of diversity are celebrated even though there may be little substantive cultural or political-economic dialogue hidden behind colorful ethnic costumes and performances. This representation is often supported at the expense of more substantive antiracist work that addresses, among other things, political-economic disparities. By participating in multicultural institutions, artists are in effect helping to maintain a racial status quo and system of economic oppression.

Ho actualizes this critique by presenting Afro Asian culture in conjunction with material concerns for people of color. Robin D. G. Kelley delineates the close ties between 20th-century black activists and the Communist Party. Black radicals understood the importance of class struggle to their communities, for they were saddled with economic inequality as much as racist violence. Most white socialist organizations treated racism as "merely a feature of capitalism—kill the latter and the former would wither away."[22] Many black radicals believed the reverse, however, arguing that uprooting racism would inevitably destabilize capitalism because of the ways race is central to its workings. The Black (and other) Nationalist ideological ties to, especially, Mao Tse Tung and the foregrounding of economic self-determination as a means toward freedom were strategies engaged to address the dual evils of modernity. Ho's work draws a similar connection between capital and race, showcasing anti-capitalist sentiment alongside the celebration of Third World cultures.

Textually, he employs popular cultural forms from the U.S. and abroad as a means to interrogate the conjunction of art and economics. As Juan Flores argues, popular culture "retains the dimensions of class and cultural capital which are so easily lost sight of in considerations of group identities and interactions along ethnic cultural lines."[23] For this reason, Ho engages popular culture by drawing on old Tin Pan Alley songs, jazz standards, and scores from popular television and film. *Railroad*, for example, features "Strange Fruit Revisited," after the Billie Holiday original, and arrangements of Duke Ellington's "Caravan," and the traditional "Auld Lang Syne," pieces that have long circulated in both industry-controlled recorded media and the oral folk tradition. There is "socioeconomic and power-defined tension implicit in the idea of the popular" and, as such, Ho exploits this tension by employing popular media forms, such as comic books and martial arts films, he feels are looked down on by dominant and elite culture.[24] For example, *Journey beyond the West* is a departure from the Chinese folk novel *Journey to the West*, and *Deadly She-Wolf Assassin at Armageddon!* is based on a series of popular Japanese manga and Samurai films. His *Dragon vs. Eagle* even explores video game technology as a conceptual and aesthetic core.

Ho refashions popular material in an attempt to bring out its more radical underpinnings, including antiracist and anticapitalist sentiments. In "Strange Fruit Revisited," for example, he presents the melody in a chopped manner and dissonant harmonization, making it almost impossible to sing along with the familiar tune. Exploiting the reedy timbre of the winds, Ho emphasizes sharp frequencies so they are harsh on the ears. Vocalist Veatrice Williams extends her singing tones to include outbursts of moans and cries. And instead of providing a unifying groove for the piece, it continually transforms from a basso continuo support to the vocals, explosions of fast, rhythmic instrumentals, and choruses of the winds that crescendo almost to the point of distortion. Instead of a beautiful song *about* lynching, the song becomes a sonic manifestation of the shock, pain, and horror of the lynching experience. As another example, the AAME has performed Holiday's classic "God Bless the Child" as a manifesto on self-determination. This message is inherent in the lyrics of the original song, but Ho also introduces this song in concert to remind audience of the theme of economic independence. In other popular culture citations, and depending on the listener, Ho's reradicalization is less easily apprehended, even though his experimentalism could still invite a new or different listening.

What is interesting about this heterogeneous source material is the overlap between forms that are considered popular and folk. Flores suggests that not only is popular culture a site through which to understand class and power differentials but, "in the case of the cultural practices of colonial and diasporic peoples, [it is a space] where the 'old' and supposedly outmoded forms of vernacular, community, and 'folk' culture—the earlier denotation of popular culture—are still very much alive."[25] For people of color, there is no clear distinction between pop and folk; in fact, that very distinction can be seen as a product of commodification and colonization. While Flores makes an argument for a temporal distinction between popular and folk, I believe there is also one of assumed connection to (or distance from) a cultural community. What Ho's compositions reveal is the ways in which progressive, community-grounded popular forms can be read as extensions of tradition versus dominant, mainstream culture that is cut off from its original sources.

Ho claims his use of popular culture as crucial to his work because it critiques the class-biased distinction between high and lowbrow culture in the modern West. He differentiates between popular culture with a "small p"—folk or urban vernacular culture—and with a "big P"—cultural material selected for the people by corporations. The two have a dialectical relationship in which the big P takes culture from the small p and then returns it to the people in a "watered-down, de-racinated, de-radicalized, de-natured form."[26] Ho describes wishing to take the small p, sometimes via the big P, and bring it back to the small p in a more progressive, experimental, creative, or challenging way. He particularly is drawn to pop cultural material that celebrates the underdog, is militant or transgressive, but might be called lowbrow by the dominant culture, such as martial-arts films.

But again questions of reception and translation arise, particularly in some of the materials Ho employs. While popular culture forms may be a site for working-class identification, they are also a product of the culture industry that has long traded in racist and sexist imagery. While he sees the use of 1970s martial-arts sources, comics, and karaoke as a nod to the "common" man and woman—finding the value in what elite society brands as trash—his full praise of some of these forms may be unwarranted. Ho has chosen martial arts as the primary movement vocabulary for his stage productions, an element he believes showcases an anti-imperialist impulse and can function as a tool to attract new and younger audiences, particularly youth of color. In his "Kickin' the White Man's Ass: Black Power, Aesthetics, and the Asian Martial Arts," he writes about the importance of martial arts films to urban black and Latino youth during the 1970s and their still-relevant showcasing of black and brown representations. These movies were spaces in which young men of color could see powerful figures that looked like them on the screen. As Kevin Fellezs illuminates in his chapter, Ho initially hesitated employing martial arts in his work because of his sense that they portrayed Asian men as "cold-blooded asexual killing machines." His friend, however, suggested that the images with which he was uncomfortable were the white popular culture industry's appropriation of true Asian martial-arts forms.

Ho resolved the issues of Asian male stereotypes by working with martial artists to present nonstereotypical—and culturally accurate—versions of their forms onstage. But the issue of female representation in his sources remains. First, the appearance of strong female characters are much fewer and far between in the movies he celebrates. And when they do appear, they are often the source of sexual titillation. Misogynist imagery abounds, for example, in the *Lone Wolf and Cub* manga and samurai film series, the source material for Ho's *Deadly She-Wolf Assassin at Armageddon!* While the narrative of the *Lone Wolf and Cub* films deals with the lead character avenging his wife's death, the films themselves are full of antifeminist imagery, very similar to the Blaxploitation films of the same era. In one scene from *Sword of Vengeance*, a townswoman's breasts are exposed as she is nearly raped by a group of thugs who have taken over her village. In another scene, the samurai is obliged to have sex with a village prostitute to save her from being killed. The earlier use of nudity and this particular plot device—in which the woman finds ecstasy but the man supposedly only performs out of duty—seemingly function to arouse the male viewer by presenting the women solely as sexual objects.

In their script, Ho and cowriter Ruth Margraff make several gestures that implicitly critique these dynamics of the earlier films: increasing the roles of female characters, having the entire story framed by a female narrator, and showcasing female performers in fighting roles. The presence of strong women in the story also results in a different moral outcome to the tale. The driving force of the original films is that the Lone Wolf will remain in perpetual violent conflict. But at the end of Ho and Margraff's retelling, after over an hour of fight sequences and bloodshed, the title character turns from the masculine violence, telling the Lone Wolf's son: "Pick up the sword to defeat the sword. But when the sword has been defeated, you must set it down. Still knowing how to use it. How to trust. To save the one with no blood on his hands." Thus, Ho and Margraff find ways to shift and comment on the male-centered phenomenon of their source, harnessing the good of the tradition while also calling out the not so good.

But are there limits to how much popular culture can be resignified? And what particular strategies work better than others? Ho's work presents examples of when this process has worked as well as when it has been less than complete. His 2009 *Celestial Green Monster* album is an engagement of the popular on multiple registers. First, he employs a twenty-person ensemble rather than his usual six or seven, stating:

> The quintessential American orchestra is not the symphony, but the big band. If so-called "jazz" is "America's classical music" (as proclaimed by the U.S. Congress, among other officiates), then its attendant large ensemble is the "jazz" orchestra. [. . .] If we apprehend "classical" as worthy of veneration

> instead of high-brow elitist or celebratory of western European bourgeois values, and imbue a dynamic sensibility to the concept of "classical" to not mean something stuck in the past, reactionary or ossified, but rather, enduring, vital and constantly relevant and revolutionary, then certainly the big band form represents the best of the so-called "jazz" tradition.[27]

Despite being historicized in the mainstream as a set of standard tunes done in rigidly set arrangements—and associated with numerous white practitioners—Ho believes the form allows a wide palette for producing aesthetically challenging work and seeks to reclaim the big band as a site of progressive music making.

Along with original pieces such as "Blues to the Freedom Fighters" and "The Struggle for a New World Suite," *Celestial Green Monster* includes two arrangements of popular pieces: the theme from *Spiderman* and a setting of "In-A-Gadda-Da-Vida (In the Garden of Eden)." The first is a brief resetting of the theme from the original television show and showcases the dense musical material composers packed into one- or two-minute sound bites (Ho's clocks in at 2:20 but feels spacious enough to highlight a fever-pitched alto saxophone solo by Jim Hobbs). In addition to "the terrific TV themes of the 1960s," Ho also grew up "infected by the contagious vamps of the late-1960s rock world," including "the popular 'jazz-rock' horn bands" such as Blood, Sweat, and Tears, and Tower of Power, and black funk bands such as Earth, Wind, and Fire and Kool and the Gang.[28] He draws out the inventive jazz roots of these popular styles in his arrangement of "In-A-Gadda-Da-Vida." In the opening movement, "Blue Planet, My Love," Abraham Gomez-Delgado sings the original lyrics in a classic rock style over a robust chorus of horns creating a rhythmic counterpoint under him. The middle of this movement opens to an electronic keyboard solo by Art Hirahara that channels both Sun Ra and Jimi Hendrix. Mary Halverson follows on electric guitar, twisting and deconstructing the melody before erupting into a cloud of distortion that sounds like the explosion of an atomic bomb witnessed through a psychedelic haze.

The sounds produced by the Monster Big Band are of a different world than the orchestras of Glenn Miller or Bennie Goodman, the swing era formation turned inside out and its strength and size pushed to the fullest. Even more, the band showcases how the ultrapop elements of television and Top 40 songs circulate in our contemporary culture, influence generations of artists, and can in many instances possess aesthetic worth despite their commodification or "low culture" status. Growing up on the East Coast in a

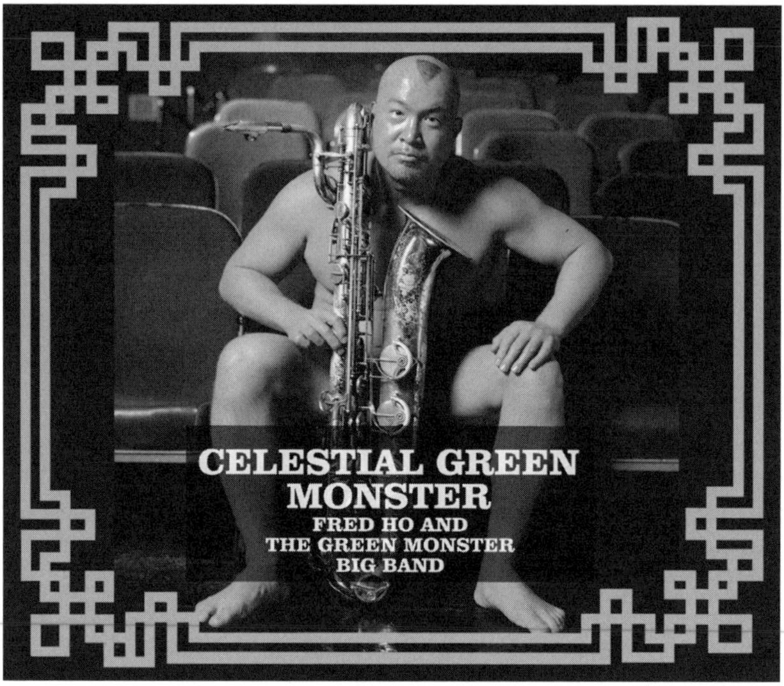

Figure 3. *Celestial Green Monster*, Fred Ho and the Green Monster Big Band, Album Cover, 2010. Credit: Robert Adam Mayer

middle-class family, it is no surprise that Ho has been greatly influenced by mainstream U.S. popular culture, and there is no escape from the industry's extensive grasp. Again, distinctions between folk, tradition, elite, and common are blurred.

But Ho's ideals fall flat in the packaging and marketing of the album's adventurous music. First, looking at the album cover and liner notes, where is the big band? The only visuals on the packaging are two photos of Ho, naked, painted green, and posing with his saxophone. The great sound and many-hued faces of his 21st-century, Afro Asian, big band are eclipsed, and Ho alone stands in as a singular Green Monster. This showcasing of the "front man" to the ensemble is further supported by quotes alongside one of the photos: "There's Shrek, and then there's Fred Ho!" and "Ho, ho, ho! Green Giant."[29] In tandem, these quotes present Ho as the latest, greatest iteration of these popular cultural figures but, again, he alone stands in for the entire band. The showcasing of the ensemble's "star" over the full group that produced the work echoes a standard marketing strategy of the popular culture industry.

The "green" of this album refers to Ho's engagement of the current ecological crisis as articulated through cultural nationalist and Marxist tenets. He proposes Afro Asian people as the original green warriors, calling out capitalism and whiteness as the source of our contemporary environmental situation. I do not wish to parse Ho's political message here, but rather suggest ways that some of his aesthetic choices impede his goals. First, the marketing of *Celestial Green Monster* slips into representations of women that tread well-worn popular culture paths of sexuality and objectification. To increase its circulation on the internet, Ho commissioned Dinorah de Jesús Rodriguez to create a music video for "In-A-Gadda-Da-Vida." The video centers on a female forest dweller—noted online as "Earth Mother's Daughter"—who is threatened by human forces such as pollution, deforestation, and overdevelopment.[30] The beautifully rendered video intercuts shots of the woman amongst the natural landscape with oversaturated bits of found footage of urban decay, Third World people, and industrial technology. The woman begins to be suffocated by these modern elements and ultimately celebrates the natural world as the site of her liberation.[31]

But despite her presentation as a strong, female persona, she is wearing skimpy clothes (a few strategically placed leaves), dancing and writhing on the forest floor, sensually eating fruit, and straddling tree trunks. These images could be read as a brown, curly-haired woman in touch with nature and comfortable in her body. But they simultaneously trade in the same fetishized imagery of women found in mainstream music videos. Most resonant with typical pop culture misogyny is that the woman repeatedly gazes seductively at the camera—including the classic pin-up girl over-the-shoulder "come-hither" look—inviting the viewer into the scene through the gateway of a potential sexual encounter. Earth Mother's Daughter parades in front of the viewer as eye candy—politically motivated or not—while the male singer croons

> In a gadda da vida, honey
> Don't you know that I love you
> In a gadda da vida, baby
> Don't you know that I'll always be true

Unlike *She-Wolf*, however, there is no readily intelligible commentary to mitigate these images. Further, by circulating in a viral video, these images can be completely detached from any kind of contextual framing, merely adding to the parade of sexualized women pervading the media.

Interestingly, Ho has employed the green cause as a tangible rallying point for his matriarchal socialist beliefs and uses the image of women and notion of matriarchy as the antithesis and/or answer to our ecological plight. Yet his same showboating results in his becoming the face for this ideology. A promotional video for the full album made by Queen Gidrea mixes images of Ho, green popular culture figures (Shrek, Kermit the Frog, the Jolly Green Giant), and green-hued stills of radicals such as Malcolm X, Mao, and Rachel Carson.[32] Green intertitles suggest that harm to the earth, such as chopping down forests, predates "crowns, currency, and capitalism." The images move alongside the *Spiderman* arrangement, with the final proclamation: "We are the green matriarchy. The golden-green femme Dragonist! The green revolutionary, luddite, Socialist." In the same moment, multiple images of Ho appear, in effect proclaiming him as the vision of the world-saving green *matriarchy*. Again, Ho alone stands in for the greater cause and is presented as the male savior.

Ultimately, Ho's works do much to blend high and low culture and to trouble the division between them. In addition, they actively call out the radical within the dominant while also seeking to infuse the mainstream with new aesthetic messages. At the same time, however, Ho employs marketing strategies straight from the same mainstream industry that he wishes to critique. Rather than fully reject these tactics, he uses the tools of stardom and provocation as a means to draw consumers. In fact, Ho is open about his decision to do "for-profit" arts and attempt to compete with large arts corporations such as Disney. He sees the nonprofit sector as a space in which artists play it safe in order to court granting institutions to fund their work. A more effective political strategy, he reasons, is to make use of the freedom afforded to corporations and infuse them with, what he calls, "guerilla tactics."[33] Reconciling the capitalist versus anticapitalist conundrum I posed above, Ho believes running a for-profit production company is "a means to have independence and self-sufficiency under the terms of capitalism."[34] At the same time, as the next section makes clear, it is his marshaling of community—which is difficult to monetize—that most greatly supports the political potential in his work and will provide for its endurance.

A New Left Vision

The space in which art actively incites politics can be varied and difficult to pinpoint. How exactly does Ho's work transform from discourse about race and class to something tangible? How can sonic representation engender structural change? Ho's political journey is not just one of creating work but of cultivating communities that can create and consume it. It is through shaping the bodies of performers, building spaces for new musical dialogues, and attempts to retrain listeners that Ho's project has the greatest potential to alter the sociopolitical landscape. Ultimately, he becomes one node in a broader conglomeration of people that stretches beyond his physical body and singular accomplishments. In fact, his central goals would and will be impossible to achieve without the surrounding community that supports his work and helps to actualize it in the world.

On an individual level, Ho describes his approach to performing music as a physical, intellectual, and emotional-spiritual exploration in which he aims to push beyond existing boundaries. The stamina, skill, and improvisation involved in Asian martial arts is an important inspiration to his musical praxis. "As Bruce Lee would put it," Ho says, "'the ultimate technique is to have no technique,'" and in his playing he wishes to reach a level of transcendence in which he is not conscious of technique. This state of oneness with the music—similar to less-mediated states of consciousness induced by meditation, for example—requires a rigorous practice. Much like Lee's improvisatory *jeet kune do*, which simultaneously blends and moves beyond a number of martial arts traditions, Ho incorporates new saxophone fingerings, kung fu breathing, and other techniques in order to push beyond historic instrumental limitations. He boasts about how he broke the two-and-a-half octave register on his saxophone as primarily a physical feat but also one that required significant intellectual and emotional stamina. At the very basic level, Ho sees this personal mastery as an anti-imperialist tool that can build strength and pride.

Technical prowess is part of how Ho sells himself, yet he pushes his collaborators to new technical heights as well. His music is unquestionably complex to perform, highly experimental—meaning there are few models to study—and he is an exacting director. Multiple members of the AAME have told me one of their primary reasons for joining the ensemble was the high level of musicianship fostered in the group. They also comment on the intensity of focus—technical and emotional—required to perform Ho's work, joking sometimes about how playing a bebop or pop tune would be a welcome "break." In addition to extended harmonies and frequent dissonances, Ho makes use of complex rhythms, including meters less frequently found in Western classical and popular traditions such as 7 and 9, polymeters (the combination of or changing between meters), and polyrhythms derived from traditions such as West African drumming. Ho foregrounds compound meters, believing they are a musico-political rejection of the dominant music canon that uses simple and, primarily, duple meters. By challenging those who play his pieces to perform composed patterns *and* improvise solos over complex vamps, he pushes them to think musically in new ways and find their own voice in conversation with his adventurous arrangements.

But this rhythmic play does not come at the expense of beauty. Ho's music grooves, and he does not eschew aesthetic enjoyment as many antiestablishment avant-gardists do. I have sat with numerous musicians after performances and have found the AAME members to be some of the most consistently excited; they love to play the material and feel a great satisfaction after doing so. Ho writes compelling themes that one can move to, rather than feeling stilted or irregular. Take as an example the main theme from the eighth movement of *The Black Panther Suite*. The horns play a two-measure pattern that repeats three times, followed by a single measure (with 16th pickup) that drives back into the downbeat. While in $\frac{7}{4}$—thus featuring an odd number of beats to a measure—the syncopated 16ths create a compelling tension over a strong backbeat pulse of eighth notes that drives the tune. The punctuation of the backbeat gets accentuated later in the piece when the rhythm section drops out and the horns play the riff accompanied only by steady handclaps on the offbeat, a pleasurable moment in which audiences will often clap along, excited by the chance to more fully engage the music.

Ho's pieces do not only require strong manual technique, however; emotional output and conviction is also required to play his music appropriately. In fact, "soul" is both an aesthetic and technical concept for him. About performing Third World cultural material, he says: "It's just not about notation. It's really about how to interpret these melodies. And the stories inside these melodies. It's not just you gotta play this bend here or you gotta do this kind of drop or fall or lift here. It's not about this kind of pitch alteration there. It can't be dissected in that type of way, it has to understood from the point of view of meaning."[35] Musical performance does not simply reside in the replication of technique or cultural codes but in infusing the performance with the ethos and politics informing the root tradition. "Expressive culture is both a musical and sociological phenomenon. You have to live it. You don't have to be genetically of it. But it's an understanding, it's a consciousness, a sensibility, ethos."[36] Understanding the experiences of the people who forged these traditions and the intention to right injustices they have faced are, for Ho, as important as rendering combinations of sounds or fancy musical flourishes. These beliefs form the backbone of the Afro Asian Marxist ideology he espouses.

This holistic technique requires a certain amount of cultural knowledge in order to be properly executed, requiring players that are fluid in various forms and/or have the ability and flexibility to learn new things. In fact, the working out of Ho's musical philosophies and the success of his projects has depended almost entirely on his musical and artistic collaborators. The AAME provides an excellent example of a particularly productive long-term community in which he is instrumental but not self-sufficient. Most writing on Ho focuses exclusively on his biography, and his voice is singled out as driving force of the group.[37] While Ho is without question a consummate composer, his ability to successfully incorporate so many styles into his pieces is also due to the diverse lives and expertise of his longtime colleagues, incomparable jazz players who also share a combined knowledge of numerous traditions from Africa, South Asia, and East Asia. Drummer royal hartigan, for example, earned a doctorate in ethnomusicology and is an expert in West African, Korean, Filipino, Latin American, South Asian, and Chinese percussion traditions, alongside his massive jazz drumming experience. Ho exhibits his own musical prowess by cultivating a space that makes use of the AAME members' intercultural musical knowledge and challenges them to put various Afro Asian traditions into dialogue through compositions that draw on these styles in combination. Ho brought them together but it is only through their integrated interests and particular cross-cultural musical training that his aesthetic vision can be realized.

The symbiosis exemplified in Ho and his bandmates extends into his other artistic relationships. He has worked with countless other musicians, writers, choreographers, directors, and activists on their projects or to produce his own work. In fact, he describes some of his biggest accomplishments as having collaborated with other radical artists, helped to further the careers of longtime friends, and nurtured the next generation of cultural workers. In this volume, essays by Peggy Myo-Young Choy, Ruth Margraff, Magdalena Gómez, Kalamu ya Salaam, and Salim Washington all illuminate the unique dynamics of collaborating with Ho. But what they most importantly reveal is that collaboration can be as much about dissent as it is about agreement—and that this friction can be productive. Many of these artists share political ideals with Ho; but the ways in which they choose to activate them aesthetically and socially are varied and, at times, areas of contention. For example, while Ho himself often is critical of the sexism in cultural nationalist or racism in labor organizations—factors he sees as leading to their ineffectiveness or demise—his collaborators at times launch similar criticisms of him. The essays here present an ethnographic glimpse into these collaborative processes and the ways in which Ho's associates have challenged him to tangibly stand by the beliefs he espouses.

Of course, the artistic tree Ho has planted also bears political fruit, modeling in aesthetic coalition potential ways of also doing activism. In fact, through the collaborations Ho has fostered, he is redefining the notion of a movement for the 21st century. The mass political actions of the mid-20th century gave way to more isolated and specialized organizing, the aging or "selling-out" of members and leaders, and ever-increasing social and political conservatism, including the former rallying ground of the Democratic Party. At the same time, the rise of neoliberalism has led to the increased dominance of multinational corporations, privatization of public resources, growing economic polarization, rolling back of hard-won civil rights legislation, and continual threats to labor rights, producing a landscape in which power seems both uncontestable and decentralized. The search for political mobilization through a collective has become a challenge with the dissolution of a strong, organized Left alongside a political-economic climate that impedes the growth of mass organization. This new era requires a different kind of movement building, perhaps without formal organizations or hierarchical structures.

Ho and his compatriots forge this movement for social and economic equality; a flexible, hyperlinked community of artists and activists that can form temporary, multiple, or varied clusters around specific needs and projects. While Ho has cultivated numerous projects with a variety of individuals toward a similar political end, the varied projects form a web of radical activity without a central institution. This type of structure may seem unremarkable from an artistic perspective but can be revelatory as a model for coordinated political action. Even more, the dialogue between individual and group, improvisation, and necessity of listening that are key to jazz performance prove similarly useful as tools for activists. Ho's ensembles exemplify the need for ongoing conversation and education in order to conduct cross-cultural and cross-racial political work; they are not simply the showcase of a happy merger but long unfolding laboratories for this type of experimentation. By no means a finished product, Ho's community continues to explore the possibilities of this ensemble-as-movement model.

And the communal spirit inspired by Ho goes beyond both arts and politics. In the summer of 2006, he was diagnosed with stage 3B colon cancer. Not one to sit idly by while Western medicine took its reactive course, Ho embarked on a proactive path of education, collecting medical wisdom from around the world to employ in his struggle. At the same time, numerous friends, fellow artists, and family members—the Warriors for Fred—stepped in to provide food, home care, and emotional support. In his chapter, Bill Mullen discusses Ho's cancer as an example of commodification and oppression at the level of the cell—the impact of living in a toxic economy. What the surge in dialogue and action inspired by Ho's illness shows, too, is that cancer impacts a community as much as the sick individual. The ways in which, for years, so many people rallied around Ho's battle stands as the greatest testament to his beloved person, valued artistic and political work, and the engaged and committed circle he has fostered. Even more, Ho in turn became a resource for the others, delivering mass emails that extolled his discoveries in homeopathic healing, healthful living, and freeing oneself from the toxic capitalist grind. Always on the lookout for better ways to live, Ho now waxes poetic about his newfound interest in farming and community-supported agriculture, all the while inspiring those around him to live more full lives on all fronts.

This last item points to a final component of Ho's community-building strategy—a desire to expand consciousness. Having an appreciation for creative or challenging music, he seeks to foster the same in listeners, desiring his music to open audience ears to new sonic possibilities and give them "a different musical nutrition." Listening to Ho's work exposes one to new timbres, instrument combinations, temperaments and modes, rhythms, languages, and subject matter; in all cultivating new musical experiences that push beyond the status quo. Engaging the music thus becomes a step in a larger process of transformation: improving aesthetic innovation, developing political consciousness, and actively constructing and consuming culture that promotes the same. This three-prong model is very much like the BAM goal of creating a new kind of critic or listener, with the specific tools to properly hear and analyze their countermodern output. As Amiri Baraka says, "because the majority of jazz critics are white middle-brows, most jazz criticism tends to enforce white middle-brow standards of excellence as criteria for performance of a music that in its most profound manifestations is completely antithetical to such standards; in fact, quite often is in direct reaction against them."[38] To support the consumption of his work, Ho works to build a listenership with ears open enough to hear his and others' sonic innovations.

But what exactly is required in this day and age to impart aesthetic innovations and their political potential to an audience? How is this historical moment different than the civil rights era in terms of the richness or vapidity of the media that pervades our ears? Ho's desire to establish new audiences presents the issue of translation and how exactly his revolutionary sentiments are to be comprehended. A major strategy Ho has employed to aid in this transmission is the use of descriptive titles that illuminate the political intention behind his compositions. Some names refer to revolutionary subject matter, such as *The Black Panther Suite: All Power to the People* and "Blues to the Freedom Fighters." Others refer to well-known movement catchphrases, like "Act Up! Before It's Too Late!," a dedication to the AIDS organization ACT UP, or the feminist "Yes Means Yes and No Means No, Wherever She Is, Wherever She Goes!" More humorously, other titles illuminate concepts central to Ho's work, such as "The New World Odor: The Huge Farts of Red Meat-Eating Imperialists Foul the Earth" or his description of *We Refuse to Be Used and Abused* as "an anti-bourgeois boogie-woogie." Additionally, in live performance, he often gives spoken introductions to pieces before the band kicks in. Ranging in length from a mere stating of the piece's title to a several-minute-long explanation of, for example, the colonial history of the Philippines to usher in "An Bayan Ko," Ho does much to set the stage for the politics that inspired his work and to provide a guide for uninitiated ears.

These titles and introductions provide guidance and an entrée into the sonic world his ensembles create so that a listener might glean more from the music. Even more, these remarks serve as hails that invite audience members into a shared political space; listeners familiar with the political subject matter will feel welcomed by the discourse, while newer listeners will be exposed to some of the main principles. These verbal descriptions do, however, lead me to question whether his music may not always speak for itself as much as he would like. Why do the political messages need to be spoken if the music *is* the politics? They are needed precisely because the music, especially for the "untrained" listener, can only go part of the way in promoting a clear ideology. In fact, it is conceivable that Ho, in essence, selects an audience of "the choir" to which his music preaches, failing to engage those who do not already ascribe to his beliefs. But in this return to the question of discourse and labels, I wonder too about how these titles might limit the possibilities of aesthetic and political meanings in his work. While colorful, these names are often quite specific and concrete. They make clear his political grounding but also narrow the room for interpretation of the music or, at least, lessen this potential by bringing the ineffable to a material level. Words indeed wield a power. But talking to Ho, at times, can almost feel like listening to a prerecorded speech because he is so invested in the catchphrase. His challenge, in moving forward, will be to exceed the very words that he claims.

Chapter Outline

This book presents a mix of voices—scholars, artists, and activists—because Ho himself is all three. Each of these perspectives illuminates different aspects of his life and work although, as it will become clear, these realms are not mutually exclusive. Divided into three main sections, the book covers the gestures Ho uses in his musical and theatrical work, his political theory and activism, and how his personal experiences relate to his career trajectory. The book offers an intimate engagement with the entirety of Ho, emphasizing his unique contributions to integrating art and politics while illuminating the communities he has formed through his numerous collaborations.

In the first part, "Revolution in Music," Kevin Fellezs in his chapter takes as his starting point the innovative martial arts dramas Ho has created. Drawing connections between Ho and one of his heroes, Bruce Lee, Fellezs discusses Ho's musical and theatrical work as part of a "popular avant-garde." No stranger to provocative creations herself, Ruth Margraff writes about the process of fashioning several operas with Ho, detailing their work from the inside out. Discussing her at times intense feelings of discomfort during their collaborations, Margraff reveals the particular emotional challenges and eventual triumphs Ho can inspire in those with whom he works. Arthur J. Sabatini rounds out this section by chronicling a broader swath of Ho's theatrical work, paying attention to the variety of themes, styles, and media he incorporates. Detailing several of Ho's major productions, he highlights the ways in which Ho creates a central space for the productive dialogue and negotiation between diverse entities. In the end, Sabatini defines Ho's collage aesthetic as not a disjointed postmodern pastiche but a variegated, holistic world based on dialectic relationships.

The second part, "The Aesthetics of Politics," features pieces that engage Ho's artistic output as part of a larger personal body of activism and his substantive contributions to antioppression movements. Diane C. Fujino analyzes the role that Ho-produced culture played and plays in the Asian American movement and socialist organizations such as the League of Revolutionary Struggle. Salim Washington follows with an essay and interview that gives a glimpse of a young Ho, coming of age as a radical while at Harvard. Bill V. Mullen completes this section with attention to a new terrain of political struggle for Ho, his battle against cancer and reclaiming control over his own body and health. Thinking through the body as a site of political engagement, Mullen offers insight into the ways in which Ho's illness revealed the harmful oppression of capitalism.

In addition to scholarly analyses, unique to this book are the contributions of artists who have collaborated with Ho and poets who have created work inspired by him. Part 3, "A Life in Community," features chapters that highlight the inner workings of the collaborative process and provide a firsthand account of the ways in which Ho has often shifted his seemingly unswerving convictions. Magdalena Gómez and Peggy Myo-Young Choy chronicle their decades-long friendships with Ho, redefining this type of relationship as one founded on shared "outsider" politics and the affinity for creating controversial art. At the same time, both women express differences they have had with Ho and how, in the end, even these disagreements have proved productive. Miyoshi Smith follows with an interview conducted with Ho, giving readers a chance to hear how he relates his own life experiences to his artistic output. Finally, Kalamu ya Salaam presents a reflection that draws connections between his fears of Ho's illness and the deaths of other friends and family members. By the end, however, he turns sadness and fear into a call to action, challenging cancer to take on the mighty Fred Ho. It is clear from all of these personal reflections that Ho's struggle with cancer was an important landmark in these contributors' lives. Their refusal to ignore this seemingly private matter is a testament to the ways in which Ho himself constantly strives to integrate all elements of his artistic, political, and individual, corporeal life.

Integral to this anthology are the poems interspersed throughout, providing a means to infuse the volume with music through text. Prominent poets—Jayne Cortez, Richard Hamasaki, Esther Iverem, Robert Kocik, and Genny Lim—all contributed original works inspired by Ho. These pieces provide intimate visions of the emotional marks Ho has left on fellow artists and friends. They also showcase a performative means to interpret the impact of Ho's work on the broader cultural landscape. The book concludes with several appendices featuring a comprehensive discography and Ho's curriculum vitae.

For over 25 years, Ho and his collaborators have interrogated the experiences of injustice faced by people of color, studied their associated cultural traditions, and fought amidst their struggles in continually innovative ways. In Ho's work, we see the continued legacy of Afro Asian music and politics, forged in the interracial cultural nationalist spaces of the 1960s, but melded with a contemporary strategy for reradicalizing Left politics. Through an examination of his works, the essays in this volume show how politics and identity are ultimately the sum of parts that unfold at the nexus of individuals and larger structures. Contributors trace a singular figure and collectively show how idiosyncratic, shifting, contradictory, and even accidental an artistic and political life can be.

While his flashy dress and in-your-face creations present Ho as larger-than-life, in truth he is only as large as any one life. Yet as the following essays interrogate his unique story, they also allow for a view into the broader

Figure 4. Afro Asian Music Ensemble: Fred Houn, Carleen Robinson, Taru Alexander, Al Givens, Richard Clements, Jon Jang, Sam Furnace, Kiyoto Fujiwara, Sayyd Abdul Al-khabyyr. Credit: Stephanie Myers

histories of the U.S. Left, jazz and creative music, and experimental "high art." These new insights into key political and artistic movements come at a most needed time. The fervor of the Arab Spring revolutions, the spirited Occupy Movement—these popular uprisings bespeak a desire for change stretching long before Afro Asian decolonization or the civil rights era. Yet they also lack the strong musical mouthpieces that drove campaigns of previous generations. This book looks into the strategies and gains Ho has made in trying to build a new musical Left, while simultaneously revealing where there is still work to be done.

Notes

Some of the statements and ideas in this introduction are from my "Revolutionary Aesthetics in Fred Ho's Afro Asian Music Ensemble," in Musicking at the Crossroads of Diaspora: Afro Asian Musical Politics, PhD diss., Northwestern University, 2009.

1. Fred Ho, "What Makes 'Jazz' the Revolutionary Music of the Twentieth Century, and Will It Be Revolutionary for the Twenty-first Century?" *Wicked Theory, Naked Practice: A Fred Ho Reader*, ed. Diane C. Fujino (Minneapolis: University of Minnesota Press, 2009), 91, 92.

2. Ibid., 54; interview with Fred Ho, November 13, 2005, Brooklyn, New York.

3. Fred Ho to Tamara Roberts, email July 12, 2010.

4. The cartoon was designed by Chanel Matsunami Govreau.

5. The AARW is an organization supporting the empowerment of Asian Pacific Americans, through programs such as arts promotion, historical documentation, and antiracist training. The League of Revolutionary Struggle was a multiracial Communist group founded via the merger of the Asian American organization I Wor Kuen and the August 29th Movement, a Chicano-Latino organization.

6. Ho, *Wicked Theory, Naked Practice*, 54.

7. Ho's biography has been covered extensively elsewhere. See Ho, *Wicked Theory, Naked Practice*; Bill V. Mullen, *Afro-orientalism* (Minneapolis: University of Minnesota Press, 2004); Deborah Wong, *Speak It Louder: Asian Americans Making Music* (New York: Routledge, 2004); and Wei-hua Zhang, "Fred Wei-han Ho: Case Study of a Chinese-American Creative Musician," *Asian Music* 25.1–2 (1993/1994): 81–114.

8. Paul Gilroy, *The Black Atlantic: Modernity and Double Consciousness* (London: Verso, 1993), 38–39.

9. Max Roach, "Musicians Should Choreograph the Minds of Our Youth," *Unity*, 12 September 1980.

10. I use "Third World" in its original meaning, as exemplified by the 1950s Afro Asian movement. The term was used by African, Asian, and Latin American political workers to indicate a desire to be independent from the First (United States) and Second (USSR) worlds.

11. Fred Ho, interview, November 13, 2005, Brooklyn, New York.

12. Ho, *Wicked Theory, Naked Practice*, 54–55.

13. See, for example, Claire Jean Kim, "The Racial Triangulation of Asian Americans," *Politics and Society* 27.1 (March 1999), 105–38; Helen Jun, "Black Orientalism: Nineteenth-Century Narratives of Race and U.S. Citizenship," *American Quarterly* 58.4 (2006), 1047–66; and David Palumbo-Liu, *Asian/American: Historical Crossings of a Racial Frontier* (Palo Alto, Calif.: Stanford University Press, 1999).

14. Vijay Prashad, *The Karma of Brown Folk* (Minneapolis: University of Minnesota Press, 2000).

15. *City Sun*, 1985; *San Jose Mercury News*, 1986; *City Sun*, 1986. Accessed in the Fred Ho Papers, Archives and Special Collections at the Thomas J. Dodd Research Center, University of Connecticut.

16. Unusual sonorities: Fred Ho, interview, November 13, 2005. My forthcoming manuscript, in part, treats Ho's use of these sounds and the challenges of disrupting racial assumptions connected to them.

17. Elaine Song, Asian American Resource Workshop newsletter, Fred Ho Papers.

18. Micaela di Leonardo states: "Neoliberalism, as developed over the second half of the twentieth century, is an intellectual/political stance that presumes that capitalist trade 'liberalization'—the end of all state regulations on business, and indeed, the end of all state-run business—will lead inevitably to market growth and, *ceteris paribus*, to optimal social ends." "Introduction: New Global and American Landscapes of Inequality," *New Landscapes of Inequality: Neoliberalism and the Erosion of Democracy in America*, ed. Jane L. Collins, Micaela di Leonardo, and Brett Williams (Santa Fe, N.M.: School for Advanced Research Press, 2008), 5.

19. Jason Stanyek, "Diasporic Improvisation and the Articulation of Intercultural Music," diss., University of California, San Diego, 2004, 5.

20. Ho, *Wicked Theory, Naked Practice*, 54.

21. Ibid., 55.

22. Robin D. G. Kelley, *Freedom Dreams: The Black Radical Imagination* (Boston: Beacon Press, 2003), 41.

23. Juan Flores, *From Bomba to Hip-Hop: Puerto Rican Culture and Latino Identity* (New York: Columbia University Press, 2000), 13–14.

24. Ibid., 14.

25. Ibid., 14.

26. Ho, interview, November 13, 2005.

27. *Celestial Green Monster*, Mutable Music/Big Red Media, 2009, liner notes.

28. Ibid.

29. Ibid. (Album cover photo credit: Carin Fortin.)

30. The video can be found online at www.youtube.com/watch?v=8WwrD19yFeI. Accessed October 16, 2011.

31. There is no strong linear narrative to the video. Rather, it is a collection of moving images that roughly explore this transformation.

32. This video, *Fred Ho! The Celestial Green Monster*, can be viewed online at www.youtube.com/watch?v=9QNmEXanTQo&feature=related. Accessed October 16, 2011.

33. Ho, interview, November 13, 2005.

34. Ibid.

35. Ibid.

36. Ibid.

37. Currently the band features bassist Wes Brown, royal hartigan on percussion,

Bobby Zankel on alto saxophone, pianist Art Hirahara, and Salim Washington on tenor saxophone.

38. Quoted in Lorenzo Thomas, "Ascension: Music and the Black Arts Movement," *Jazz among the Discourses*, ed. Krin Gabbard (Durham, N.C.: Duke University Press, 1995), 266.

PART I

Revolution in Music

IT REMAINS TO BE SEEN

Only the drums
And yells of yay!

Only the drums
And yells of yay!

Because we are alive in this place.
Because we grew up on Now-or-Laters,
Candy necklaces and Cocoa Puffs
And we are still here.

Here to bear witness, to stomp, holler, love, scream
To declare that *it remains to be seen*, to fight.

Surely Bush and his crew are no worse
than McKinley and his crew
And my people survived!
Surely Colin Powell and Condi Rice are not worse
Than Booker T. and Stepin Fetchit.
And my people survived!

Surely the latest no-lye relaxer and hair weave
Are not worse than the conk, process or *hard press.*
And my people survived!

Bring my armor
Fuse with me the collective spine
Of Middle Passage bones
Raising from the ocean bottom.

Bring conga, djembe, kalimba, steel pan.
The deepest well pitch of Paul Robeson,
The most makes-you-cry note of Marvin Gaye,
Bring big pots of black-eyed peas, injections of melanin
Bring the mass choir from Mississippi
Mahatma Ghandi's prayerful walk
But don't forget Harriet Tubman's pistol!

Because the polar caps are melting now
And our farms are nearly all gone.
They put pig genes in our collards and tomatoes.
Horse piss into our wombs.
Smallpox, anthrax and Ritalin in our veins.
And, into our hands, either a rifle, a corporate card
Or some license to entertain.

Only the drums
and yells of yay!

Only the drums
and yells of yay!

Because I am here
in this place.
Because we are here

Because we—who weren't supposed to be . . . anything
From North Philly, the South Side, Southeast, and Compton—
Have survived Nixon's forehead, Reagan cheese,
The Bushman's smartbombs and now
The Bushmaster's do-it-yourself terror.
Survived cordons of gangs, crack, crackheads
And our cut buddies turned predators and capitalist tool.

Only the drums
And yells of yay!
Because I am here, alive
In this place
Because we are here
And we weren't supposed to be . . . anything

Go on—take me to the river.
Go on—take it to the bridge!

Because Rumsfeld, Ashcroft, Cheney and Rove
Are on the loose! Trying to code my life
in orange, red and yellow alerts.

Wanting me to be afraid as I peer at the TV screen
Exploding with lies and myth.

And my people have survived!

Because the polar caps are melting now
And our farms are nearly all gone.
They put pig genes in our collards and tomatoes.
Horse piss into our wombs.
Smallpox, Anthrax and Ritalin in our veins.
And, into our hands, either a rifle, a corporate card
Or some license to entertain.

C'mon. Bring conga, djembe, kalimba, steel pan.
Make thunder.
Go on—take me to the river.
Go on—take it to the bridge!
Because we have survived
And we are here,
In this place all bathed and in our armor.

And ready.

—Esther Iverem

1

Enter the Voice of the Dragon

Fred Ho, Bruce Lee, and the Popular Avant-Garde

KEVIN FELLEZS

> I am trying to create a new American opera that appeals to today's youth—particularly inner city youth—who think of opera as something conservative and exclusionary [. . .] I at least want my artistic/theatrical concept to be more exciting and captivating, and for the martial arts to demolish the aesthetics of grade-B action films, boring Broadway and moribund modern dance.
>
> —FRED HO, "Beyond Asian American Jazz"

> I believe that I have a role [. . .] the audience needs to be educated and the one to educate them has to be somebody who is responsible. We are dealing with the masses and we have to create something that will get through to them. We have to educate them step by step.
>
> —BRUCE LEE, *Words of the Dragon*

Fred Ho's *Journey beyond the West: The New Adventures of Monkey* (1996) is an "Afro Asian score for ballet," an eclectic brew of high and low culture, as well as Afrodiasporic and Asian American cultural elements. *Journey beyond the West* is a reinterpretation of popular Chinese Monkey King tales, a figure who protects the lowly and oppressed from evil spirits and the caprices of the gods. As Susan Asai notes, "Within the socialist framework of Ho's politics, The Monkey King can be thought of as the equivalent of a working-class hero defying the capitalist, bourgeois forces that oppress the masses."[1] Through all of his works Ho has built an aesthetic informed by political histories as well as his insistence on the efficacy of music to serve as a revolutionary tool of "the people."

It is not only Chinese mythology that inspires him. In the composition, "Monkey Decides to Return Home 'To Right the Great Wrongs'" from *Journey*, Ho's voicings for the horns recall Chinese opera themes, assisted in no small part by the use of instrumentation borrowed from Chinese operatic ensembles. Another work, *Voice of the Dragon: Once upon a Time in Chinese America* (1997), is a reinvention of ancient Chinese myths, the Chinese martial-arts tradition and its popular-culture form, the martial-arts action film, as well as Asian and Afrodiasporic musical influences Ho describes as "Afro-Asian new American multicultural music."[2] We can hear this merging of political acumen and musical hybridity throughout his work.

His work is thus positioned in "already hybrid" spaces complicated by his use of elements gleaned from popular culture. Understanding his own work as operating within a tradition he terms the "popular avant-garde," his use of popular-culture elements is both aesthetic strategy and political advocacy. Defining the popular avant-garde as an aesthetic program dedicated to "elevating standards, promoting the necessity and importance of experimentation but at the same time being rooted, grounded and vibrantly connected to the people," Ho castigates accessibility in art as a needless "dumbing down, a pandering" to popular audiences.[3] He is also wary of various connotations of "avant-garde" because "it can be both purveyor of change or perpetuator of privilege, solipsism and snobbish elitism [particularly if it implies] the completely anti-political position of *l'art pour l'art* (art for art's sake, which I and others would assert, *is* political by asserting the autonomy of art and ideas as standing above society and thereby tacit acquiescence and accommodation to the status quo)."[4]

While Ho's work operates within a context of an historical Asian American jazz movement and its set of political commitments, I pursue a slightly different tack in this chapter, focusing on Ho's articulation of a popular avant-garde. A key element of his aesthetic that has been largely overlooked is the martial-arts film and, in particular, the philosophical texts (films and writings) of actor Bruce Lee as a way of representing Asian American struggles for recognition, thinking about Asian American sources of spiritual knowledge and aesthetic sensibilities, and as an example of the contradictory impulses Ho gathers together in the creation of the popular avant-garde.

In ways similar to the journey *hua pen* narratives took to become valorized as literati cultural production, Ho appropriates the work of Bruce Lee and the marital-arts action-film genre in the creation of his popular avant-garde in order to educate his audiences, provide models of revolutionary and liberatory political action, and to give voice to counterhegemonic perspectives.

Because engendering a revolutionary consciousness in his audiences remains Ho's primary goal, not merely entertaining them with high-concept spectacle (though he assuredly accomplishes that, as well), his creative work remains rooted in a dialectics of education and entertainment, popularity and populism, and tradition and innovation. Through his engagement of the martial arts action film genre, Ho also taps into a longer historical continuum that stretches back to Ming era literature. As Bruce Lee asserted, "In fact tradition is nothing but a formula laid down by experience. As we progress and time changes, it is necessary to reform this formula . . . box-office success is a formula, but will I forget my food and sleep for this dead formula? I, Bruce Lee, am a man who never follows those fearful formulas."[5] Fred Ho is also a man who has chosen to "not forget his food and sleep for a dead formula," forging instead his own unique aesthetic.

Music, Manga . . .

Antonio Gramsci understood "the popular" as a locus of intersecting interests, rhetorics, and representations, a space of both conformity and opposition to elite culture.[6] Similarly recognizing popular culture's hybrid nature, yielding both conservative as well as radical energies, Ho channels his creativity into recognizable forms he can then implode from within, challenging audiences' expectations even as they are entertained. Because Ho's extravagant creativity and unapologetic embrace of consumer cultural signs occurs in tandem with his stated agenda of revolutionary creative production, he interrogates popular culture's commodification of creative work through a provocative set of inquiries into the meanings of various idioms, traditions and cultural hierarchies, especially as he points to "the people" for their tastes and legitimation. For example, Ho's admiration for *Lone Wolf and Cub*, a manga (Japanese comic book) and the movie series it inspired, is not only to participate in *otaku* (manga and anime fan) culture but is also an expression of his political and cultural solidarity with popular audiences.[7]

Ho has written about his idea of revolutionary art and its relation to popular culture, setting a four-point agenda—speak to the people, go to the people, involve the people, and change the people—and emphasizing the need to engage popular audiences, not as an effort to merchandise his art more effectively or to lessen the political impact of his art, but to increase the effectiveness of his creative work in creating a revolutionary consciousness in his audiences.[8] His views echo those of Angela Davis, who has argued that "as Marx and Engels long ago observed, art is a form of social consciousness—a special form of social consciousness that can potentially awaken an urge in those affected by it to creatively transform their oppressive environments. Art can function as a sensitizer and a catalyst, propelling people toward involvement in organized movements seeking to effect radical social change. *Art is special because of its ability to influence feelings as well as knowledge.*"[9] Ho's idea of a popular avant-garde is fundamentally anchored to Davis's idea of popular culture engagement as a means to motivate audiences to question normative assumptions and ideologies.

Ho has been working toward this idea of the popular avant-garde for most of his career. Indeed, decades before he explicitly theorized the popular avant-garde, he looked to some of the most popular forms of jazz in order to drive his aesthetic, with a special attentiveness to the transcultural orientation jazz has long offered the perceptive listener. A robust muscularity energizes Ho's creative energies, and his hypnotic cover of Duke Ellington and Juan Tizol's "Caravan," a composition whose title speaks to cross-cultural exchange and whose dominant modal flavor connects jazz to non-Western musical traditions, speaks directly to a legacy of a "popular avant-garde" in jazz. Ably demonstrating his sympathies and abilities within a jazz tradition, Ho's arrangement of the song from *The Underground Railroad to My Heart* (Soul Note, 1990) highlights the centrality of cross-cultural fusions in Afro-diasporic music and, in particular, within jazz.[10]

The political tenor of jazz artists such as Charles Mingus, Max Roach, or Archie Shepp, who drew equally from the past as well as from their own individual musical aesthetics, were models for Ho's own developing sense of purpose for his music.[11] But it is not only African American precedents Ho recognizes. He cites earlier Asian American cultural expression, writing, "Other early Asian American folk cultural forms include oral tradition of folk stories, ballads, chants and folk songs brought over by the early Asian laborers from their peasant oral traditions." Importantly, "the great body of the Asian American cultural tradition emanates from the working class Asian communities and is [created and performed in] the Asian languages and dialects."[12] In fact, early Asian American folk culture was shaped by the structural racism Asians faced, and their poetry, music, and other cultural activities expressed their "feelings and experiences of separation, loneliness, disappointment, bitterness, pain, anger and struggle."[13] He has also detailed the musical and political histories of an earlier generation of Asian American musicians such as Frank Chin and his group, A Grain of Sand, as well as the folk rock group, Yokohama, California.[14] Ho has tapped into these reserves of Asian American culture in forming his Afro Asian new American multi-cultural music, the musical component of his popular avant-garde.

As ethnomusicologist Wei-hua Zhang observes, "Diversity is [one] of Ho's musical qualities. He likes to synthesize different musical styles and genres and mold them. His expanding use of elements from a variety of musics such as West African, Latin, reggae rhythms, Filipino kulintang, Chinese and Korean instruments, Arabic and Japanese modes, has become characteristic of his compositions. Almost all of his works are marked by multiple sections and changing meters and moods."[15] More importantly to this chapter, the development of Ho's multicultural music increasingly took shape as not only Asian instrumentation and musical aesthetics were blended with Afrodiasporic musical traditions, particularly jazz and rhythm 'n' blues, but took place in conjunction with his idea of the popular avant-garde, utilizing links to Asia that were not bound to the high art cultural traditions such as Japanese Noh or Chinese Peking Opera, but to popular culture forms such as manga and samurai and kung fu film genres.

. . . and Martial Arts

Ho's interest in cultivating a youth audience partially motivated his incorporation of the martial-arts action film, a genre he once found demeaning for its depiction of Asian males as cold-blooded asexual killing machines—a representation of Asian masculinity Ho described as nonhuman at its most basic level.[16] However, Ho was admonished by black Cherokee activist Day Star to recognize the martial arts as part of his tradition and to not allow how it had been "appropriated and misrepresented [in films] influence you because then you're just reacting to it. Take it back! Make it something revolutionary."[17] Her advice forced him to recognize the liberatory possibilities of the martial arts and, by extension, martial-arts movies. In fact, *Voice of the Dragon* was part of Ho's program to "de-Europeanize" the world, fueling his search for alternative models and forms onto which he could transpose his larger creative ambitions.[18]

Soon after his conversation with Day Star, he began incorporating martial-arts choreography and, similar to classical Chinese literary works such as Luo Guanzhong's *The Romance of the Three Kingdoms*, from which martial-arts movies have also taken their narrative cues, Ho's use of Chinese folk tales and mythology has linked these two traditions in his work since the mid-1990s. Significantly, his scores, which are a blend of African American musical practices and instrumentation with Chinese instrumentation and musical aesthetics, form a kreolized accompaniment to his martial-arts-themed works. Ho asserts: "Martial arts and music, for me, have many parallels. Each is a metaphor for the other. Music is about developing a sound that will bring down the walls of Jericho, it's about finding *chi*. Martial arts [also develops] a way to transform form so that it becomes highly individual, agentive and impactful."[19]

For Ho, a compelling component of the Chinese martial arts is the willingness of martial artists to confront and contemplate conflict, particularly confrontations situated beyond emotional, interpersonal antagonisms. Quoting from Bruce Lee's film, *Enter the Dragon*, Ho recalled Lee's words as the final battle commences between Lee and the film's archnemesis Han: "You have offended my family. And you have offended a Shaolin temple." As Ho noted, "[Martial arts] did not *deny* human conflict as so much of the [arts] but deals with real human conflict. [Most artists] want to deal with conflict on the level of emotions but not physical conflict." Importantly, Ho is drawn to the martial arts for his theater productions not only because it appeals to youthful audiences but because modern dance "aesthetics and politics are in complete denial to the real physical world. It has an idealized view of the body and an idealized view of physical reality in which conflict doesn't really exist [. . .] I mean, you can't explain war (or imperialism or colonialism) simply by [pointing to] emotions and interpersonal conflict. [But] the martial arts offers that dimension to movement/performance that modern dance can't."[20]

It is Ho's insistence that the benefits of martial-arts training are not merely manifested in the physical realm but are manifested in its inculcation of self-discipline and a finely tuned sense of ethical, even moral, standards that motivate his utilization of kung fu in his theatrical productions. Ho argues that while conventional action heroes such as James Bond act in "heroic" ways, Bond is not only motivated by self-interest but also works for the state—a conservative, even reactionary, "hero." Bruce Lee, on the other hand, operates on the basis of honor and ethical principles. Ho notes, after quoting Lee's line to Han about offending his family and the Shaolin temple, "[Lee] didn't say, 'You have offended *me*'! His motivation [stemmed] from principle, he's fighting for principles [. . .] Otherwise you're just an opportunist, a hired gun, a mercenary."[21] Importantly, Ho reminds us that blacks and Latinos embraced the martial arts, as well, because it revolutionized, to use his term, their sense of identity by fostering camaraderie and self-discipline.

We can see the ways in which conflict moves beyond the merely personal in order to engage a larger ethical dimension explicitly in *Deadly She-Wolf Assassin at Armageddon!* Ho based *Deadly She-Wolf* on the Japanese manga series *Lone Wolf and Cub*, which recounted the travels of a lone *ronin*, or masterless samurai—the Lone Wolf of the title—and his infant son, Cub. They are on "the road to Hell" in Lone Wolf's efforts to avenge his wife's murder. The series ends with Cub finally killing the man who planned his mother's death. Inspired by Kazuo Koike and Goseki Kojima's tale of vengeance, Ho and Margraff produced *Deadly She-Wolf at Armageddon!* as a parable about an individual's journey toward self-awareness by characters whose destinies are bound by interpersonal as well as larger social histories.

Ho's attraction to Japanese samurai and Hong Kong kung fu films as creative models increased as he began to note these genres' oppositional aesthetics. Additionally, using popular forms such as the martial-arts action film as inspiration and foundation for his aesthetic principles, Ho created works openly celebrating their populist origins.[22] Similar to writer Lu Xun's revolutionary use of woodblock prints in early twentieth-century China, Ho chose to appropriate a degraded form of commodified culture, such as the martial-arts action film, in order to create revolutionary works that subvert hegemonic or corporate-economic signification and authorization.[23] The martial-arts movie *Enter the Dragon* and, in particular, its star, Bruce Lee, influenced Ho's aesthetic and political vision for *The Voice of the Dragon*, a work he describes as a "music and martial arts cantata," ironically citing a high art musical form in tandem with the martial arts.

An example of the value of Lee's work for Ho is his borrowing of Lee's iteration of "the art of fighting without fighting" as an ideal. In *Enter the Dragon*, Lee's character is challenged to a fight by another martial artist, known simply as Parsons, after Lee answers a question about his fighting style with the aphoristic "My style is the art of fighting without fighting." Unable to avoid his challenger, Lee points out that the ship's deck is too small for a fight and suggests taking one of the lifeboats to a small island nearby. Parsons agrees and steps into a lifeboat. Without getting into the lifeboat himself, Lee lets out its lead line, stranding Parsons as he and the lifeboat separate from the larger ship. Handing the line to Chinese ship workers who had suffered abuse from Parsons earlier in the scene, Lee cleverly "fights without fighting."

Clearly echoing Lee's dialogue, Chen Jack, a character in Ho's *Voice of the Dragon*, declares, "To subdue your enemy without fighting is the highest skill." In Ho's popular avant-garde, popular culture is the repository of "folk" knowledge and the subaltern epistemes of "the people," who, he recognizes, are no longer the peasants of rural seventeenth-century China (the period in which *Voice of the Dragon* is set) but are, to varying degrees, cosmopolitan subjects whose common ground can be found in popular culture. Thus, Ho positions his music and creative work within the same discursive turf populated by devalued popular culture forms such as the martial-arts film genre in order to reach those audiences he is most interested in educating—people, particularly the young, who are marginalized and oppressed because of their skin color, class, and/or gender positioning.

Defending his decision to use martial arts films as a creative template, Ho cited an introductory scene in *Enter the Dragon* of a conversation between Lee and his Shaolin master teacher to illustrate how Lee was a philosopher-fighter whose martial-arts skills had "gone beyond the mere physical level [to reach] the point of spiritual insight."[24] When asked to name the highest technical level he hopes to achieve, Lee replied, "To have no technique." Ho views this intuitive, "down to the cellular level" act of *immersion* in an aesthetic and technical tradition acts to *transcend* conventional limits and, as his self-taught musicking attests, mirrors his own immersion in jazz through working with established jazz artists such as Archie Shepp as important first steps that enabled him to work through the jazz tradition and eventually transcend it.

The idea of going "beyond technique" in order to educate, enlighten, and perhaps, provoke audiences to "fight for righteousness" also speaks to Ho's ideas about the nature of aesthetics in the twenty-first century. Keeping in mind V. I. Lenin's dictum, "Ethics will be the aesthetics of the future," he writes, "[Musical] notation is not the enslaver, the oppressor of spontaneity and improvisation. Calcification, de–African Americanization, co-option is not caused by musical deviations and practices, but, in my view, by *ethical violations* [. . .] As a non–African American, but a person of color (oppressed nationality in the US), *I was drawn to and inspired and revolutionized by [Afrodiasporic] music's* musical and—possibly more profoundly—*extramusical qualities*."[25] In other words, the fusion of musical and dramatic materials function not as an aesthetic end in itself but to serve liberatory goals.

Ho further links the martial arts and black music by asserting that Lee was "the Asian John Coltrane."[26] In order to understand this comparison, it helps to recall Amiri Baraka's assertion (writing under the name LeRoi Jones) that "John Coltrane [. . .] is an example of the secular yearning for the complete change, for the religious, the spiritual."[27] Coltrane, recognized widely in the jazz world as one of the most visible advocates for the spiritual impulse running through jazz music, cast a wide influential net. For his part, Coltrane recognized music's affective powers and looked for ways in which to focus his music toward benevolent ends. Coltrane explains:

> I've already been looking into those approaches to music—as in India—in which particular sounds and scales are intended to produce specific emotional meanings [. . .] I would like to bring to people something like happiness. I

> would like to discover a method so that if I want it to rain, it will start right away to rain. If one of my friends is ill, I'd like to play a certain song and he will be cured; when he'd be broke, I'd bring out a different song and immediately he'd receive all the money he needed. But what are these pieces and what is the road to travel to attain knowledge of them, that I don't know. *The true powers of music are still unknown. To be able to control them must be, I believe, the goal of every musician.* I'm passionate about understanding these forces. I would like to provoke reactions in the listeners to my music, to create a real atmosphere. It's in that direction that I want to commit myself and to go as far as possible.[28]

Ho views the creation of an Afro Asian multicultural music in the same way, declaring, "I was profoundly drawn to and inspired by African American music as the expression of an oppressed nationality, for both its social role as protest and resistance to national oppression, and for its musical energy and revolutionary aesthetics," commenting further on the various ways African musicians transformed various Western European musical practices and assumptions through their own aesthetic frameworks to create vital African American music cultures and traditions.[29] As stated earlier, Ho, like Coltrane, believes the shamanistic power of African music—and by extension, African American music—enables the music to "reach down to the cellular level" and empower both musician and listener.

He further supports his comparison of Lee and Coltrane by noting that both were iconoclastic innovators. In 1960, Coltrane recorded *The Avant-Garde*, announcing his immersion in free jazz aesthetics, which did much to legitimize the style for some jazz critics due to Coltrane's proven stature within mainstream jazz. In Lee's case, his "total system," as Ho calls it, known as *jeet kune do* was a break from traditional kung fu, incorporating not only martial arts techniques but a philosophy with a strong Taoist influence, as well. Furthermore, Ho points to Lee's assertion that, using self-discipline and a high degree of intuition, an individual who has been "trained" by philosophical ideas found in Taoism and Buddhism, must often act in opposition to hegemonic interests in order to maintain her political, ethical, and artistic integrity.

Traditions of Change

Tradition has its uses, though the contradiction of using traditions to break away from traditions further problematizes the use of popular culture elements. Lee consciously utilized Chinese literary tropes in the subversion of stereotypes of the Asian male in the film *Enter the Dragon*—a move Ho would also initiate for his multimedia martial-arts stage extravaganzas. Lee was aware of the philosophical underpinnings of this engagement and used Chinese philosophy, particularly Taoism, as a way to subvert Chinese traditional culture as well as Western representations and misrepresentations of Chinese ethnicity. Two Ming novels involved with the martial arts and the uses of tradition, including religious ones—*The Romance of the Three Kingdoms* and *Outlaws of the Marsh*—also inverted the traditions they faced, forming a tradition of Chinese letters that periodically "turned on itself." In his attempt to raise the level of discourse in a Chinese martial-arts film, Lee used strategies that earlier Ming novelists employed and for the same purpose that would inspire Ho in his revolutionary works, namely, to create works that challenged hegemonic interests and questioned normative assumptions held within dominant ideological positions.

The idea of connecting a creative artist to philosophical, spiritual, and/or political interests is foreshadowed in Chinese letters by Luo Guanzhong, the author of *Three Kingdoms*. Chinese literature scholar Andrew Plaks writes about these dual roles in the Ming period: "Many of the individuals who were prominent in the sparkling successes of various fields of literati culture in the sixteenth century, including drama, were directly involved in one way or another in the formation of the vernacular novel genre. . . . We may recall, by the way, that Lo Kuan-chung (Luo Guanzhong) was also a man of the theater; in fact, what little we know about him derives from this connection alone."[30] The fact that these novelists drew on older historiographical works is another indication of the periodical reframing of Chinese literary signification.

Still, for all his philosophizing, Lee placed a high value on the utility of martial-arts skills; namely, the ability to physically attack and counterattack adversaries. This is not the usual position of philosophers—they may argue vehemently with one another, but there is a low tolerance for physical negotiation. Lee addressed this martial-arts ideal:

> I say that if you want something beautiful, take modern dancing. What good would it do a boxer to learn to meditate? He's a fighter, not a monk. It's all too ritualistic, what with bowing and posturing. That sort of Oriental self-defense is like swimming on land. You can learn all the swimming strokes, but if you're never in the water, it's nonsense. These guys never fight. They all want to break three-inch boards or two bricks or something. Why? That doesn't make them fighters.[31]

This emphasis on utilitarian values separates Lee from what he perceived as a false reliance on tradition or an overemphasized valorization of historical precedent. Lee was explicit about the need to remain flexible, stating, "At present I am working on the script for my next film. I haven't really decided on the title yet, but what I want to show is the necessity to adapt oneself to changing circumstances. *The inability to adapt brings destruction.*"[32]

The emphasis on practical—educational, transformative—agendas for their creative work connects Ho and Lee to earlier Chinese philosophical traditions, as well. Chinese historian Ronald G. Dimberg writes of Confucian practice, "Confucius was not interested in the Way of Heaven as an abstract concept, but in its practical application in the realm of human endeavor."[33] When a disciple of Confucius told him a hermit was teaching people to renounce the world, Confucius answered, "If I am not to be a man among other men, then what am I to be? If the Way prevailed in the world, I should not be trying to alter things."[34]

Likewise, Ho envisions his creative works as performances of social change, as ways to create new social relations. For instance, for *Warrior Sisters: The New Adventures of African and Asian Womyn Warriors*, he "encouraged a 'Third World' cross-cultural casting [of African and Asian women], *hoping to encourage greater 'Third World' consciousness and solidarity*."[35] He went beyond merely casting African and Asian women, however, by insisting on having "singers of African descent perform Asian roles and singers of Asian descent perform African roles," clearly demonstrating the realization of a multicultural perspective that is not rooted in essentialist notions attached to race or nationality.[36] He further complicated the high/low cultural hierarchical divide by mixing singers of both Western opera and "pop-soul" backgrounds.[37]

Adaptability and flexibility also resonate across both men's work in their relationship to improvisation. Ho argues that Lee was a master improviser, stating unequivocally that Lee's "*Jeet Kune Do* is a manual and a manifesto for improvisation. [Lee] says, for example, the point of technique is to have no technique. [Lee] talks about learning to be intuitive. He says, yes, you can study forms and so forth but you can't be a prisoner of them."[38] Ho has claimed that the same attitude pervades his artistic work, arguing that "tradition is not something you go back to—it's something you build upon and hopefully [you are able to] make an innovation. Tradition doesn't go backward, it goes forward because it has a lot of struggle in it."[39] As I have been arguing, both artists operate within a devalued popular idiom, the martial-arts action genre, and must negotiate between the Scylla of attracting and entertaining popular audiences and the Charybdis of the hegemonic interests that authorize and legitimize cultural production of any kind (or, at the very least, significantly impact the ideological and discursive positioning of both popular culture and its audiences).

Similar to Ho, Lee saw "backwardness" in strict adherence to Chinese tradition. "What is *Jeet Kune Do*? Chinese martial art, definitely! It is a kind of Chinese martial art that does away with the distinction of branches, an art that rejects formality, and *an art that is liberated from tradition*."[40] Lee tackled hegemonic power by subverting what had been fetishized by colonial powers, namely, traditional arts frozen in an exoticized, pre-European contact past. "The classical man [Lee's term for a tradition-bound subject] is just a bundle of routine, ideas and tradition. When he acts, he is translating every living moment in terms of the old." Moreover, "[If] you follow the classical pattern, you are understanding the routine, the tradition, the shadow—you are not understanding yourself." He also asks, "How can one respond to the totality with [a] partial, fragmentary pattern?" His answer is that "[when] one is not expressing himself, he is not free. Thus, he begins to struggle and the struggle breeds methodical routine. Soon, he is doing his methodical routine as response rather than responding to what *is*."[41]

Lee also criticized the nativist view that maintains that "preserving" a cultural essence is an act of resistance showing, instead, that it is merely a posture of acquiescence to hegemonic discourse. Lee addressed the real world of negotiation: "In daily living, one must follow the course of the barrier. To try to assail it will only destroy the instrument [the fetishized object]. And no matter what some people will say, barriers are not the experience of any one person, or any one group of persons. *They are the universal experience.*"[42] Lee's martial art "non-style," *jeet kune do*, had as one of its defining tenets this goal of "liberation from tradition."

Ho has also refused to remain tied to either external political and artistic trends or even to his own political stances. As the Asian American movement began to fracture, he began associating with younger activists who criticized the earlier Asian American movement for its sexism and unexamined patriarchal notions regarding gender relations. He admitted, "Many twenty-something womyn activists educated me about the question of patriarchy," and his studies of Marxist and radical feminist theory eventually led to a collaboration with Ann T. Greene on *Warrior Sisters: The New Adventures of African and Asian Womyn Warriors*, an "action adventure opera about the escape from a New Jersey prison of Black Liberation Army leader Assata Shakur told as a myth-epic."[43] Ho's use of current popular culture to educate audiences to "hidden histories" such as the story of Shakur echoes the Neo-Confucian *hua pen* storytelling legacy of the Sung and Ming dynastic periods, a popular form of oral storytelling among children and peasants as well as elite adults that was officially circumscribed as folk culture and thought unworthy of the serious attentions of elite literati of the period.[44]

Ho's "irreverent" use of both high and low cultural elements—indeed, his reengineering of cultural elements—is predicated on his four-point agenda of speaking to, going to, involving and, ultimately, changing the people. In his ironic use of the term *opera* to describe his multimedia works, Ho, like Lee and their antecedent storytellers, fixes his sights on two aspirational ideals. The first is the innovative extension of tradition, that is, using traditional elements but in reconfigured ways that speak to contemporary realities rather than reinscribing hidebound dogma. The second involves the movement of vernacular traditions into valorized art forms that follow from the refiguring of prior tradition. It is this cycling and recycling movement of innovation, sacralization, and back again that marks the dialectical dance between popular artists and high cultural legitimation. Ho's formulation is all the more powerful for not simply invoking an "eternal return" but a spiraling "changing same," to borrow Amiri Baraka's term for black cultural variation that retains a unique, core aesthetic perspective. While strategically essentialist, Baraka's formulation explains the continuing power of Afrodiasporic culture and helps us comprehend Ho's use of popular cultural forms that in their articulation of radical politics constitute an "avant-garde."

Ho uses this idea of cyclical innovation and cultural reinvigoration in his use of popular forms such as martial arts and samurai films—and particularly their international appeal—as a means to "capture and evoke the spirit of folk music" in his shaping of an Afro Asian new American multicultural music.[45] Arguing for their value in opening up spaces of opposition to and recalibration of cultural norms *that are embedded within the forms themselves*, Ho creates manga-inspired operas that express both a populist desire for a better vision of reality (heroic tales of the individual overcoming institutionalized adversity, for example) as well as his own political ideas that might be harnessed to such a vision. Or, as he succinctly put it, "My goal is a radical unity of form and content." Similar to Bruce Lee's admonition that swimming on land is a nonsensical exercise, Ho is uninterested in enacting a "methodical routine as response." In fact, challenging routine allows Ho to reconfigure martial-arts narrative tropes in ways that recall Ming period literary aesthetics.

Conclusion

Daniel Inosanto, a martial-arts student of Lee's as well as an expert *karateka*, noted in an interview, "[Bruce Lee] felt very strongly that if he could get people to appreciate something in the Chinese culture, then they would appreciate something in other cultures as well. He felt that he was doing his small part in establishing something toward world peace and harmony and understanding among other people of different cultures."[46] Lee, himself, states unequivocally, "Although others may disagree, to me, racial barriers do not exist in reality. If I say that 'everyone under the sun is a member of a universal family,' you may think that I am bluffing and being idealistic. But if anyone still believes in racial differences, I think he is being too backward and narrow in his perspective. Perhaps he still does not understand man's equality and love."[47]

Ho's Afro Asian multicultural music is an aural complement to the idea that a multicultural ethos might arise to subdue or overcome the divisive idea of "pure" cultures or the unyielding allegiance to conservative notions of culture. While using the characterizations and scenarios that have been handed to him from the Ming novels, *The Romance of the Three Kingdoms* and *The Outlaws of the Marsh*, via the martial-arts film genre, Ho has used them to show the inability of tradition *by itself* to give contemporary Asian Americans a voice as well as to reveal how tradition can be used to evoke a multicultural perspective that transcends the limits of race, gender, and nationality. As Rey Chow writes, "In the 'third world,' the displacement of modernism is not simply a matter of criticizing modernism as theory, philosophy, or ideas of cognition; rather, it is the emergence of an entirely different problematic, a displacement of a displacement that is in excess of what is still presented as the binarisms of modernism-postmodernism."[48]

Indeed, it is Ho's innovations on the myriad set of influences and traditions through which he creates that lend his work such remarkable power. The popular avant-garde, then, is more than a means to educate—it is a powerful cultural adjunct to revolutionary action. Ho asserts, "Many would say: Fred, let's focus on what's possible. Or, Fred, your ideological and political predilection seems to preclude propensities for the here-and-now possible reforms. But I will only quote Sun Ra in response: Everything possible has been tried and nothing has changed. What we need is the Impossible. The music we make must embrace the Impossible in the arduous journey to make the music a true force for social revolution."[49]

Figure 5. Asian American Art Ensemble, 1985. Credit: Ken Shung

Figure 6. Asian American Art Ensemble. Credit: Unknown

In sum, Ho's popular avant-garde is a masterful blend of Afrodiasporic and Asian musicking, Chinese martial arts and the martial arts action film genre and draws its counterhegemonic power from its ability to reach audiences without having to dilute its revolutionary message or massage its transformative ideological impulse. Asian martial arts such as *kung fu* and *karate*, after all, originated in the practical strategies for confronting elite power by oppressed populations who had been stripped of weapons other than their bodies and intellects. Binding the popular avant-garde to his iteration of an Afro Asian new American multicultural music, Ho's creative works demonstrate the inherent power of subaltern cultural production despite its marginalization, occlusion, and/or defamation by dominant cultural hierarchies by voicing truth to power. By placing these "impossible" examples of multiple multicultural perspectives within his hybrid cultural productions, Ho ably demonstrates the possibilities his popular avant-garde art hold for advancing progressive, even radical, social transformation.

Notes

1. Asai, "Cultural Politics," 98.
2. Ho, "'Jazz,' Kreolization and Revolutionary Music for the 21st Century," 142.
3. Interview with the author, September 5, 2007.
4. Ho, "Imagine," original emphasis.
5. Lee, *Words*, 119.
6. See Antonio Gramsci, *Selections from Cultural Writings*, trans. William Boelhower (Cambridge, Mass.: Harvard University Press, 1991, c1985).
7. Interview with the author.
8. Ho, "Revolutionary," 289.
9. Davis, "Art on the Frontline," 236, added emphasis.
10. For a cogent investigation of Ho's work in relation to jazz, see Asai, "Cultural Politics." She also provides a succinct biography of Ho's early activist and musical activities. For a more detailed biographical sketch, see Zhang, "Fred Wei-han Ho." Ho provides an autobiographical outline of his public activities in his "Beyond Asian American Jazz."
11. Ho mentions Mingus, along with Ellington, John Coltrane, and Archie Shepp, as musical influences in an interview with Fiona Ma, "Talking about a Revolution."
12. Ho, "Revolutionary," 384.
13. Ibid.
14. See Ho, "An ABC from NYC."
15. Zhang, "Fred Wei-Han Ho," 96.
16. Ho is aware of other U.S. popular culture misrepresentations of Asian males such as the emasculated laundry boy and cook, employed in the domestic tasks gen-

dered female under U.S. patriarchy. See R. Lee, *Orientals*, for a cogent study of the ways in which Asian males have been represented and misrepresented in popular culture. Lee addressed other stereotypes of Asian males in a response to an offer to portray Charlie Chan's son in a television series that was to be titled *Number One Son*. Lee, in rejecting the offer, said, "It's about time we had an Oriental hero. Never mind some guy bouncing around the country in a pigtail or something. *I have to be a real human being*. No cook. No laundryman" (Lee, *Words*, 98, added emphasis). His constant struggle was to "be a real human being." This was not just an internal struggle but a battle that he waged in the world, in the society of men, much like the heroes of *Three Kingdoms* and *Outlaws*. As noted in the text, Lee placed himself within a contemporary perspective that transcended historicism or an overly reverential reliance on tradition.

17. Interview with the author, September 5, 2007.

18. See Kyle Gann, "Monkey Business."

19. Interview with the author.

20. Ibid.

21. Interview with the author.

22. See B. Lee, *Tao of Jeet Kune Do*, a journal of Lee's philosophical and aesthetic thoughts.

23. For more on Lu Xun and the historical context in which he operated, see Spence, *Gate of Heavenly Peace*.

24. This quotation begins the conversation between Bruce Lee and his master teacher under discussion. This scene was cut from the original theater and video releases of the film.

25. Ho, "Revolutionary Asian American Art," 288–89, emphasis added.

26. Ho, interview with the author.

27. Baraka, *Black Music*, 198.

28. Quoted in Porter, *John Coltrane*, 211, emphasis added. I am indebted to Porter's explication of these interviews for the information contained in this paragraph. The chapter titled, "So Much More to Do," from which this quotation is taken, deals at length with Coltrane's interconnected interest in spirituality and music.

29. Ho, "'Jazz,' Kreolization and Revolutionary Music for the 21st Century," 135.

30. Plaks, *Four Masterworks*, 44.

31. B. Lee, *Words*, 65.

32. Ibid., 138, added emphasis. The film to which Lee refers, *Game of Death*, was uncompleted at the time of his death, and the ending was constructed from the footage that was already shot. However, it is highly unlikely that the *Game of Death* film one sees today is a product Lee would endorse, as it abandons much of his philosophizing.

33. Dimberg, *Sage and Society*, 3.

34. Quoted in ibid., 3.

35. Ho, "Beyond," 49, emphasis added.

36. Ibid., 49.

37. Ibid., 49.

38. Ho, interview with the author.

39. Ibid.

40. B. Lee, *Words*, 127, added emphasis.

41. B. Lee, *Tao*, 16, 17, 16–17, original emphasis.

42. Little, *Warrior Within*, 47, added emphasis.

43. Ho, "Beyond," 49.

44. For informative surveys on the Ming and Sung literary traditions, see Hsia, *Classic Chinese Novel*, and Hsun, *Brief History of Chinese Fiction*.

45. Ho, "'Jazz,' Kreolization and Revolutionary Music for the 21st Century," 140.

46. Little, *Warrior Within*, xxxiii.

47. B. Lee, *Words*, 82.

48. Chow, *Writing Diaspora*, 57.

49. Ho, "Imagine," n.p.

Works Cited

Asai, Susan M. "Cultural Politics: The African American Connection in Asian American Jazz-based Music." *Asian Music* v36n1 winter/spring 2005: 87–108.

Baraka, Amiri (LeRoi Jones). *Black Music*. New York: Apollo-William Morrow, 1968.

Chow, Rey. *Writing Diaspora: Tactics of Intervention in Contemporary Cultural Studies*. Bloomington: Indiana University Press, 1993.

Davis, Angela. "Art on the Frontline." *The Angela Davis Reader*. Ed. Joy James. Malden, Mass., and Oxford: Blackwell, 1998.

Dimberg, Ronald G. *The Sage and Society: The Life and Thought of Ho Hsin-yin*. Honolulu: University Press of Hawai'i, 1974.

Farquhar, Judith, and Mary L. Doi. "Bruce Lee vs. Fu Manchu: Kung Fu Films and Asian American Stereotypes in America." *Bridge: An Asian American Perspective* fall 1978: 23–40.

Floyd, Samuel, Jr. *The Power of Black Music: Interpreting Its History from Africa to the United States*. New York and Oxford: Oxford University Press, 1995.

Gann, Kyle. "Monkey Business: Fred Ho De-Europeanizes Opera With Martial Arts," *Village Voice* 19–25 Nov. 1997.

Guanzhong, Luo. *Three Kingdoms: A Historical Novel*. Trans. Robert Moss. Beijing and Berkeley: Foreign Languages Press and University of California Press, 1999.

———, and Shi Nai'an. *Outlaws of the Marsh*. Trans. Sidney Shapiro. Beijing and Bloomington: Foreign Languages Press and Indiana University Press, 1981.

Ho, Fred. "An ABC from NYC: 'Charlie' Chin: Asian American Singer and Songwriter." *East Wind* spring/summer 1986: 29–31.

———. "Beyond Asian American Jazz: My Musical and Political Changes in the Asian American Movement." *Leonardo Music Journal* v9 1999: 45–51.

———. "Imagine the Impossible! Perpetuating the Avant-Garde in African American Music." Keynote address for the Fourth Annual Interdisciplinary Jazz Studies Colloquium, "What's Avant-Garde about the Avant-Garde," University of Kansas, 30–31 March 2007.

———. "'Jazz,' Kreolization and Revolutionary Music for the 21st Century." *Sounding Off! Music as Subversion, Resistance, Revolution.* Ed. Ron Sakolsky and Fred Wei-Han Ho. Brooklyn, N.Y.: Autonomedia, 1995.

———."Revolutionary Asian American Art: Tradition and Change, Inheritance and Innovation, Not Imitation!" *Legacy to Liberation: Politics and Culture of Revolutionary Asian Pacific America.* Ed. Fred Ho, Carolyn Antonio, Diane Fujino, and Steve Yip. San Francisco: AK Press, 2000.

———. "What Makes 'Jazz' the Revolutionary Music of the 20th Century, and Will It Be Revolutionary for the 21st Century?" *African American Review* v29n2 1995: 283–90.

Hong, Terry. "Rebel Yellow: In his Bold Multimedia Performance Pieces, Saxophonist and Composer Fred Ho Combines Politics, Prose and a Dash of Revolutionary Fervor." *A. Magazine* 31 March 1998: 78.

Hsia, C. T. *The Classic Chinese Novel: A Critical Introduction.* New York: Columbia University Press, 1968.

Hsun, Lu. *A Brief History of Chinese Fiction.* Peking: Foreign Languages, 1959.

Kim, Jungwon. "Intersections." *A. Magazine* Feb./Mar. 1999: 39+.

Lee, Bruce. *Tao of Jeet Kune Do.* Santa Clarita, Calif.: Ohara Publications, 1975.

———. *Words of the Dragon: Interviews 1958–1973.* Ed. John R. Little. Boston: Tuttle, 1997.Lee, Robert G. *Orientals: Asian Americans in Popular Culture.* Philadelphia: Temple UP, 1999.

Little, John. *The Warrior Within: The Philosophies of Bruce Lee to Better Understand the World around You and Achieve a Rewarding Life.* Chicago: Contemporary, 1996.

Ma, Fiona. "Talking about a Revolution: Fred Ho's Monkey Orchestra Shakes Up the San Francisco International Jazz Festival" *AsianWeek* v20n11 11 Nov 1998: 21.

Ming, Lai. *A History of Chinese Literature.* New York: Day, 1964.

Plaks, Andrew. *The Four Masterworks of the Ming Novel.* Princeton, N.J.: Princeton University Press, 1987.

Porter, Lewis. *John Coltrane: His Life and Music.* Ann Arbor: University of Michigan Press, 1999.

Rolston, David L., ed. *How to Read the Chinese Novel.* Princeton, N.J.: Princeton University Press, 1990.

Shatz, Adam. "New Seekers in Jazz Look to the East." *New York Times* 23 Nov. 1997.

Spence, Jonathan. *The Gate of Heavenly Peace: The Chinese and Their Revolution, 1895–1980.* New York: Penguin, 1982 [1981].

Thomas, Bruce. *Bruce Lee: Fighting Spirit.* Berkeley, Calif.: Frog, 1994.

Zhang, Wei-hua. "Fred Wei-Han Ho: Case Study of a Chinese-American Creative Musician." *Asian Music* v25n1/2 1993/1994: 81–114.

2

"Oh the Hilt, the Hilt Again Please"

A Glimpse Inside the Making of Operas with Fred Ho

RUTH MARGRAFF

I used to think jazz sounded expensive, until the day I met Fred Ho in 1997. He put on a recording of *Journey beyond the West*, and I remember the force of his music trembled a stained-glass fish lamp against the Park Slope sunshine in Brooklyn, streaked in darkness. Fred had asked my beloved mentor Aishah Rahman to recommend a radical writer who could "kick his ass." I had studied playwriting with Aishah at Brown University, and Fred played music for her *Lady Day* Billie Holiday musical back in 1972. Fred says that at first Aishah told him there was no one, and then she thought of me.

So Fred grilled my politics that day, as we dreamed up a vampire that would become the central character in our first collaboration, *Night Vision: A Third to First World Vampyre Opera.*[1] Fred said "the first shall be last" and I said, quietly, "that won't change anything." I believed form was more radical than content because any message can fit into the capitalist system but we came to agree that artists should be radical in form and content both. Fred would ask me who my enemies were and I would say I didn't want any enemies—not knowing there were at least three standing closer than a brother, undermining my every move. When we returned to these debates later, maybe because I bought him dinner, Fred once made me so mad I told him I'd eat out of a dumpster if we could get along. We were changing in proximity by then—both of us warriors.

I was forever trying to write the swords I heard in Fred's music. In writing "Red Sheath for the Modern Revolutionary Peking Opera" that ends my play

Red Frogs, I described the ornaments of a sword with "rage uncircumcised in jaded dragons that would melt against your fist." I wrote about a warrior's name that was "gilt in a thrust of waists, ungirded to the underside of our suspended mounts, so binded to the double edg'ed edge" . . . I tried sometimes, as yin to Fred's yang, to "weep the porcelain to silk, gunpowder into tea."[2] For *Night Vision*, I laid out photocopies of blood magnified 300× all over my basement apartment—some of which looked like negatives of suburban trees or telephone wires coming out of the back of a house, some like the painted chaos of Jackson Pollock. I became obsessed with stealth bombers, crusader art, Iraqi Bedouin songs, and Disney Davids. For my "Heartsong Aria" of *Night Vision*, I wrote the electricity of a vampire's heart transfusing blood with darkness:

> Claiming to preserve us as the sacrifice goes limp
> You knew a thousand years ago my pulse would stir your fetus
> To the thrall sealed shut against the wide-eyed glottis (dragging
> me down like an arrow) . . . when I open up my heart
> When I open up my heart
> Made like slaughter in the dark I seem to you? My lamb shorn
> to the breast?
> Stripped to the murmur?
> Thus you lust the savage by mistake. (*Night Vision*, 2000)

I always heard the swords there, striking and flashing in Fred's music—not for the martial-arts choreography on stage, but drawn of the much deeper scarlet of revolution. I came to Fred almost cavalier in the privacy of my own innate rebellions on form that he called "white downtown." He challenged me to think more politically, which I had evaded, because I was a pacifist and the son of a Baptist preacherman, having once converted scores of people to what I no longer believed. I remember one of Fred's syllogisms as "If you are white in a white supremacist society, you are a white supremacist." This stopped me in my tracks and made me read a lot of Marxist theory, including Butch Lee and Red Rover's *Night-Vision: Illuminating War and Class on the Neo-Colonial Terrain* (1993), which Fred loaned to me.

Because of Fred, because of traveling to war-torn Bosnia in 1999, because of teaching remedial English in Crown Heights, Brooklyn, to adults who would miss class because they were in jail, pumping drugs in the broom closet, or getting a restraining order—the proscenium of my world imploded around the time I was writing *Night Vision*. I had been writing *The Cry Pitch Carrolls*, which I called a nativity operetta set in a nostalgic nuclear winter. Looking back, I realize the *Carrolls* contain a parody of the whiteness of the New York downtown experimental theater world in which I worked at the time, in addition to being an allegory of the snow globe I lived in from ages five to nine in Ishpeming, Michigan. *Night Vision* marks a point of departure or point of origin in my work that probably has most to do with my collaborations with Fred Ho. I found myself in the crucible every American should acknowledge—that of Ralph Ellison's *Invisible Man*. I felt myself growing resistant toward what I have come to understand as a U.S. proclivity to "overidentify"[3] cultural subjectivity as singular and exterior.[4] Slovenian philosopher Slavoj Žižek claims "You are always split between what you are as subject . . . and the external place where the truth about you is inscribed."[5] I felt this invisible split in my sociopolitical identity that I have recently been writing about as a marking of a "self" in alliance with an "other" or as a swollen antagonism that must resist the swollen [white] protagonism of our dominant U.S. narratives.

In *Night Vision*, we wrote this resistance as an "en-Nightenment" to challenge the Eurocentric enlightenment that brought us imperialism and what I call evangelical capitalism.[6] The "en-nightenment" of *Night Vision* calls for us to acknowledge who we are in the platforms of social power and nature, and how we will identify in the seams of Self and Other that are not visible, but make up our own private and public actions, alliances and desires. In the intimate duet of "Incomplete Blindness," the Troubadour is nearly seduced to understand the point of view of 'Ajlinna id-Dibayih, our Vampyre, but finds that he would have to give up too much of his own privilege to go further into this abyss:

And when
It's deathly quiet in the shadow
When I listened to—
I thought your velvet voice
En-nightened by the night
I thought about your fresh temptations
Pressed dark in the vinyl (by the needle). (*Night Vision*, 2000)

In my notes, I have the transcription of a phone call with Fred from around 1998, after writing for a year on *Night Vision* and hearing the first rehearsal tape of the partial score we recorded at New Dramatists:[7]

FRED: What did you think?
RUTH: Do you have a minute—are you in the middle of something?
FRED: No. I have to leave in 10 minutes. (*Silence*) You didn't like it.

RUTH: No. I liked it.
FRED: Well then what, what are you saying? What do you mean, just say it.
RUTH: Well I thought I heard something when it was live. I was afraid to listen to the tape. I almost couldn't listen to it at first.
FRED: Why? Why not?
RUTH: I've been up all night, just staring at the wall, I haven't moved since I came home and the tape is still in the—in the . . .
FRED: Why? You don't like the music? You don't like the tape?
RUTH: That's not the problem. I thought I heard something there when it was live that I haven't heard in any of your other music. Something that doesn't exist.
FRED: What do you mean? What are you saying?
RUTH: It's irrational. I'm fine now.
FRED: This is a very good piece.
RUTH: I know that.
FRED: We have to let everyone feel that. You have to stay focused. You have to stay on track. You have to call the directors and finish writing this. We have to think bigger.
RUTH: I know. I am on track. I'm fine now.

It was one of the times in my life where I could see all the way down into the bones of the music. I could feel something there that was arresting in a way that made it unbearable for me to move because I knew it would inspire me for years. It was unlike anything I had ever heard. I couldn't articulate what it meant but later could see it was prophetic; it was dangerous. A work of art, it was both ancient and before its time.

When we presented the first concert of *Night Vision* at the Cooper Union's Great Hall, the opera police descended on us like hounds, saying the libretto and the music were far too dense to be an opera.[8] We had transgressed the genre of opera with a text too poetic to be set to music, and much too irreverent. And the music was too formidable also, fighting the velocities of the text. In short, this opera was radical in form and content both, and this would be why we had to start working in reverse; Fred would write the music first and work with me in weekly story meetings, a process we have used throughout our *Voice of the Dragon* trilogy. This method was a necessity in order to continue to control the means of our own production in a climate growing to a stranglehold of conservatism after 9/11. *Night Vision* was never produced again after its premiere in a downtown black box of Here Arts Center in New York, while our *Voice of the Dragon* trilogy has been commercially successful, touring nationally to critical acclaim. From this, I learned that sometimes I must work more stealthily to subvert my radical aesthetics in order to reach a broader audience with radical content. I always keep at least one project close to my heart that is uncompromised while I am doing this so that my instincts will survive the hostile terrain.

I used to say I work 18-hour days and that the only person I know who works 21-hour days is Fred Ho. I know this because I was privy for years to Fred's inner circle and have eaten many meals in which Fred gets up to take a call, pick up a fax, or the doorbell rings. It is 100,000 percent always about Fred's work. But, at the same time, Fred also instigates many adventures that stretch beyond the standard conception of work. A few unforgettable glimpses:

- Fred's cowboy boots, designed in Austin, Texas, with Black Panthers on them in vibrant color
- Buckwheat pancakes with blueberries and the way Fred makes a spinach salad
- Walking home from the Revolution Bookstore planning a future uprising for cities across America
- Eating at Sun Lok Kee with a dozen different casts of shows before it burned down
- Finding a boxed set of *Romance of the Three Kingdoms* in English at a hidden bookstore in Chinatown
- Looking down at clear jelly fish that washed ashore on Jones Beach and Fred telling me deadpan that they were silicone breast implants
- Reading hundreds of graphic novels standing in comic book stores all over New York City, many of which don't exist anymore
- Strolling all over Chinatown, especially the boutiques on Mott Street that sell the gorgeous decorated jackets I still wear, textile stores with bolts of gold cloth dragons, kimono shops in the East Village. And wearing hand-me-down Fred Ho designs (!)
- Screening thousands of bootlegged videotapes of Hong Kong cinema favorites sharing Fred's tapes and DVDs back and forth for years, many without subtitles and from a few stores in Midtown that kept shifting to different corners
- Dinner with Mary Sharp Cronson upstairs in the hourglass restaurant over by theater row[9]
- Hanging out on the second floor of the old Pearl River store, where the Peking Opera bootlegs used to play continuously on the VCR
- Packing up millions of books when Fred sold his loft

- Triple-fortune sandalwood soap
- The pencil mark on the wall of Fred's Greenpoint apartment from when he first moved in, about where to make a chamber for playing his baritone sax

In the past ten years, I've almost learned to read the mind of Fred Ho. Cowriting more than seven operas and various songs, we have worked for years almost daily together to create, imagine, and produce works that fly in the face of the numbing mainstream, that press against the riptides pulling down a maelstrom of coopted complacence, dulling the blades of instinct in the spawn of benign imitations from our proactive generation.

What I have come to love about Fred Ho is that he knows inherently the art of the struggle, the sheer labor, the defiant will of what it takes to live the hour of the wolf. When we wrote the title character of *Deadly She-Wolf Assassin at Armageddon!*, we created a female wolf who was raised as a weapon with "no name, no art, no trace but shadows." When she discovers that her lifelong target is in fact her father, she says, as she fights him to the death, "I could always feel your strength. Across the fields. I forged my rhythms to your own. In the silhouettes of my inferno, distilled upon my soul. You were always there, preying on the fangs of the corrupt that threaten the survival of the pack. Without vengeance, without doubt."[10] I feel this way about Fred—that I will always feel his strength in the world now, no matter how far apart we might live or sojourn. I think the Lone Wolf[11] legacy of Japanese manga, films, and novels that influenced Fred's concept spoke to me because our She-Wolf is struck by fate rather than by a conventional American dream. First, in being given the bloody office of counterassassin and, then, by being hunted and hated by the empire and all its minions in eventual exile. This is the loneliness of an instinct that moves beyond institutional intuition, beyond monolithic acceleration of opportunism, to the rare and radical way of the Wolf. I see Fred and even myself as having been given, likewise, not the American pie-in-the-sky dreamy sort of lives or careers—we have been given virulent swords. We have been charged with striking out fiercely against the grain, in defiance against impenetrable and often invisibly massive streams of power.

When I drove Fred to his first chemo session, I was unprepared for how he would try to carry on the meeting we were having as they hooked him up to the port that would, at the end of a very long day, make him have a reaction that turned him scarlet and stopped him cold. I had pretended to go have lunch so he wouldn't see me cry hysterically in the parking lot. I used to think about hand-to-hand combat sometimes, watching him play the piano, trying to hear a new score in a way that is difficult because he sometimes sings off-key. One time, at the Congee Village restaurant, I looked down at his hand beside his food, and it later appeared to me in a dream where he was chopping up ordinary food into beautiful squares and there were the most gorgeous origami insects moving slowly in the corners of the room. I knew I'd had written this recognition in "Coin #7" when I wrote the last scene of *Red Frogs*:

BEATIFICA: Deep in the insignia there are entire hemispheres of vengeance just like yours. I try to improve my calligraphy all day. There are strugglemarks on the walls where I have dragged things heavy and cursed under my breath with no strong arm to haul these things for me.

PENNY: Do you have any support anywhere now? Or will you be leaning on my footing for that?

BEATIFICA: I have none. I have no support anywhere.

PENNY: Are you still in love with the torso's hand? The one you thought had a gentleness as it rested on the piano or beside a plate of food he carved for you?

BEATIFICA: It seems to have thickened now, thrashing in the sea, set apart from himself.

PENNY: You knew it was thick, that it would always be thick.

BEATIFICA: It had a blunted force. Hammering at my will.

PENNY: It can still pound the keys for what it wants them to do. It can shape its students with one welt of flotsam to the brow.

BEATIFICA: You stand still in a place beside the proletariat.

PENNY: You're not divine, that's final now. You seem the same and I'm the same. I am beside myself. (*Red Frogs*, 2002)

What I heard on the first recording of *Night Vision*, when I stared at the wall all night, was not only a force I've always felt inside of Fred's music—the weaponry, the genius, the crisis and combat, the struggle—but I think I tried to explain it later to him as a "side of you." And that it does exist in a sort of gentleness, revealed only fleetingly, and with an innocence almost too pure for this world. This side of Fred makes all of us who know him feel like we are part of his parallel universe, third and first worlds in transfusion—it makes our hearts spring to our throats. As if we all are part of the legacy of his political allegorical vision, grander than any of us alone. Fred told me one time, probably just to get me to write faster, that I was Ng Mui.[12] I came rushing

Figure 7. Cast members, *Once upon a Time in Chinese America, 1999.*
Credit: Steven Reinhard

back with the ending of *Dragon vs. Eagle*, sprung from a piece of organic fruit he gave me, the juice running down my hands and all over the G train.

Notes

1. *Night Vision: A First to Third World Vampyre Opera.* Libretto/lyrics by Ruth Margraff, music/concept by Fred Ho. Autonomedia/Big Red Media, December 2000.

2. Ruth Margraff, *Red Frogs: A Burlesque Mirror for the Summer Purgatorio, American Theater Magazine* 19, no. 9 (TCG), special issue *The Future of New Work*, November 2002.

3. *Overidentification* is a term Slovenian philosopher Slavoj Žižek coined to describe the aesthetic effect of early 1980s Laibach punk performances, which tried to critique "the obscene superego of the ruling ideology" in the former Yugoslavia socialist society by associating with industrial, martial, and neoclassical music. However, when Laibach, together with a Neue Slowenische Kunst (New Slovene Art) collective, tried to combat the Big Other by overidentifying with nationalist symbols, which included swastikas and black crosses, they quickly ran into controversy as they couldn't seem to disassociate their ironic meaning with the meanings already inscribed within these cultural conventions.

4. I have written about this "split" more theoretically in my chapter "Hidden Fires: PeaceWorks' Invocation as Žižekian Response to the Gujarat Massacres of 2002 (Calcutta, India)."

5. Quoted in Peter Canning, "The Sublime Theorist of Slovenia" (an interview with philosopher Slavoj Žižek) *Artforum International* (March 1993): 84–89. Žižek explains the theories of Jacques Lacan regarding political ideologies suggesting that communication between nations is necessary for cultural unity as individuals cannot communicate with themselves because of an eternal internal split.

6. See also Ruth Margraff, "An Evangelical Capitalist Message in a Bottle to the Next Millennium of Robinson Crusoes in Proscenium," in *Theatre in Crisis? Performance Manifestos for a New Century* (Manchester, U.K., and New York: Manchester University Press, 2002), ed. Maria Delgado and Caridad Svich.

7. This was recorded around 1998 live in a rehearsal hall at New Dramatists, a playwrights service organization of which I was a member. See also www.NewDramatists.org.

8. The *opera police* is my term for conservative and cowardly potential producers, funders, and critics who had power over the fate of our production but who possessed no imagination.

9. Mary Sharp Cronson is the founder and producer of the Guggenheim Museum's "Works in Process" performance series, which has presented *Voice of the Dragon* and other works by Fred Ho.

10. See Ruth Margraff and Fred Wei-han Ho, "Deadly She-Wolf Assassin at Armageddon!," *PAJ: A Journal of Performance and Art—PAJ 86* 29, no. 2 (May 2007): 94–107.

11. *Lone Wolf and Cub* (子連れ狼 Kozure Ōkami) is a well-known *gekiga* or manga created by the writer Kazuo Koike and the artist Goseki Kojima. First published in 1970, the story was adapted into six films starring Tomisaburo Wakayama, four plays, a television series starring Kinnosuke Yorozuya, and is widely recognized as an important and influential work. *Lone Wolf and Cub* chronicles the story of Ogami Ittō, the shogun's executioner who uses a dōtanuki battle sword. Disgraced by false accusations from the Yagyū clan, he is forced to take the path of the assassin. Along with his three-year-old son, Daigorō, they seek revenge on the Yagyū clan and are known as Lone Wolf and Cub.

12. Ng Mui is the last of the five ancestors from the *Voice of the Dragon* trilogy, Element: Earth—to strengthen bones. Tiger-style hand-to-hand boxing with invincible body armor, close-quarter combat.

3

Fred Ho's Operatic Journey

ARTHUR J. SABATINI

In 2008, Fred Ho launched into creating a new work, *Mr. Mystery: The Return of Sun Ra to Save Planet Earth!* Ho calls it an Afrocentric science fiction opera, and it begins on a spaceship in the not-too-distant future. The legendary musician, Sun Ra, receives a message for help from a desperate planet on the verge of total annihilation as a result of catastrophes caused by the human race. Written with poet-author Quincy Troupe, the libretto spins with complications that are typical in Ho's productions. Sun Ra considers the plea from Earth and argues about his options with his crew. An imperfect hero, Sun Ra is persuaded to revise his thinking before making a decision. A work in progress, the music, set, and costuming in *Mr. Mystery* pay homage to the late Sun Ra and his versions of improvisation and big-band performance.

As with all of Fred Ho's collaborations, the result will evolve into an operatic, multimediated spectacle that will be musically inventive and politically charged. Following productions such as *Dragon vs. Eagle!* (2006), *Deadly She-Wolf Assassin at Armageddon!* (2005), and *Night Vision: A New Third to First World Vampyre Opera* (2000), *Mr. Mystery* revolves around grand, apocalyptic themes. Those who are familiar Ho's topically driven music and performance work, such as *The Black Panther Suite* (1999) and *Turn Pain into Power!* (1991), might ask how he has shifted from his concentration on the material history of Asian and African Americans to such fantastic, allegorical theatricalizations. Has he forgone his social activism, avowed revolutionary stance and historical consciousness? Does this recent work indicate a change from multicultural music theater and opera rooted in myth and traditional forms to outrageous, comic experimentalism? Is he on a creative adventure, now in space, that signals a more mystical, unearthly tone for his work?

Of course, no one can foresee the future. However, for over two decades, as an artist dedicated to "multimedia creative expression" and collaboration,

Ho has uncompromisingly created mixed performance genres and elaborate narratives that represent and advance his visionary artistic and political ideals.[1] This was evident from his efforts in the 1980s at synthesizing African American jazz with Chinese and pan-Asian music to his large-scale performances incorporating dance, martial-arts choreography, and video. In fact, Ho's music theater productions and operas—the focus of this essay—have aimed not only at fusing but at amplifying the possibilities of multidisciplinary theater and operatic performance. Ho's conceptions of music and the arts, as this collection demonstrates, are integrated with his overarching ideological thinking. This applies to his performance practices, approach to composition, collaborative sensibility, and, above all, a highly developed, individualized musical style emerging from the African American jazz tradition. Ho's work pursues themes related to a multicultural worldview and consistently engages the interplay among politics, art, music, performance, and, as he often writes, "revolution" as "the way" of liberation.

Although there are experimental dimensions to Ho's work in theater and performance, they persistently revolve around a few selected themes, dramatic situations, and heroic characters in epic struggles. Though each work varies in tone from urgent and serious to slapstick and operatically extravagant, they all share common elements: one or multiple journeys, physical confrontations between characters, sustained rhetorical dialogues, and fantastic scenarios. Ho's musical aesthetic also adheres to artistic choices and practical decisions that fulfill the aims of his producing organization, Big Red Media Inc.

So, Ho's new work on Sun Ra is neither mysterious nor indicative of a change. If anything, the journey into space and polemics and meditations on myth, music, and saving the planet are emblematic of Ho's deepest personal concerns and lifelong musical and theatrical preferences. In essence, Sun Ra resembles characters in Ho's early theater work, such as Filipino immigrants and the Chinese trickster, Monkey, who are participants in and representative of the powerful and recurring theme of the journey.[2] In many contexts, as this essay shows, representations of actual and mythical, fantastic and psychic journeys function to shape the narratives and structure of live performances. These journeys are inevitably marked with political, ethnic, racial, and aesthetic significance and, overall, chart nothing less than a non-Eurocentric construction of world history. That is, they center on Chinese, Chinese American, pan-Asian, American, and African American histories, experiences, social, and aesthetic genres and sources. Moreover, while each of Ho's productions is either complete in itself or part of a series, they are also interrelated. In this sense, the location of his narratives and the travels, trials, and adventures of his characters constitute an imaginative universe—a cosmos, actually—with a fervent musical aesthetic at its core and trenchant performative energy emanating out in all dimensions. Ho's productions contain worlds within worlds that transport audiences and challenge them to reimagine existence through music, live performance, and renewed political understandings.

A Dialogic Approach

In order for us to characterize the performances and styles of representation in Ho's work, it will be useful to refer to dialogic concepts derived from theories of Mikhail Bakhtin.[3] Briefly, dialogic categories critically address the interplay of social and artistic genres and other factors relative to historical, social, political, and aesthetic practices. Dialogic studies demonstrate how particular images or forms combine to resist, undermine, or otherwise expose oppositional tendencies and subversive meanings in texts. Consider, for example, the very title of Ho's opera, *Once upon a Time in Chinese America*. The phrase juxtaposes the obvious generic opening of a classic, European fairy tale with a construction that seemingly exists in collective, historical memory: "Chinese America." However, "Chinese America" has never been an originary place as either part of pre-Columbian America or any social conceptualization. Superficially, the phrase implies a hybrid entity that conjoins two different realms: a conventional literary formula, derived from oral tradition, and a plausible but fictitious social, historical category. In Ho's use, however, each term is meant to be complexly singular. The title does not suggest a place of fantasy, but a critical, ambiguous concept requiring interpretation. Thus, the very phrase "Once upon a Time in Chinese America" simultaneously discloses unsettled meanings and critical relationships to problematic social, political, and historical realities. This occurs throughout Ho's work, in which there are no final blendings or fusion of ideas—or, in performances, an "organic" wholeness in them—that does not also produce tensions demanding interpretation.

Another fitting trope from Bakhtinian theory is carnivalization. In *Rabelais and His World*, Bakhtin explores medieval carnivals, during which extreme, grotesque forms of play and exhibitionism became the seeds of social satire and, often, incipient rebellion.[4] In the contemporary world, Mardi Gras or Chinese New Year are similar occasions for wildness, though without the political significance of medieval carnivals. For Bakhtin, when the grotesque, comedic, or carnivalesque images, forms, or music appear in the arts and society, they can retain a symbolic value and function to critique the status quo and suggest alternative possibilities.

In every dimension of Ho's music theater and performance work, the elements he selects produce carnivalesque relationships. Consider, first, his interweaving of Asian instruments, songs, and musical forms with African American jazz and matching them to martial-arts dance.[5] Or, Ho's mixing of political ideology with mythical subjects (e.g., Monkey is a revolutionary!). In these and other instances, Ho combines *and* contrasts multiple systems of performance, practice, history, and materials. His intent is to enrich and ideologically reaccentuate genres, music, dance, and narratives in order, ultimately, to urge a reappraisal of the existing order of things. And, while not all of the work is comically carnivalesque, Ho's productions invariably engage in derision of dominant social structures, forms, and reigning powers while offering an imaginative and provocative alternative.

Ho's music has always displayed a dialogic and carnivalesque depth. His playing and compositional style has been described, by him and others as, variously, a synthesis, hybrid, fusion, and blend. But it is more than that. In a 1994 speech, "Kreolization and the Hybridity of Resistance vs. Cultural Imperialism," he identified his music as "Afro-Asian New American Multicultural Music."[6] As such, Ho creates music that absorbs multiple traditions and affirms itself as resistant while undermining the stability of culturally dominant genres. His music also presents itself as an example of a transformative aesthetic proposition that, as Ho emphasizes, is also political.

In Ho's opera-theater and multimedia productions, music is never in the background or for purely aesthetic effects.[7] For Ho, the Afro Asian New American multicultural sound functions simultaneously in tandem with the dramatic action and movement to call attention to sociohistorical and political factors in the narratives. Ho's music is performed while live action is occurring, and the choice of particular musical materials takes on critical extramusical significations (along with the librettos, costumes, and the mise en scène). Compositionally, since Ho's jazz inspired language and performance practices involve improvisation, with some musicians playing non-Western instruments, any moment in a production can allude to a number of historical times, places or events, such as Shogun-era Japan or ancient China.

The opening scene in Ho's *Warrior Sisters* provides a rich example of Ho's dialogic conception. The setting is China and West Africa in the colonial era, around 1890, but then quickly segues to 1902 San Francisco. Sounds of Morse code, shouts in German, English, and other languages erupt as crowds march across the stage. Musically, footsteps lead to drumbeats and low chords, led by Ho's saxophone, before a short ensemble motif is heard and male voices in chorus emerge. A military, work routine beat returns, and a call and response chant begins: "Foreign devils steal our land / This would never happen in the dynasty of the Ming!" Thus, within less than two minutes, Asian, African, operatic, militaristic, and 20th-century colonial and postcolonial sonic and musical materials weave together and establish a narrative current that will both convey the action and keep its meanings suspended. The music functions as a definitive voice that reaccentuates the significance of the on-stage action. That is, although the music "fits" the movement of the actors, it also positions the audience to hear it as sound converging dialogically on the moment from different historical and social times, posing questions about the function of the music in historical contexts. When, later in the drama, African dances and song styles along with Chinese opera intonations are heard, Ho reinforces the interplay of sounds, and it becomes clear that music has its own integrity and contemporary significance as both part of the performance for the audience present and as social history.

The Journey and Ho's Cosmos

The characters and the plots of Ho's work feature journeys into the future or past or through all time. They are globalized, transhistorical, with events taking place on earth and beyond in a cosmos of Ho's invention. In this sense, Ho reconceptualizes the archetypal and classical idealizations of the journey as pilgrimage, quest, or odyssey. His parodic reformulation urges an understanding of journeys as international, thoroughly politicized and specifically interpolated through provocative renderings of historical pasts and futures in relation to Asia, the Pacific Rim, Africa, and America.

Thematically, the journey has several dimensions for Ho. It can be at once real and historical, referencing Chinese laborers, African slaves, and others; and metaphorical, in the case of the time-traveling Warrior Sisters or Sun Ra in orbit. Journeys epitomize the intensely conflictual life experiences and consciousness of the masses; and, simultaneously, the internalized experience of heroic individuals who choose, or are called upon, to respond to oppressive political and material conditions. In Ho's cosmos, as Sun Ra orbits, there are also references to Celestial Heavens, Magical Mountains, the Undersea World and mythical realms. Characters journey to "Mother Earth" and such exact places as the Euphrates River, premodern Ghana, and the Clinton Correctional Facility for Women in New Jersey. In the era of internet and cinematic time travel, such aesthetic transportations are not remarkable. But, in the context of staged and musical performances, Ho's far-flung places function not merely as a backdrop for exotic adventures, but as markers for recurring sociopolitical dramatizations, rehistoricizations, and aesthetic extrapolations. In Ho's cosmos, Chinese and other Asian, African, and African American people play prominent roles. Human, animal, and imaginary figures such as a she-wolf assassin also mingle in journeys, many of which lead to confrontations and combat with oppressive forces. Moreover, as the various works are cross-referenced in relation to each other in terms of musical sources and social groups, they imply interconnected, intertwined realities, histories, and myths.

The multiple journeys represented in Ho's theater unfold accompanied by his fluid, propulsive baritone saxophone playing and his band's improvisations. This creates a distinctive sound that also instantiates artistic proposition and a forceful ideological statement. That is, from "Celestial" settings (*Journey to the West*) to the Shaolin martial arts saga based in rural China (*Voice of the Dragon*) to scenes occurring in the Middle East, the musical beats and forms derive from Afro Asian sources and a 20th-century performance aesthetic. By incorporating Asian and non-European instrumentation (as well as scales, rhythms, and performance practices), Ho establishes a critical, dialogic relationship with historical events, actual people, myth, and fantasy. Led by his emotive and lyrical playing, stories are told episodically, with improvisatory plasticity in real time. In each staged work conflicts are literally played out in music whose fundamental energies derive from Ho's ensembles' bop-jazz idioms as refashioned with folk-based, cross-cultural sources. In effect, sonically, Ho is asserting that the texture and pulse of human experiences happens alongside a vernacular music, the historical summation of which is his multicultural big-band sound. Of course, as with his construction, "once upon a time in Chinese America," Ho realizes that the hypothesizing of music as if it were occurring in real life and in nonmusical situations is the stuff of established practices—chiefly in cinema and opera. However, his positioning of sound and his performance style and compositional choices are meant to question conventional musical materials in "exotic" situations and the implicit (aesthetic) "colonization" of others who, in traditional performance, are represented by music that is not their own.[8]

In his many productions, Ho has demonstrated an astonishing artistic range and an ever-maturing aesthetic that serves his political and ideological commitments. He has also forged a number of working collaborations and a form of opera and multimedia performance that is uniquely his own. What follows traces the development of Ho's overall theatrical conception by discussing Ho's work chronologically from a performance perspective.

A Chinaman's Chance (1989)

The first journey represented in Ho's oeuvre occurs in *A Chinaman's Chance: A New American Docudrama.*[9] With Ho's libretto and poetry by Genny Lim, the production focuses on the experiences of "Chinese laborers in America" and is to be performed "in the tradition of Chinese opera and with larger-than-life rendering." Ten characters (including "a dual persona/bilingual god of war and literature"), two choruses, and the musicians fill the stage, recalling Chinese opera presented at pre–World War II U.S. Chinatown theaters.

The on-stage musicians are called "The Celestial Orchestra (pantheon of gods and god-like entities)." The setting is cited as "Spanning between the Celestial Heavens and Earth (i.e., southern China peasant village, contract labor ship, California, Detroit)." The time as "From the Dawn of Creation to the mid-1800s to 1982." Presented as "docudrama," everything in the performance is based on folk sayings, poetry, ballads, and historical texts. Musically, Ho adapts and extends Chinese song forms and includes Chinese instruments such as the *erhu* and *sona*. Songs and spoken lines are in English and Chinese (directly and "in narrative chant").

The characters in *A Chinaman's Chance* recount their journey from China to the United States to seek work. Men sing of leaving their families and of their degrading treatment as workers; young women sing of their lives as prostitutes. Racist characters appear and stereotype the Chinese immigrants. Midpoint in the performance, there is a long narration on the Great Railroad Race, a historical episode in which Chinese and Irish workers competed to finish a section of the railroad.

A Chinaman's Chance presents an implausible scattering of places, temporalities, performance genres, and human relationships. It asks an audience to participate in a journey that traverses the heavens to the land and sea and, simultaneously, time travel from the "Dawn of Creation" to precise moments in the late 1800s in the U.S. West. They hear Chinese poetry, witness characters in colorful period costumes and one dancing, baritone-sax-playing god. The entire production proposes a negotiation of diverse imaginative worlds, artistic styles, and cross-cultural and historical material. While in Ho's later work these elements are more narratively structured, *A Chinaman's Chance* succeeds in creating an interpenetration between Ho's Afro Asian musical ideas and the remote material of a prejazz era.

In the European picaresque tradition, a single character embarks on a journey and, through his experiences, the reader sees people from all strata of society. Ho parodies this formula by neither selecting a representative character nor establishing a single point of view. He also mixes history and myth into a form of magical realism. In *A Chinaman's Chance*, the journey is conveyed as a collective one and musically by a god-narrator-musician. A character, Kwan Gung, the God of Literature and War, announces that "ever since the mighty giant Pangu wielded his chisel and hammer to carve order from Chaos, the Chinese have ventured into new lands," and, as if in response, a few scenes later, a worker heading to California cries, "Why do I leave my family and new bride to set out on a voyage across the ocean to a foreign land?" To which, an older man sings, "Welcome, fellow countrymen, to China Camp! Some of you have just come from the Sandalwood Mountain, where you were treated worse than dogs."

The mix of cosmic, heavenly, and historical realms reaches its apex in the middle of the production when Kwan Gung reappears as "a virtuosic solo baritone saxophone voice. His 'spirit' plays the sax in the heavens. His 'physical' being is on earth, dancing. A monstrous railroad train looms/stalks him." This image is extraordinary: a celestial, yet earthbound, god-human-musical figure playing and dancing under the shadow of a train, which is also one of the paramount symbols of the journey. In this performance, the train functions as an external, predatory force. It is the repository of labor (the Chinese "coolies"), and ethnic and racial "competition" (between Irish and Chinese workers), and economic advancement (for the railroad baron). Of course, in African American poetry and music, particularly the blues, trains are, unforgettably, symbols of the flight to freedom from slavery and, equally, are a source for rhythmic pulse of music and song. All in all, this image presents a reckoning with history, social forces, myth, and art woven together. Yet none of the threads dissolve into a singular nor acceptably integrated form. The image proclaims to an audience that there is a perspective that can reveal music, godliness, magical transformation, and a complicated historical narrative of a people all at once. This presentation of a dense, multiple, concurrent trope will occur again in Ho's works and will be sustained by the live performance of music and Ho's compositional dynamics, as conveyed by Ho and his various bands. To comprehend and respond to these dense tropes, Ho asks that audiences engage their imaginations, and in succeeding works he presents a way to read his work.

Bamboo That Snaps Back (1986) and *A Song for Manong* (1988)

Not every musical theater or opera by Ho is set in the vastness of the cosmos. The journeys in *Bamboo That Snaps Back* and *A Song for Manong* are more concentrated in time and space. Following the practice of "docudrama," the instrumentation and interpolated jazz compositions resonate with Asian musical forms and significations. Manong is a Filipino endearment for "elder brother," as the single immigrant men came to be known. They carried musical instruments, songs, and sacred chants from their homeland as they traveled to Hawaiian sugar plantations in the early 20th century and, later, to California farms and cities.

Conceived as multimedia theater, the work is in three parts and relates the vicissitudes of Chinese, Filipino, and Japanese people who reflect on leaving their homelands. The music, texts, and performances represent journeys that are supported by projected images, stylized costumes, and on-stage movement. Both *Bamboo That Snaps Back* and *A Song for Manong* use extremely individualized and personal statements that localize Asians and Asian American life. For example, in "Survivor/For My Father," poetry by Janice Mirikitani (performed by Jodi Long), Japanese and Japanese American experiences of separation between a father and daughter are conveyed.

As in all of Ho's work, musical materials are dialogized through an interplay of traditional song forms with jazz and period music. Rock and roll melodies and rhythms from the 1950s appear in another song, "The Earth is Rockin' in Revolution/Drowning in the Yellow River." Tensions and heightened commentary made by the compositional forms and improvisations by musicians and ensemble produce a charged sense of a universe in motion, a journey that remains ongoing.

Journey beyond the West: The New Adventures of Monkey, a Trilogy (1989–97)

Commissioned in 1989 to write music to accompany an episode from the classic Chinese novel, Wu Ch'eng-en's *Monkey*, Ho undertook what would become nearly a ten-year project called *Journey beyond the West: The New Adventures of Monkey*.[10] A 16th-century satirical epic, *Monkey* derives from folk traditions and was often adapted in Chinese opera. It relates the comic adventures of Monkey and his companions on their quest for secret Buddhist scriptures in India. On his journey, Monkey encounters a Dragon King, demons, monsters, and supernatural forces. In Bakhtinian terms, *Monkey* is the consummate carnivalesque tale. The Monkey character subverts authority, pokes fun at religion, and indulges in drunkenness and revelry. For Ho, the gesture of creating a staged, musical production with an Asian trickster figure in its center became a vehicle for cross-cultural aesthetic and political statements.

The creative development of *Journey beyond the West* (also called *The Monkey* trilogy) resulted in the formation of the Monkey Orchestra and two albums. In program notes, Ho remarks that "the work is a synthesis of Chinese folk music and opera, with African-American music, radical political allegory, and American popular culture."[11] The few staged performances were full of artistic innovations. Ho envisioned the performance as "a 'living comic book' akin to the old silent movies with continuous live music visuals and movement on stage (with lots of grand battle scenes of dazzling martial arts) with no spoken lines."[12] The score eventually intertwined Chinese and Asian scales and motifs. And, when staged, the Monkey Orchestra, composed of Asian, African, and European instrumentation, was elevated ten feet above the players, as if in the "heaven." *The Journey Begins* and *Monkey Meets the Spider Spirit Vampire Demons* also introduced José Figueroa's martial arts reconceived as movement (then choreographed by Rebecca Lazier and later by John Carrafa). With characters in resplendent and comic costuming, performances featured solo and ensemble dancing, stylized stick fighting, sword play, and fan dances.

Suggesting that *Journey beyond the West* be called "trickster jazz," Bill Mullen provides a cogent analysis of its themes and music.[13] Relying on recordings, he emphasizes its political and allegorical elements and Ho's conceptualization of Monkey as a revolutionary figure, with references to the African American trickster, the "signifying monkey." In performance, the relationship among the diverse elements of narrative, character, dance and movement, and text, conjures an experience that raises other questions about the selected story elements and its politicized meanings. That is, the performance style and musical materials, modified from their respective traditions, serve to not only signify as themselves, albeit blended by Ho, but, dialogically talk back to the discursive dimensions of the text as rich symbols of aesthetic and social practice in their own right. All the performers revivify the inherent spirit of Afro American and Asian jazz, Chinese opera, martial arts, dance, and Western dramatic forms. The high spirits and power of performance itself becomes liberatory and, in effect, critiques the politicized elements in text. Infused with Chinese musical instrumentation and form, and equally drawing on big-band jazz, as one reviewer indicated, the music plays off "Ellington for the sultry chromatic chords and unhurried swing and on Mingus for sinewy riffs and an assertive bluesiness. There are touches of Leonard Bernstein, too, particularly in fight scenes of Jets-and-Sharks syncopation."[14] Thus, although the music supports a revolutionary text, it retains a fidelity to deeply rooted Asian, African, and American sources showing the unexpected politics of the older musical materials.

The use of martial arts in performance raises similar issues. When Ho and his collaborators create "martial arts dance and choreography," it can, once again, be seen as an attempt to synthesize two different types of performance practices that clearly emerge from very different realms of society and social, ethnic, and cultural histories. Read closely, "martial arts dance and choreography" constructs a paradoxical convergence of an activity that was once militaristic but is now regarded as sport or exercise, and a source for artistic activity. In performance, for Ho, the simultaneous representation of dance as martial arts and martial arts as dance is meant to be maintained, though highly stylized. Importantly, the two practices are on display and neither is privileged nor subsumed by the other. This allows Ho's work to sustain a tension and not become purely entertainment, even as it is theatricalized. Dialogically, the combination of Ho's music and his chosen martial-arts performance style exemplify an aesthetic that he presents as revolutionary. This also creates what will become a consistent issue in Ho's work: the critical interplay between art, performance, and political awareness.

Monkey's journey begins in *Journey beyond the West: The New Adventures of Monkey*, in act 1, *Uproar in Heaven*, at "The Dawn of the Earth to circa 100 A.D." After being imprisoned for 500 years, Monkey travels from the heavens to towns and fishing villages to the Himalayas, into India, and to the magical Flower and Fruit Mountains. These wild leaps across time and space to imaginary and real places, with mythic and heroic characters, also become a signature for Ho's subsequent music theater productions. Moreover, the concept of interconnected epic stories, with the same or similar characters, will occur in the three-part collaboration with Ruth Margraff, beginning with *Voice of the Dragon: Once upon a Time in Chinese America . . . The Martial Arts Epic*.

With its themes and tropes of a journey, and as a dialogic transgeneric, postmodern production, *The Monkey* trilogy is also marked by theatrical innovations and an extraordinary lyricism. It transports Ho's art into different theatrical and imaginary vectors and establishes working relationships with a number of other artists. By drawing on an extended literary form, the novel, and engaging a more physically comedic and popular, carnivalesque tone and performance style (including choreographed martial arts), Ho added to the depth of his sense of African American and Chinese musical materials. He also accented their potential for complex overlappings, social commentary, and sheer exuberance.

Warrior Sisters: The New Adventures of African and Asian Womyn Warriors (1998)

The two exceptions to Ho's myth-based spectacles are *Warrior Sisters: The New Adventures of African and Asian Womyn Warriors* (1998) and *All Power to the People: The Black Panther Suite* (1999). In these works, the journey theme is evoked but treated with a distinctly different tone. The journeys unequivocally occur on earth, in recent history with, as in *A Chinaman's Chance*, documentable sources. Such use of historical realism suggests a counterpoint to the allegorical and fantastical settings in the other productions and underscores the wide range of Ho's artistic and sociopolitical commitment.

In "Theses on the Philosophy of History" Marxist thinker Walter Benjamin, whose work has affinities with that of Mikhail Bakhtin, wrote,

> To articulate the past historically does not mean to recognize it "the way it really was" (Ranke). It means to seize hold of a memory as it flashes up at a moment of danger. Historical materialism wishes to retain that image of the past which unexpectedly appears to man singled out by history at a moment of danger. The danger affects both the content of the tradition and its receivers. The same threat hangs over both: that of becoming a tool of the ruling classes. In every era the attempt must be made anew to wrest tradition away from a conformism that is about to overpower it.[15]

This applies to Ho, Ann T. Greene, and Mira Kingsley's production of *Warrior Sisters: The New Adventures of African and Asian Womyn Warriors*. With realistic, transcontinental settings and historically based characters, *Warrior Sisters* seizes "moments of danger" and replays heroic actions in order to envision a rewritten past as a prelude toward a concept for the future. The work is not without a touch of the fantastic, since the entire plot turns on the adventure of four women who traverse time and space. But since it is a single, transparent conceit, it serves to unify the narrative and functions to create a fluid dialogue among the ostensible subjects of the opera—"womyn warriors" and colonial practices and attitudes. The female revolutionaries in the production are the Chinese Boxer rebel Fa Mu Lan; Nana Yaa Assantewa,

Queen Mother of the Ashante nation; Sieh King King, a Chinese feminist who lived in San Francisco around 1900; and Assata Shakur (born JoAnne Chesimard), a leader in the Black Liberation Army in the 1970s. Such a grouping would, to paraphrase Benjamin, "wrest tradition" into a new perspective as Ho attempts in all of his music theater.

The story in *Warrior Sisters* contains elements common to Ho's political and theatrical vision, although the dramatic events are completely situated in definite times and places. The opera also inaugurates what will become central to succeeding work, female "sheroe" characters who lead rebellions, seek secret teachings and texts, and avenge the wrongs against women and the oppressed. Although they "time travel," the women in *Warrior Sisters* possess neither super powers nor superior skills. Instead, they draw power from their legal and royal roles, leadership capabilities and moral convictions, and belief in a feminist history and revolutionary values. As for journeying through time, or "tearing a hole the universe" (as stated in the opera's program notes) so they can work together, that is accomplished by "Earth Mother's magic," an unquestioned force that becomes infused with ideological significance.

As staged, *Warrior Sisters* has driving musical energy and choreography that swiftly propels the narrative.[16] The set consists of platforms and open scaffolding, with stairways on both sides of the stage that frame encounters among the characters in a village, a warehouse, a courtyard, a prison, and homes in Florida and rural Cuba. Center stage, in the back, the eight-member Afro Asian Music Ensemble plays.

The opera opens in China, circa 1890. Dancers and other performers, some of whom sing as a chorus, portray workers and peasants. Wearing red outfits, they fold the Union Jack and the Stars and Stripes under the watchful eyes of armed guards. It is the time of the failed Boxer Rebellion and, within minutes, a fight breaks out and dozens of the members of the chorus, holding long sticks, chant in protest. A young woman, Fa Mu Lan, is assaulted, then escapes momentarily only to return, all in white and wearing a startling white headdress (as if on a white horse), to sing encouragement for the revolt. The lighting turns blood red and the second scene commences. It is Kumase (pre-Ghana), in the same era, and British officials are demanding payment in the form of a royal Golden Stool from the leaders of the Ashante nation. Dressed in period costume, the Queen Mother, Nana Yaa Asantewa, admonishes the men for negotiating with the British just as a war dance begins. The scene then quickly switches to San Francisco's Chinatown, 1902. We are introduced to Sieh King King, a stowaway from China who advocates feminism and protest among the Chinese merchants and laborers.

What follows ties the women together: Nana Yaa Asantewa is transported to a cell in the Seychelle Islands in the Western Indian Ocean, and she will be freed by Fa Mu Lan, who appears on her horse "in a blinding apocalyptic burst of light." Together, they leap to San Francisco to meet Sieh King King, who is speaking to an audience of workers in a Chinese theater. The three then seek the fourth women warrior, Assata Shakur (Joanna Chesimard), a Black Panther fending off the police in Harlem in 1973. The last acts of the opera include a shooting, a chase scene, the capture of Assata Shakur, her sentencing, and her incarceration in the Clinton Correctional Facility in New Jersey. There, a pregnant Shakur is rescued by her warrior sisters, and collectively they foment revolution. The opera ends in Cuba, as Shakur, joined by the spirits of Fa Mu Lan, Nana Yaa Asantewa, and Sieh King King, all hear of news of street protests in New York, which prompts them to sing in chorus "All power to the womyn! / Daughters of the Earth! We who have been last / We shall be first."

Despite the improbable sequence of events, in performance, the balanced dynamics of the music, the interspersing of solos, duos, trios, and choral singing, and the dance and movement create a work that is more low-key than Ho's other operas. The stage action is not overdramatized, and there are no special effects to enhance the magical transportation of the warrior sisters across time. (In fact, the audience laughs at the appearance of Fa Mu Lan and Nana Yaa Asantewa in San Francisco at the Chinese theater as if it is patently a mere stage trick.) Movement and choreography in *Warrior Sisters* draws seamlessly and appropriately on Chinese martial arts, West African dance, African American popular dance, and Chinese opera, while Ho's compositional structures and ensemble's playing support the plot throughout.

Overall, there is a consistency of aesthetic effects in *Warrior Sisters* that never sensationalizes the narrative or thematic material. The audience witnesses the succession of events as logical and rhetorical, albeit operatic. Yet it is clearly not a typical opera in which the characters develop psychologically or are entangled in a plot with unexpected turns. Walter Benjamin, a champion of Brecht's epic theater, would have recognized the episodic and openly imagined reinvention of historical "moments of danger" in *Warrior Sisters* as Brechtian. He would also have seen the attempt to create an association of shared meaning through feminine rebellion as a rejection of the "conformism" to which women's history is too often circumscribed.

As Benjamin remarks in the quotation above, history "really was," but in retelling it, there are also reasons "to seize hold of a memory," which is no news to women. In other contexts, Benjamin often calls on art and writing to create "illuminations" of the past and for ourselves. For Ho and his collaborators, that has meant shining a light on actual geopolitical times and places in order to revive the lives of real figures in transhistorical contexts, as in *Warrior Sisters* (and through images in *All Power to the People: The Black Panther Suite).*

The material reality of the personages in *Warrior Sisters* serves as counterpoints to the allegorical figures in *A Chinaman's Chance*, the archetypal characters in the *Journey to the West* operas, the pop culture–inflected martial-arts heroines in *Voice of the Dragon* and *Deadly She-Wolf Assassin at Armageddon!*, and the complicated characters in *Night Vision: A First to Third World Vampyre Opera*. Populating his oeuvre with all of these characters and their voices contributes to yet another dialogic aspect produced by Ho's work. Just as Brecht related the trials of historical figures such as Galileo and Joan of Arc, the presence of "moments of danger" for the real warrior sisters (and, soon, Sun Ra), anchors the landscape in his cosmology with human lives whose facticity speaks for itself. In this sense, Ho opens his theatrical performances in history just enough to suggest a resistance to complete acts of aestheticization. He poses a critical relationship between the real and unreal and establishes an historical sensibility that makes the historical magical and the magical-mythic historical. To reckon with Ho's vision, then, is not only to grapple with a mythic monkey, vampires, "colonialists," and "workers," but to engage known lives and the historical events that surrounded them.

For Mullen, *Warrior Sisters* should be regarded as "a crucial addition to the corpus of Afro-Asian cultural texts."[17] His thorough examination of the intricacies of the opera explores the journey theme and includes a reading of its political and feminist implications. Mullen states, the warrior sisters' "journey is not primarily one beyond Western, Eurocentric conceptions of race but one that enters a new territory or Third Way beyond patriarchal conceptions of color, power, sexuality and empire." He further acknowledges that the opera "recasts *Journey to the West*'s search for an "enlightened" text into a quest for a "womenyst" opera.

Ho's collaborative works with Ruth Margraff after *Warrior Sisters* fulfills this quest. However, to consider this observation from another perspective, the presence of images and themes of light and enlightenment (though quests and martial-arts training), and darkness (in *Night Vision*), will also become important to Ho. Sun Ra, of course, is the very name of the Egyptian god and alludes to the Sun. The inclusion of light as thematic, in different contexts, intriguingly inserts and rearranges the significance of Ho's work as a whole. For Walter Benjamin, "illumination" meant historical, social, and mystical revelation. More associated with mysticism, light, like sound, is also part of the natural world. By becoming aware of light and enlightenment, in his theatricalized work, Ho's expands his art into other realms for consideration and opens a dialogue with otherness beyond the material world into the cosmos.

All Power to the People! The Black Panther Suite (1998–2003)

During the same period as the development of *Warrior Sisters*, Ho was working on a project that focused on the Black Panther Party. First conceived as a "black panther ballet," in 1995, with martial-arts choreography, the production evolved over four years.[18] Unlike his revision of operatic form and the musically thematic coherence of *Warrior Sisters*. Ho approached *The Black Panther Suite* as a collaborative, visually mediated martial-arts dance. Instead of his music being supportive of a narrative and staged action, he established another type of dialogic interplay between his and other's musical voices and historical events. Played by the Afro Asian Music Ensemble, music for *The Black Panther Suite* is entirely instrumental. Video material is synched in relation to the length of 15 one-to-five-minute sections. However, in lieu of presenting a straightforward unity or complementary relationship between music and imagery, the music provides a commentary and creates a mood of engagement and confrontation throughout. When it is performed with dancers, a third, simultaneous, element is added. Sections of the work have titles that echo Black Panther slogans, such as "All Power to the People! Serve/Organize the People!" and "Loving the People Is a Love Supreme! The Personal Is Political!!!" (a reference to a John Coltrane composition). Ho's saxophone playing alludes to the music of Coltrane and other musicians, such as Rahsaan Roland Kirk and Charles Mingus, who were active during the 1960s. It is significant that the Panthers did not invoke jazz, music, and drama in their cause (although an Oakland music group, the Lumpen, created a soul and gospel performance for them).[19]

It is the achievement of *The Black Panther Suite* that Ho ingeniously produces an association between the deeply felt and adventurous music of 1960s jazz artists and the street-level transformative politics of the Black Panthers. What Ho proposes, with music that is forceful and exciting on its own terms, is that the Black Panthers and musicians of the times were linked in their spirit and desire to call attention to the conditions of life for African Americans and to offer new ways of understanding and acting through creative rebellion, if not actually advocating revolution.

In live performances, Paul Chan's video for *The Black Panther Suite* performance is silent and consists of an overlapping, dissolving, and quick-cutting flow of documentary photographs, archival film, television clips, graphics, and montages of headlines. Ho's score, and the free, dynamic improvisatory ensemble playing, respond to the shifting imagery. When performed with dancers, costumed in Black Panther outfits, the work has a synergetic explosiveness that invokes the passion of the 1960s and resonates across similar historical eras (though it is never quite a ballet). The music is not a soundtrack in the conventional sense, but an orchestrated series of pulsing statements that vividly replay the Black Panther's history and sonically realize their agenda in larger contexts. The music manages to be celebratory and an homage—and a call to arms.

Paul Chan's video begins with a test screen of rippling black and white lines, followed by graphics of the Black Panthers logo, which is replaced by an antique map of Africa that burns outward from the middle, disclosing the front page of the *New York Times* in 1851. Photographs of slaves and documents about slavery appear. Chan intersperses the material with distorting video effects and, later, cartooning of faces amidst colorful abstract washes, which make the viewer aware that this is a contemporary artistic statement and not a standard documentary. It is not without humor and, overall, the video is carnivalesque, maintaining an underground zine quality. There are excerpts of ads showing such stereotyped figures as Uncle Ben and Aunt Jemima, and unflinchingly brutal clips of police beating protestors, along with visual citations referencing Vietnam, East Timor, and the Zapatistas. In each section, the music pops in tandem with the imagery and, in performance, live-video mixing adds to the equally improvisatory energy.

Photographs and news clippings of the Black Panthers Huey P. Newton and Bobby Seale flash by, as do images of Malcolm X, Martin Luther King, Angela Davis, and John Coltrane. Animated distortions of the faces of Supreme Court justice Clarence Thomas and New York Mayor Rudolph Giuliani and others add a mocking tone. One sequence in the video intersperses scenes from D. W. Griffith's racist epic, *The Birth of a Nation*, with incidents of violent police actions against the Panthers. Another sequence, "Political Power Doesn't Grow Out of a Sleeve of a Dashiki or X-Cap, But from the Barrel of a Gun!," parodically snipes at the Black Panthers' signature leather jackets, berets, and sunglasses. The outfits are offered for "sale" in a pseudo late-night TV advertisement. Throughout, Chan's free associations become visual variations on themes, making it a jazz video riffing along with Ho's impassioned but tightly whipped music, the whole bounding from anger to tribute to compassion.

The martial-arts choreography, including video projected during live performance, and the elimination of actors and singers in *The Black Panther Suite* represent a creative transition for Ho. Clearly, it stands in relation to the "docudrama" projects in *Bamboo That Snaps Back*, *A Song for Manong*, and *A Chinaman's Chance*; it also collapses on a "moment of danger," as in *Warrior Sisters*. Nevertheless, after *The Black Panther Suite*, Ho's work will not focus on such identifiable historical material. It will be no less filled with ideas and political vision and, musically and theatrically, no less complex and powerful. But, the scope of his work will increasingly become, first, triumphantly engaged with the legends of the martial arts, then wildly transhistorical and apocalyptic, before leaving for space with Sun Ra for and his possible return to Earth.

Ho and Ruth Margraff in Collaboration: *Voice of the Dragon* Trilogy (1999), *Night Vision: A New Third to First World Vampyre Opera* (2000), *Deadly She-Wolf Assassin at Armageddon!* (2005)

In contrast to the comedic style of *Monkey* and the realism of *Warrior Sisters*, in *All Power to the People!* dancers glare while cycling through martial-arts routines, periodically jutting their fists into the air in the Black Panther salute. In the next series of operas, *Voice of the Dragon*, and for *Deadly She-Wolf Assassin at Armageddon!*, Ho's work fully expands martial-arts dancing, and interweaves it as central to the themes, stories, and characters in each work. In another move, Ho and collaborator Ruth Margraff restage Western actor–based performances by introducing a single narrator to relate the dramas. Neither actor, nor musician, nor dancer, the Narrator becomes part spectator, part impersonator, and part interpreter of the play's contents. In a detached voice, he or she tells the story directly to the audience, as do the narrators and storytellers prevalent in Asian theatrical traditions. This technique constructs another notable dialogic relationship in that, along with music and new media, the Narrator's voice allows Ho to range even more imaginatively over ideas and artistic genres that figure in the cosmos of his art.

Margraff and Ho collaborated for over a decade on five productions, all of which display a shared intensity of vision, textured narrative concentration, and a parodic romp through popular genres and sources. Their work draws on martial-arts history, vampire tales (*Night Vision*), and such media-based forms as video games and Japanese cult films (*Deadly She-Wolf Assassin at Armageddon!*). When choreographed by José Figueroa, Margraff and Ho's productions take on an animated spirit and re-present journeys that span epochs and cultures, known and fantastic realms.[20] The operas in the *Voice of the Dragon* trilogy, for example, trace an arc from a time "in a place beyond History and Fantasy" and evoke allegories of apocalyptic confrontations and redemption in futuristic dimensions.

Ruth Margraff is an inventive playwright with an international reputation. Her sense of plot and character and her crisp, poetic, eclectic language resulted in work with tight, dramatic sequences suited to Ho's musicianship on the baritone saxophone as well as to his sense of orchestration and improvisation. Writing of Margraff's text (in *Shaolin Secret Stories*), a reviewer noted that "the Narrator shifted between high-flown storytelling and slangy retold dialogue, with glints of humor."[21] In other work, Margraff and Ho plunged into darker themes and harsher tones and language.

In three parts, *Voice of the Dragon* traces the legend of mythical Shaolin monks who specialize in different martial-arts practices and achieve magical powers. In wise, storytelling voices the on-stage narrators (male and female) provide backgrounds and verbalize the character's thoughts and, like a ventriloquist, speak for them. This structuring for performances frees the martial artists and other actors to engage physically and mime their roles while the Afro Asian Music Ensemble plays on stage.

Musically complex, with choreographed combat sequences and moments of pageantry, *Voice of the Dragon* has a hip tone and excited pacing. *Once upon a Time in Chinese America* and *Shaolin Secret Stories* were pitched for general audiences (the former successfully toured more than forty U.S. cities). Of *Shaolin Secret Stories*, a reviewer acknowledged the "nearly nonstop display of leaping, punching, somersaulting," commenting that the tale "was delivered with melodramatic relish by an elegantly costumed narrator (Marina Celander)."[22] After seeing *Once upon a Time in Chinese America*, another reviewer underscored its appeal to young people: "the action was kung fu, tai chi, and boxing, seasoned with hip-hop and some electric boogaloo. The accents may have been Chinese, but the cadences were rap."[23]

Since there is no singing, *Voice of the Dragon* is equally dance and theater. With two-to-twelve-minute scenes, there is an improvisational excitement as the musicians key in during on-stage fights. Ho's Chinese and Western instrumentation establishes associations through motifs and rhythms, between the identities of characters and the music. For example, when he is introduced, Li Wen Mao, a fighter from a family of actors, typical melodies and percussion riffs from Chinese opera accompany him.

The narrative in *Voice of the Dragon* is meant to be epical. Part 1, *Once upon a Time in Chinese America*, recounts the fate of the key figures and main plot of the saga. Characterized as "revolutionaries," five "legendary ancestors" and their nemesis, Gar Man Jang, are introduced. Each character possesses extraordinary martial-arts skills that have been shaped from their personal histories and in relation to natural and mythic symbols. Chen Jak, a "Visionary Strategist" whose fighting style is Tai Chi Chuan, is like the animal "dragon—to ride the wind." Gee Shin, "raised by a pack of leopards," becomes a Long Pole expert and is associated with wood. Li Wen Mao emerged from the world of opera and fights Crane kung fu style. Each figure has an aphoristic philosophy. Li Wen Mao's is "Opera is warfare without bloodshed. Warfare is opera with bloodshed."

The sisters, Ng Mui and Gar Man Jang, are the other fighters. They will eventually confront each other in the final battle in *Dragon vs. Eagle!* (2008). Gar Man Jang is malevolent, "a poisoned soul," who is the destructive force.[24] Aligned with "an Imperial devil by the name of Eunuch Chow Mae Ngai, she is a hermaphrodite who becomes a feared fighter and vicious leader. Fierce and independent, Gar Man Jang rejects attempts to humble her into learning the teachings of 'Shaolin Way.'" Ng Mui is tutored by Gar Man Jang but then develops into a "healer, philosopher, revolutionist" and renowned hand-to-hand boxer.

Once upon a Time in Chinese America relates the overall story of the Five Ancestors and the rise of Gar Man Jang. *Shaolin Secret Stories*, although written later, is a prequel that details the childhood backgrounds of Gar Man Jang and the five fighters. As the Narrator traces their stories, each character appears on stage as gangly and untamed, all "outcasts, misfits, freaks and juvenile delinquents." Opera orphan Li Wen Mao is sickly and weak; Chen Jak is an impudent street urchin. During the fifty-five-minute performance, each figure transforms into poised fighters in their various styles.

Shaolin Secret Stories concludes where *Once upon a Time in Chinese America* begins. *Dragon vs. Eagle!* also features a narrator but does not continue the tale in a straightforward fashion. Adding to the original ancestors, there are other characters and a complex, highly allusive structure that combines ancient legends with alchemical lore and contemporary Asian popular forms, including Hong Kong action cinema and Japanese anime. As proposed by Ho and Margraff, it is "a multi-media music theater work exploring the technology, new science, and imaginative storytelling techniques of the burgeoning online gaming genre with cross-cultural themes between Chinese and American theatrical and music culture."[25] The setting replicates the architecture of interactive games and includes role-playing options and virtual characters who will populate the stage environment.

Dragon vs. Eagle! takes place in the future. Eagle, a Western superpower "of bio-techno modernism," is motivated by "fundamentalism and evangelical capitalism" and seeks to overtake the Dragon East superpower, which is "ancient, imperial and ethnocentric." For protection, a Magistrate of the Dragons uses sorcery to resurrect Gar Man Jang as a savior, only to witness her run amok. Gar Man Jang seizes power and, in possession of Secret Scrolls, battles "the White Barbarian Eagle Clans" and Eagle characters named Jockstrap and Terror Master. A battle occurs, which results in "mass acquiescence" and an assimilation of the both Dragons and Eagles. Gar Man Jang continues to rule until she faces Ng Mui, her lost sister. A half century before, Ng Mui had retreated to a cave and taught her student, Yim Wung Chun, all she knew. Yim Wung Chun will defeat Gar Man Jang and discover the last secret scroll and its revelations.

Creating a martial-arts ballet and multimedia performances with dance had long been an artistic goal for Ho and represents another dimension of his creative energy and aesthetics. In the *Voice of the Dragon* trilogy, Ho achieves that goal and, with *Dragon vs. Eagle!* and *Deadly She-Wolf Assassin*, surpasses it through amalgamation of multiple contemporary and historical sources and media. Intriguingly, *Voice of the Dragon* and *Deadly She-Wolf Assassin* are works that are overtly metatextual and, despite some of the descriptions above, only vaguely allegorical. In fact, notes for *Shaolin Secret Stories* include this statement: "While combining aspects of Chinese history, martial arts legends and myth, with American multi-cultural concepts, the VOD trilogy is set 'in a Place Beyond History and Fantasy' and is not intended to be a period historical interpretation."[26] This disavowal suggests reading the works as acts of imagination and artistic display in ways that differ from Ho's previous productions. In effect, Ho is revising historiography with art, myth, and performance, implying a pursuit of imagination as a deeper form of knowing.

This is reinforced when we consider José Figueroa's martial-arts choreography in *Voice of the Dragon* and the choreography by Tsuyoshi Kaseda in *Deadly She-Wolf Assassin*. Unlike social and modern dance and ballet, martial arts is meant for self-defense. Adapted over the centuries for the purpose of exercise and for athletic competitions, the martial arts have evolved through long, specific traditions of discipline and training (e.g., karate, kung fu). When portrayed in action films, the martial arts are subject to extensive editing and stylization. The fighting styles and their significance are keyed to the story and actor's roles. In *Voice of the Dragon* and *She-Wolf*, however, the live martial-arts action is an embodied, visual, kinetic language in itself. Characters are depicted as types (snakelike or tiger), and their movement is coordinated with Ho's music. More saliently, Ho asserts that martial-arts styles are related to the archaic Asian experience and culture as well as the Western remediated interpretations over the past several decades. As Ho and his choreographers employ actual martial artists in performance, some of whom have dance and actor training, the effect is a presentation of on-stage action as a material event, closer to live competitions than to martial arts in the movies (which seem to be implicitly critiqued).

Ho's music, of course, supports, punctuates, and conveys the action while the narration sustains the story and advances psychological insights. In performance, moments of incredible simultaneity occur—between dancers and the music—as well as sequences where the multiple art forms (including the martial arts) flow and weave into patterns that are at once discordant or contrasting. In other words, each of the dominant art forms momentarily articulates itself dialogically in relation to the others, allowing the audience to see the warping and weaving of interdependent elements.

Through its immersion in popular (and some esoteric) realms of Asian martial-arts mythology and contemporary media representations, *Voice of the Dragon* is less about a specific journey than a reminder of the eternal, universal themes of the battle between forces of good and evil and the succession of generations. Nevertheless, the journey of Gar Man Jang and the training of the martial artists can be read as Ho's reminder of the persistence and dedication to a way of life and commitment to a social or political cause. In his larger, cosmic vision, this is a new idealization. Gar Man Jang's evil soul and her nefarious doings are set against the goodness and "revolutionary" teachings of "the Way" defined by the Shaolin Temple. (The conflict in *Dragon vs. Eagle!* also bypasses the Shaolin way.) *Once upon a Time in Chinese America* ends with the lines, "And so and so on goes on the pirating of the poisoned souls against Shaolin. Every passing century, every once upon a time, and every ever after." At the conclusion of *Dragon vs. Eagle!*, however, Ng Mui discovers the meaning of the final Secret Scroll, which rejects all divisions and fighting. It "leads to all life forms interacting, to transformation, spontaneous origin, and a future where truth can never be destroyed." More significantly, "It will exist forever once it is imagined."

The scrolls themselves pass to Yim Wing Chun, and they "transform into the most beautiful translucent fruit." This leaves her to ponder why the powers of imagination and knowledge have been so obscure for humanity. She asks, "Where is the hidden seam of great and common, center and periphery, human and nonhuman that can collide and dance the tracks of birds?" Grand music follows, and the stage directions indicate: "Hero of heroes children's choir; the whole world sings with several generations of children and adults blending Eastern and Western instruments, and then goes wild and free, jubilant and holds together in a celebratory carnival."

This triumphant vision seals a cycle that originated with the purity of the teachings of the mythical Shaolin Temple. In the context of Ho's cosmological journey, it creates a realm of meaning and possibility, not least of which in the very moments of performance on any given evening. But, as noted above, since this occurs "in a Place Beyond History and Fantasy," it is wholly an act of imagination, an aestheticized reality, a performance, emerging from the already imaginary—but completely, eternally human—spheres of myth and art. Of course, the very act of creating such a work—the idea of art and live performance—is to bring into the world new types of experiences and meanings.

Deadly She-Wolf Assassin at Armageddon! (2005) and *Night Vision: A First to Third World Vampyre Opera* (2000)

In a total of ten works for the stage (including two trilogies, *Monkey* and *Voice of the Dragon*), Ho has introduced a cast of dozens of real and fictional characters. Musicologically, there is an extraordinary amount of material to explore concerning his musical choices, compositional approaches and strategies, and his evolution as a composer and musician. In relation to theater and performance, Ho's treatment of genres and their combinations for each production could be assessed both in and of themselves and in terms of the dynamics of contemporary performance.

As I have suggested, Ho's work conjures a proliferating, creative life in a cosmos that encompasses the imagining of supernatural beings and events yet the work does not avoid social and political issues. There are, as in *The Monkey* trilogy and *Night Vision*, fantastic creatures and folkloric elements drawn from the abundance of sources in world culture. In other contexts, from *A Song for Manong* to *The Black Panther Suite*, actual voices, clear ideological positions, and known events are represented. Myth appears frequently (as in *Voice of the Dragon*) and parody and metacommentary on music, the arts and culture are evoked (see below on *Deadly She-Wolf Assassin at Armageddon!* and *Night Vision*). In short, Ho is neither nostalgic nor thoroughly idealistic: instead, he presents an epical vision of human life in its complexity and boundlessness.

And this must be stated emphatically: there is the music—performed live at every performance, with Ho and musicians on the stage, never in an orchestra pit. It is composed, rehearsed, played, and recorded with longtime members of the Afro Asian Music Ensemble and other musicians who know Ho well. The absolute, inimitable originality of his musical artistry is at its core and resonates throughout all of his work. Ho's musical heritage is from the Afro American tradition of the period of the 1960s and his blendings and amalgamations of the musics of Asia and Asian Americans are at the foundation of his aesthetics. In the end, Ho's cosmos is musical, with a big-band, baritone-saxophone-led sound that allows, invites, encourages multiple voices, instruments and an ever-expanding repertoire. As a cosmos—that is, as a universe understood philosophically and aesthetically—it is joyously inventive, self-reflexive, dense with echoes of tradition, and heading on a path toward reconciliation for humans of difference and a deeper understanding of the possibilities of human life.

As a sign of his versatility, though, Ho's collaborations with Margraff often resulted in explorations of darker and more mature themes, with shifts in his musical tone and psychological complexity. *Deadly She-Wolf Assassin at Armageddon!* is set in Japan and is full of bloody vengeance; and *Night Vision: A First to Third World Vampyre Opera* takes place now, although the nightmare of historical traumas ripples through it. In both works, Ho's imagination takes on a different musicality and engages yet other artistic genres, earthly worlds, and meanings.

In *Deadly She-Wolf Assassin at Armageddon!*, Ho and Margraff's tale telling derives from the 1970s Japanese cult-genre film hits, *Lone Wolf and Cub*, manga books, anime, and other sources. The films are known for quick-cutting cinematography and eclectic scores that often include jazz combined with traditional Japanese music. They have an air of graphic novel starkness and contain exaggerated, highly stylized samurai sword fighting.

In notes on his score, Ho says that the music for the films is comparable to the classic soundtracks for black exploitation movies, spaghetti westerns, and TV series like *Mission: Impossible*. For the production, his music has "virtually no melody. Rather, texture and rhythm abound."[27] One reviewer caught the intent of Ho's compositional approach, remarking that in "a climactic swordfight, for instance, Ho swings his band out into full staccato structures as potent as cinematic scoring."[28] By making live performance seem cinematic, Ho creates a dialogic relationship with his materials and sources that overtly emphasizes mediated and cross-cultural interpenetrations.

At once a period piece and a consciously wrought music theater work, *Deadly She-Wolf Assassin at Armageddon!* reveals Ho's engagement with crossover artistic, pop, and cult genres. And, like in *Voice of the Dragon* and *Night Vision*, history is represented as rife with sinister conspiracies and the complex human relations. The plot is multilayered and there is a sense of horrific fate propelling all the characters. The She-Wolf, who recalls the Warrior Sisters and Gar Man Jang, is psychologically compelling and fully realized. In performances, the Narrator (played by Marina Calendar), stands close to all the actors and, particularly when speaking for the She-Wolf, becomes emotionally entwined with events. Overall, the work has a sinister, tragic mood, and the Samurai style sword, pole fighting, and boxing take place with a crispness that differs from martial-arts scenes in Ho's other productions.

Ho and Margraff's first collaboration was *Night Vision: A New Third to First World Vampyre Opera*, which they started in 1998.[29] It is an ambitious project that featured live video and sound mixing, singers, and choruses in a convoluted tale of cross-cultural vampirism, mysterious musics, and haunted lives. Uncharacteristically for Ho, the band includes electric keyboards and guitars, and, musically, the production in infused with rock and hip-hop. However, this is not unexpected for two reasons: Margraff has an interest in rock music, and *Night Vision* is the story of a 2000-year-old female vampyre who evolves into a pop music superstar with the aid of a maniacal techno-producer, the Spin Doctor. Equally anomalous for Ho, the work does not directly reference Black culture, Asians or Asian Americans. Instead, the characters and sources originate in the Roman Empire, the Renaissance, and the Middle East. Hong Kong action movies inform the video imagery, and, eclectically, the music and texts derive from "Iraqi Bedouin desert songs, Crusader art, and Times Square erotica."[30]

Like the *Warrior Sisters*, who reappear throughout history, and the resurrection of Gar Man Jang in *Voice of the Dragon*, *Night Vision* turns on a journey of return of a woman who is reincarnated, 'Ajlinna id-Dibayih. A Roman Centurion hired to murder Moors, she gorges on the hearts of infants and becomes a vampire. She eventually develops an uncanny singing voice that resonates with the sounds of the First and Third Worlds. "Her songs are so compelling that she rises to fame in every century," the CD program notes explain, "only to disappear suddenly in a black chariot when her killings are discovered."[31] This pattern continues into the present; 'Ajlinna id-Dibayih finds herself controlled by the Spin Doctor until the Centurion's descendants reappear to reclaim their stolen hearts.

With twenty scenes, the production runs over ninety minutes as this twisted tale is sung and chanted. Margraff's extravagant libretto coos and explodes, rants and proclaims. The set is a nightclub-turned-recording-studio called Limousine. It was staged with "a wall-sized video screen with two televisions on either side of it, a faux-DJ setup on the front chassis of a limo with working headlights, several closed-circuit video cameras and mixers, a bunch of microphones, loud music skipping through every pop genre from the last 30 years, and boisterous acting and singing styles."[32]

Night Vision references a dizzying set of characters, including a Crusader Moorish Boy and a Troubadour Rory Boy. Songs and lyrics slide between demotic riffs, rock hymns, and stream of consciousness poetry. One is titled, "Psalm 23 Home Movie," another is "Sling Your Arrowhearts." In the end, as the notes explain, 'Ajlinna thwarts all who exploited her and causes an apocalyptic breakdown of "First World evangelical capitalism. Leaving only her original bulrush basket in the hands of a true-heart-ed shepherd boy."[33]

As with the She-Wolf and Rogue Assassin, the Vampyre diva is manipulated by fate and evil forces in a society, ostensibly like ours, that destroys itself because of malignant practices and the reign of unchallenged powerful figures. But, as this is taking place in Ho's cosmos, wickedness and the total destruction of the world are not to be regarded as a final statement. All will be renewed, and heroic figures of great promise—like Monkey, the Warrior Sisters, and Ng Mui—provide reasons for hope, joy, and affirmation.

Resolutions and the Future

As we look back on all of his music, theater, opera, and other work, we see that Ho's life's journeys affirm a form of redemption through art, thought, and imagination as a prelude to transformation. It is a deep, hard-won, and joyous declaration of the power of music, storytelling, dance, the martial arts, performance, writing, and artistic collaborations—with its roots in Asia, Africa, and Afro Asian American cultures and experiences. Importantly, his work is remarkable for going beyond cultural borrowing and synthesis. His overall aesthetic is defiantly individual and emerges from within a severe critique of the destructive forces that have operated throughout the oppressive journeys stemming from forms of slavery, imperialism, and forced migrations in human history. For Ho there may be a resolution of past injustices, decimations, and an end to horrific journeys. It would have to be with hope that recognizes past wrongs and provides a meaningful conception of the future. This can occur, he shows, as music and performance combine with polemics and political, social, and historical knowledge—so that, as the last words in several productions proclaim, humanity can create "Revolution!," "Victory!," and a "New World!"

Ho's music, writing, and theatrical productions will likely encompass—and contest—whatever emerges in the 21st century. Moreover, his engagement with multicultural forms of performance and collaborations stand as a model for artists. His theatrical and operatic productions outline how to create a vision and a cosmos drawn from the world's inexhaustible histories, myths, music, and performance traditions. So, too, does his treatment of traditional and current narratives and his participation in what he calls the "diasporic continuum." As for Ho's next productions, his chosen themes, political values, and musical materials are established though seem infinitely elastic and capable of becoming richer and more penetrating.

Of course, everything will not happen at once, and change is inevitable. Over the decades Ho's call for renewal has itself transformed. Earlier works call for commitment and combat. *Warrior Sisters*, for example, ends with the lines: "All power to the womyn!" Later, in *Deadly She-Wolf Assassin at Armageddon!*, the vengeful assassin's sword is passed on from the father to the son. But, intriguingly, the last lines in *Dragon vs. Eagle!* intimate a more mystical resolution of human journeys and for the fate of the world. After her great battles, the heroic Yim Wing Chun, opens ancient, secret scrolls that magically flower into "the most beautiful translucent fruit." She tries to grasp the secret as the "entire world becomes translucent, clear and then vanishes." The vision entrances her. Is there a way, she ponders, to recognize "the bright abundance overflowing" of the world as it is? And, "How can we defeat the monstrous terrors of the world with art, beauty, compassion, honor and intelligence?"

Perhaps, to end this essay where it began, Sun Ra will find an answer after orbiting in Ho's cosmos, or discover, as the real Sun Ra used to say, that "space is the place." In either case, our dialogues must continue, and while the earth may not be saved, the cosmos—Ho's and ours—can be imagined with enlightenment and everything Yim Wing Chun desires and, always, the music, the music, the music.

Figure 8. Cast members, *A Chinaman's Chance*. Credit: Unknown

Notes

My thanks to Professor Roger N. Buckley for assistance, patience, and permission to use the Dodd Collection at the University of Connecticut, which provided support and access to Ho's papers (Fred Ho Papers, Archives and Special Collections at the Thomas J. Dodd Research Center, University of Connecticut). Thank you to Tamara Roberts. Finally, deepest thanks to Fred for supplemental material, corrections, and for decades of life changing and challenging ideas and music.

1. "Multimedia creative expression" appears on http://www.voiceofthedragon.com/, Ho's Web site. Throughout this essay I identify each work by title but also as music theater, opera, multimedia, or performance. All of these terms are meant to describe live performances with on-stage musicians, dancers, voices, and electronic media. However, genre classifications are less important for my discussion than the overall thematic interrelationships among the work. I am also writing of "Ho's work" with full understanding that it is always highly collaborative. My apologies to any collaborators and persons involved in Ho's productions I have failed to mention.

2. See Bill Mullen, "Making Monkey Signify: Fred Ho's Revolutionary Vision Quest," *Afro-Orientalism* (Minneapolis: University of Minnesota Press, 2004), 163–206. Mullen reads Ho's work as an allegory of a personal journey, with an emphasis

on the development of his political and ideological thought through 1998. My approach to the journey theme does not consider Ho's personal life or experiences.

3. Mikhail Bakhtin, *The Dialogic Imagination: Four Essays*, ed. Michael Holquist, trans. Caryl Emerson and Michael Holquist (Austin: University of Texas Press, 1981); and Mikhail Bakhtin, *Problems of Dostoevsky's Poetics*, ed. and trans. Caryl Emerson (Minneapolis: University of Minnesota Press, 1984).

4. Mikhail Bakhtin, *Rabelais and His World*, trans. Helene Iswolsky (Cambridge, Mass.: MIT Press, 1968). My dialogic reading is aimed at consideration of all elements of Ho's productions and how they interrelate and contribute to his aesthetics and ideological statements.

5. Although Bakhtin did not write of the blues, jazz, hip-hop, or other music of African Americans, they thoroughly embody the carnival spirit and dialogic elements.

6. Fred Ho, *Wicked Theory, Naked Practice: A Fred Ho Reader*, ed. Diane C. Fujino (Minneapolis: University of Minnesota Press, 2009), 119 (113–20).

7. In this essay I am responding as much to the actual performances and staged histories of each work as to scripts, scores, recordings, videos, and manuscript drafts. As such, what I write may be a projection of unrealized aspects of actual performances and, perhaps, suggest more than any single audience would have experienced in a given performance.

8. By contrast, consider European orchestral music in films set in non-European countries, amid ancient civilizations, or in outer space. Audiences have grown accustomed to this musical texture and its coded emotional coloring. The drama inherent in Eurocentric orchestral music has become so conventional that it goes unnoticed by audiences. Thus, characters and the social order of different times, and in all cultures, become subsumed—even harmonized—by the orchestral sound.

9. Quotations that follow are from Fred Ho, "A Chinaman's Chance," 1989 (typed manuscript, no pagination), Fred Ho Papers, series 38: Asian American Theatre, 1979–1995, 3:I script. Also, there was a one-time 1989 performance at the Brooklyn Academy of Music.

10. *Journey beyond the West: The New Adventures of Monkey* was performed in different versions. "The Journey Begins" and "The Journey Home" were staged at the Brooklyn Academy of Music's Next Wave Festival. *Monkey Meets the Spider Spirit Vampire Demons* became a children's ballet; and, a prequel, *Uproar in Heaven*, was recorded as a CD but never staged. Ho worked simultaneously on *Monkey* and other theater pieces along with live performances as a soloist and ensemble leader. He fulfilled commissions, wrote essays, and produced recordings, all of which contribute to how his work and ideas evolved aesthetically.

11. *Journey beyond the West*, Fred Ho Papers, series 38: Asian American Theatre, 1979–1995, 3B. *Journey to the West* took place as a performance in several stages.

12. *Journey beyond the West*, Fred Ho Papers.

13. Mullen, "Making Monkey Signify," 189.

14. Jon Pareles, "Chinese-Jazz Fusion in Monkey's Tale," *New York Times*, Nov. 28, 1997, E31.

15. Walter Benjamin, "Theses on the Philosophy of History," in *Illuminations*, ed. Hannah Arendt, trans. Harry Zohn (New York: Schocken Books, 1968). 253–64, quotation on 255. As for the affinities with Bakhtin, both writers assert the necessity of creating dialogues with history and focus on art in relation to social conditions, and both value the imagination of the artist.

16. See the Production History and Fred Ho Books appendices. My remarks are based on a video of a 2000 performance of *Warrior Sisters* at the Kitchen in New York City.

17. Mullen, 196.

18. See Fred Ho and Paul Chan, *All Power to the People! The Black Panther Suite*, DVD, Big Red Media and Innova Recordings, 2003. The DVD contains a history of the project, with poetry by Jayne Cortez. Completing and recording the hour-long, 15-movement musical composition occurred 1998, followed by Paul Chan's video production. A live video and music performance version premiered at the Kitchen in New York City in 1999, but it was not until 2003 that martial-arts choreography was added and, that same year, an interactive DVD. In some subsequent live performances, the video was mixed live by Abraham Gomez-Delgado. The DVD includes a gallery of photographs.

19. Although I have not explored it, there is much to be said about how Ho's non-theatrical music and writing broaden the ideas and material in relation to the staged performances.

20. Fred Ho, *Once upon a Time in Chinese America*, CD, American Composers Forum, (c) 2001 Ho/Transformation Art Publisher/Big Red Media Inc. Quotations and references in what follows from the CD recording and liner notes. Part 1, *Once upon a Time in Chinese America* (1999) was directed by Mira Kingsley; Terry O'Reilly directed part 2, *Shaolin Secret Stories* (2004). Except for *Night Vision* and *She Wolf*, the works feature martial-arts choreography by José Figueroa. Ho's collaboration with Figueroa and Ruth Margraff is a subject that needs to be explored in more depth.

21. Jon Pareles, "Crouching Leopard, Somersaulting Dragon," *New York Times*, Jan 10, 2004, B21. All quotations and references to *Shaolin Secret Stories* are from an unpublished manuscript, unrecorded CD, and video documentation of a performance in the Apollo Theater, New York City, 2007.

22. Ibid.

23. Elizabeth Zimmer, "Everyone Was Kung-Fu Fighting," http://www.villagevoice.com/theater/0145,sight,29877,11.html, accessed June 28, 2012.

24. Quotations and references to *Dragon vs. Eagle!* are from an unpublished manuscript provided to the author by Fred Ho.

25. Ruth Margraff and Fred Ho, "Deadly She-Wolf Assassin at Armageddon," *PAJ* 86 (2007): 94–107, quotation on 95.

26. Fred Ho supplied the script and promotional notes to the author. However, the phrase, "in a Place beyond History and Fantasy" appears on the CD version of *Once upon a Time in Chinese America . . . The Martial Arts Epic.*

27. Ibid., 94.

28. Lewis Whittington, "Peregrine Arts? Deadly She-Wolf?" *Broad Street Review*, July 18, 2006, http://www.broadstreetreview.com/index.php/main/article/Peregrine_Arts_Deadly_SheWolf, accessed June 28, 2012.

29. Ho and Ruth Margraff. *Night Vision: A New Third to First World Vampyre Opera*, double CD with libretto (unpaginated), (c) 2000 Ho/Transformation Art Publisher/Big Red Media Inc.

30. Ibid.

31. Ibid.

32. James Hannaham, "Hide Your Jugular, It's the Blood-Sucking Diva." February 8, 2000, www.villagevoice.com/theater/0006,hannaham,12357,11.html, accessed June 28, 2012.

33. Ibid.

PART II

The Aesthetics of Politics

POLITICS AND POETRY

Dear Sarah Palin,
Politics and poetry don't mix
Poets don't see black and white
The way some soccer moms see good and evil
They see all the colors in between and
the colors that go into making colors
the colors they are
Microtones between whole notes
hapa notes, mixed-blood mutts and mongrels
in polychromatic, polytechnicolor hues

"He doesn't see America the way you or I do!"

They see afterglows and
affirmations on rainbow cellar doors
Aurora Borealises bouncing off hoops
Fetuses coiled like bullets inside
wombs of teenage moms with
tattooed hips, food stamped
footsoles and walled off *barrios*
graffiti narratives
outlaw miscarriages and
21 gram dreams

Dear Sarah,
Politics and poetry don't mix
Those who live in a world of
winners and losers, saints and sinners
for whom, dogma barks
know to slice their bread
but never to cover their shit

—Genny Lim

4

"Return to the Source"

Fred Ho's Music and Politics in the Asian American Movement and Beyond

DIANE C. FUJINO

I met Fred Ho at four historic political events—all in 1998. In March, I heard him blowing his saxophone on stage at the Jericho march and rally for political prisoners in Washington, D.C. As I sat next to veteran activist Yuri Kochiyama, watching throngs of activists, young and old, primarily but not exclusively Black, greet her, and as I listened to Fred Ho, it became clear that Afro-Asian solidarity was being practiced that day.[1] I had first heard Fred perform, but did not meet him, eight years earlier at the Association of Asian American Studies conference, held at the University of California, Santa Barbara. I was blown away by the forcefulness, audacity, playfulness, and unexpectedness of his music. In May, at an Asian American Movement conference at UCLA, Fred approached me to collaborate on what became *Legacy to Liberation*, the first anthology on the revolutionary Asian American Movement.[2] The next day, we both attended, along with some 100 others, the founding meeting of the Asian American Left Forum in Los Angeles. This was part of a revival of radical grassroots political formations in the late 1990s, which included the Black Radical Congress and New Raza Left. That meeting was filled with hope for a lasting national network of veteran and newer activists, but as Ho advocated for a discussion of socialism, several women charged him with pushing his own agenda in a forceful and masculinist way. In September, after Fred performed for the hugely successful Critical Resistance conference on the prison industrial complex at UC Berkeley, Fred, my partner, and I walked the streets of Berkeley, with all eyes focused on a large Chinese man, with a tiny triangular tuft of hair on an otherwise shaved head, dressed in a flamboyant ankle-length jacket made from bright red kimono material, taking intense and purposeful footsteps just to get a bite to eat.

We see glimpses of Fred Ho through my interactions with him in that one historical year—his connection with a variety of radical movements, his music, his controversial politics and personality, his colorful style, and his intensity.[3] This essay centers on the unity of culture and politics in Ho's contributions to the Asian American Movement, to Asian American jazz, to Afro-Asian solidarities, to music making, and to political theory. I frame his work in Amilcar Cabral's words "return to the source," calling forth the need to resist the historical images of subordination created by dominant society, to return to one's cultural roots or at least to the liberatory aspects of that culture, and to develop a resistance movement that connects with the unleashed imagination and lived experiences of ordinary people.

Unity of Politics and Culture: "National Liberation Is Necessarily an Act of Culture"

> A people who free themselves from foreign domination will be free culturally only if . . . they return to the upward paths of their own culture. . . . Thus, it may be seen that if imperialist domination has the vital need to practice cultural oppression, national liberation is necessarily an act of *culture*.
>
> —AMILCAR CABRAL, *Return to the Source*

Amilcar Cabral's insistence on the centrality of culture in the struggle for national liberation, contained in his *Return to the Source*, is visible in Ho's cultural and political theory and practice. Cabral became a leader of the independence movement in West Africa in the 1950s, founding the PAIGC (African Party for the Independence of Guinea and Cape Verde), as a leading force against Portuguese colonialism. In 1970 Cabral gave a speech, "National Liberation and Culture," at Syracuse University in New York that stressed the importance of culture in the anticolonial struggle.[4] He asserted that no colonizing force or oppressor can successfully dominate without destroying the culture of the oppressed peoples. Maintaining one's culture, turning back toward one's cultural heritage, or re-creating a liberatory culture (because as Cabral emphasizes, no culture is fixed or flawless) in the face of colonialism is thus a revolutionary act. This process is what Cabral refers to as "return to the source." Rooted in Cabral, Ho asserts, "Oppressed people don't begin to fight their oppression until they resist the identity and historical image their oppressor makes of them."[5] This requires a shedding of assimilationist tendencies to become like the oppressor. Music, as one form of cultural expression, is an important medium for resisting the oppressor's symbolism and for decolonizing one's mind. Ho's approach is to create not only politically transgressive content, but also musical forms that defy Western assimilationism. Ho also designs his own clothing (dramatic hip- and floor-length jackets from second-hand Japanese kimono material or African prints) and boots (with bold colors and designs of dragons) as an individual act of cultural resistance. He shuns Western clothing encasing his body and trapping his mind in favor of ones that reflect his hybrid, Third World, Afro-Asian identity. He chooses women's kimonos, retailored into men's jackets, to link his feminine and masculine qualities. In his music and his clothing, Ho is an innovator of an Afro-Asian style.

Still, as important as cultural expression is, Cabral argued that it is insufficient by itself to transform oppressive structures. Moreover, he asserted that the anticolonial movement must connect with the culture of the masses of people, primarily because the predominant peasant base in his country, secluded in rural areas, was relatively untouched by the culture of the colonial powers. Writing in the midst of anticolonial struggles in Guinea-Bissau in the early 1970s, Cabral stressed that returning to the source "is of no historical importance unless it brings not only real involvement in the struggle for independence, but also complete and absolute identification with the hopes of the mass of the people, who contest not only the foreign culture but also the foreign domination as a whole." It is insufficient to struggle for one's own psychological, cultural, or political liberation; one must link one's individual freedom with the freedom of the masses of ordinary people, especially the most downtrodden. For Cabral then, "a reconversion of minds"—a "re-Africanization" in this case—"is completed only during the course of struggle, through daily contact with the popular masses in the communion of sacrifice required by the struggle."[6]

While Cabral's statement—"national liberation is necessarily an act of culture"—insists on the intertwining of politics and culture, which is of relative importance? Cabral's argument that a cultural "return to the source" "is not and cannot in itself be a sufficient act of struggle against foreign domination seems to suggest that political resistance is primary. It is certainly typical to think of culture as an extension of political resistance. But James Smethurst, in his rigorous study of the Black Arts Movement (BAM), asserts that "one could just as easily say that Black Power was the political wing of the Black Arts movement."[7] William Van Deburg goes even further, claiming that the

Black Power movement "was not exclusively cultural, but it was essentially cultural." He argues that culture—and not politics—was the most popular aspect of the Black Power movement.[8] Though popularity does not necessarily denote importance, many have claimed that one of the most significant legacies of the Black freedom movements is not its material gains, but rather its ideological and cultural transformation of U.S. society.[9]

While Ho would agree with the transformative power of artistic and symbolic projects, he would also emphasize its connectedness with political protest. This is why Cabral, in all his complexity and dialectical thinking, is particularly appealing to Ho. Drawing from Cabral, Ho's political theorizing, cultural work, and personal and activist practices involve a decolonizing of one's individual and collective mind, a serious engagement with the struggle for liberation, the integration of aesthetic and political resistance, and the goal of personal and societal transformation. When BAM leader Larry Neal stated, "The artist and the political activist are one," he was defining the Black aesthetic in political terms.[10] Ho, it can be argued, sought to articulate an Asian American aesthetic in political terms.

Afro-Asian Solidarities

Ho's entrée into music was sparked by the 1960s Black Power and Black Arts movements, magnetic forces that touched something deep in his soul. Foremost among his musical mentors was Archie Shepp, who captivated Ho with "his outspoken militant political views, fused with Marxist influences" combined with "his soulful and incendiary tenor saxophone playing."[11] LeRoi Jones (Amiri Baraka) said about Shepp's music and politics: "The word was, at the time, ' . . . man, that cat'll scare you to death.'"[12] Shepp was known for his audacious statements, among them "The Negro musician is a reflection of the Negro people as a social phenomenon. His purpose ought to be to liberate America aesthetically and socially from its inhumanity. . . . I think the Negro people through the force of their struggles are the only hope of saving America, the political or cultural America."[13] Shortly after acquiring his first saxophone, a second-hand baritone, at age fourteen, Ho, while still a high school student, began attending Shepp's classes at the University of Massachusetts, in Ho's hometown of Amherst. Through Shepp, Ho encountered another important influence, composer and trumpeter Cal Massey. Years later, in the 1980s, Ho was moved to conduct original research into Massey's life and music and organize a series of tribute concerts dedicated to the late Massey.[14] Ho expressed: "Massey's extended suites, such as 'The

Black Liberation Movement Suite' . . . strongly appealed to me with their thematically epic historical scope, Fanonic titles ('The Damned Don't Cry'), soulful melodies, complex and rich harmonies, Afrocentric rhythms (more African-inspired or African American interpreted than actually traditional African). It was the music of liberation and revolution . . . ; one could hear the Black Panthers marching inside the music itself."[15]

Being a decade younger than most '60s activists, Ho, born in 1957, was actually a '70s activist. This decade shift is important. The mainstream social movement historiography has come under increasing criticism for emphasizing the civil rights and early New Left movements, while denouncing and misinterpreting the turn to Black Power in the mid-1960s. But as academic and activist scholarship focuses on Black Power activism, the gap in the literature on the 1970s radical movements becomes even more glaring. Contrary to the common notion that the '60s movements died by the end of that decade, activist-intellectual Max Elbaum argues that the social movements continued well into the 1970s, largely through the turn to Marxism-Leninism. The New Communist movement and its genealogical predecessors—Black Power, the antiwar protests of U.S. imperialism in Vietnam, and the post–World War II explosion of Third World national-liberation struggles—directly shaped Ho's politics.[16]

In 1974, two changes on the national scene sparked Ho's radicalism. First, Ho first heard Amiri Baraka speak in 1974. That year, Baraka made a dramatic turn to Marxism-Leninism (and a decade before that, Baraka had transitioned from acclaimed Beat poet to Black nationalist). As an outspoken Black nationalist leader and the budding New Communist movement's "best-known figure," Baraka's latest metamorphosis sent shock waves throughout the Black and Third World movements.[17] Within the ranks of the Congress of Afrikan People (later the Revolutionary Communist League) and the African Liberation Support Committee, both national united front organizations with Baraka in the leadership, Black militants were embroiled in contentious debates over the merits of nationalism versus Marxism-Leninism.[18] In the early to mid-1970s, the *Black Scholar* captured this debate. The cultural nationalists, notably Third World Press publisher Haki Madhubuti and poet Kalamu ya Salaam, argued that Black oppression was primarily rooted in racism, racism preceded the development of capitalism, and White people were the main enemy. Madhubuti went so far as to denounce Third World solidarity, claiming that only Blacks would prioritize Black liberation. Baraka and other Marxist-Leninists asserted that racial and national oppression could not be eradicated without eliminating capitalism, that Black (and other people's) oppression was primarily rooted in monopoly capitalism and imperialism, that support for Marxism-Leninism necessitated support for national liberation, and that fighting monopoly capitalism in the United States helped undermine imperialism in Africa.[19] Ho followed the debate unfolding in the pages of the *Black Scholar* and in the Black movement.

The second change that radicalized Ho was that, in this same period, many Asian American organizations began to adopt Marxism-Leninism. In fact, Elbaum asserts that Marxism-Leninism was "the dominant left trend in the Asian American [Movement]," as it was heavily influenced by the writings of Mao Zedong and the communist revolutions in China, Vietnam, North Korea, and the Philippines.[20] In the same year as Baraka's controversial conversion, I Wor Kuen (IWK), a group that Ho later joined, turned to Marxism-Leninism. Formed in New York City in 1969, IWK merged with the San Francisco Chinatown–based Red Guard Party in 1971 to become the first nationwide revolutionary Asian American organization. From early on, IWK had declared itself for socialism in its twelve-point platform: "We Want a Socialist Society. . . . We want a society that works for the fulfillment of human needs. . . . where each gives according to his [or her] ability and takes according to his [or her] need."[21] But theirs was an eclectic socialism in promotion of revolutionary nationalism until 1974. Two years later, influenced by the Third World movement's shift to Marxism-Leninism, young Marxists at Harvard where he was then a student, and his involvement in the working-class immigrant community in Boston's Chinatown, Ho, at age eighteen, came to embrace Marxism-Leninism and joined IWK soon thereafter.[22]

In 1978, IWK and the predominantly Chicano August 29th Movement merged to form the League of Revolutionary Struggle (LRS), a leading Third World Marxist-Leninist organization. The next year, Baraka's Revolutionary Communist League (formerly Congress of Afrikan People) joined, followed by other Asian (namely, East Wind in Los Angeles), Puerto Rican, Dominican, Chicano, and African groups. LRS grew to become one of the largest Marxist-Leninist groups in the United States and was unique among the New Left by having oppressed nationalities, ethnicities, and women heavily represented not just among its members but also among its leaders.[23]

Race and National Liberation

What is significant about IWK, LRS, the Congress of Afrikan People/Revolutionary Communist League, and some other U.S. Third World revolutionaries is that their adoption of Marxism did not require them to liquidate the

National Question. The disputes about the relationship between nationalism and Marxism have been one of the key divisive issues in the U.S. Left movements since at least the 1920s. But by the 1970s, many radicals, including Ho, criticized the Old Left for supporting nationalism in theory but not in practice. Black social critic Harold Cruse, for example, rebuked the Communist Party USA (CPUSA) position as "a national question without nationalism."[24] Ho actively engaged in this discussion, advocating the need for Marxism-Leninism to uphold national liberation. These ideas are not uniquely his; he would not claim this, nor is this particularly important to him. Instead, drawing from Mao, Ho's views about knowledge production are materialist and collective. Mao's famous axiom from his widely read essay "On Practice" states: "If you want knowledge, you must take part in the practice of changing reality. If you want to know the taste of a pear, you must change the pear by eating it yourself."[25] Knowledge is produced not from books or from one's mind alone, but in the context of social practice, through reflection on the world, and through interactions with others. Significantly, the development of theory is to be used as a guide to a social practice.

Ho developed his ideas on the National Question, or the relationship between class struggle and national liberation, in the context of his study and practice in IWK, LRS, and the Third World Left in the 1970s through the '90s. He wrote "Notes on the National Question" in the first six years of the 21st century. He argues that national oppression—and not racism per se—characterizes the subordination of U.S. "oppressed nationalities" (or "people of color" in today's parlance). He defines national oppression as "the oppression of nations and nationalities. It is the systematic, historical oppression of an entire people—of all classes of the oppressed nation or nationality." National oppression includes racism but extends beyond it. Ho states:

> National oppression means oppression over nations and nationalities, and is not reducible to racism as the "race/class/gender" non-Marxists would have us think. Racism is part of the particular historical and social development of U.S. national oppression. The material basis of racism is national oppression. To reduce the national struggles as one of "anti-racism" is both wrong and objectionable for diminishing the extent of national oppression, for narrowing and limiting the political solution to be integration and assimilation as opposed to national liberation and the seizure of state power and control over territory/land.[26]

While adamantly opposed to racism, Ho's main criticism is that antiracist struggles do not necessarily demand power or land and land rights. Land provides the material basis on which to build homes, schools, hospitals, factories, and roads; land provides sustenance and food, a means to survival; and land provides an identity, a cultural compass, a spiritual, psychological, social, and physical connection to life itself. Malcolm X issued this call in the 1960s—"revolution is always based on land"—and in the 1990s, the Zapatistas revived Emiliano Zapata's rallying cry of the Mexican revolution, "tierra y libertad" (land and freedom). Ho, borrowing from Mo Nishida, contends that the Japanese American redress movement of the 1980s should have included a demand for the land taken from the Japanese Americans during World War II.[27]

Ho's second major criticism of an antiracism framework is that it does not necessarily involve the goal of national liberation, but rather often strives for racial integration into dominant society. His criticism of integrationism points to his location far outside the mainstream, including the liberal-labor "Left," but situates him squarely within nationalist ideologies. The concept of Black Power coincides with Cabral's "return to the source." Stokely Carmichael (Kwame Ture) and Charles Hamilton, in their influential *Black Power*, reason that when integration results in Black people moving into White neighborhoods and schools, then it reinforces the idea that Whiteness is superior; thus, "'[I]ntegration' is a subterfuge for the maintenance of white supremacy." Instead, Carmichael and Hamilton call for power, Black Power, so that "black people [can] become equal in a way that means something."[28]

Ho's ideas spark controversy. Many activists and academics today will disagree with his ideas, seeing his views on national liberation as outdated and his views on integration as irresponsible. Ho's ideas ring of an earlier period, when the U.S. political economy was characterized by Keynesianism; they are, some will argue, no longer relevant under today's global neoliberalism. Ho would agree that ideas from another historical period or geographic location should not be mechanically applied. Instead, "[T]he dialectic must itself be analyzed dialectically. This is no embarrassment; rather it is a necessary awareness for self-criticism."[29] Still, to Ho, the theoretical ideas of national liberation continue to characterize the subordination of oppressed nationalities today and ought to be used as a guide for social change. Hugo Chávez's efforts in Venezuela, he argues, provide a stunning example of a current struggle for socialism and national liberation taking place within a single nation-state, as it is shaped by and influences international events and movements. The state of race relations has certainly changed from the 1970s. With the advent of multiculturalism, many contend that integration does not merely proceed from Black to White neighborhoods, as busing did in the 1970s. With the existence of more multiracial neighborhoods, schools, and workplaces, Carmichael and Hamilton's argument linking integration to White supremacy is less relevant today. Still, like Vijay Prashad, who critiques today's "bureaucratic multiculturalism" for limiting antiracist struggles to the promotion of diversity, Ho criticizes the kind of celebratory multiculturalism that dominates U.S. culture today—what he calls celebrating the five Fs: food, fashion, fads, festivals, and famous people.[30] To move beyond bureaucratic multiculturalism and racial inclusion into the capitalist state, Ho asserts that national liberation, and not merely antiracism, remains a critically important arena of theoretical and practical struggle today.

While I address critiques by mainstream academics and activists, Ho was targeting a different audience. His primary objective in writing his essay on the National Question was to motivate Marxist-Leninists to support U.S.-based movements for national liberation, specifically as the Left group he joined briefly in the early 1990s moved toward, in his view, socialist integrationism. Ho's essay is influenced by the writings of fellow LRS comrade, Amiri Baraka, who contends that proletarian internationalism, misinterpreted by some Leftists as the repudiation of nationalism, requires a simultaneous movement toward national liberation, socialism, and internationalism. More pointedly, Baraka chastises U.S. Marxists for failing to actively oppose national oppression: "Marxists cannot be so involved with theoretically upholding internationalism that they dismiss their own nation's concrete national liberation struggle."[31] Ho's other major objective was to influence the nationalist movements to move toward Marxism-Leninism. Ho's reason for supporting Marxism-Leninism, and not revolutionary nationalism per se, is that the latter "pulls up short in the revolutionary process of eliminating all classes, for unqualified support for the leadership of the proletariat over all other classes."[32] Still, he supports national liberation because "it's just these struggles for democracy, in all areas of U.S. life that will bring the masses of all nationalities to revolutionary positions."[33]

Cultural and Political Radicalism in the Asian American Movement: Creating an Asian American Jazz

Given the power of creative projects to express social conditions, to stir the soul, and to inspire protest, it is not surprising that such works blossomed alongside the Asian American Movement (AAM) as it emerged in the late 1960s. Frank Chin, Janice Mirikitani, Tomie Arai, A Grain of Sand trio (Nobuko Miyamoto, Chris Iijima, and "Charlie" Chin), Dan and June Kuramoto, artists at the Kearny Street Workshop, and many others created plays, poetry, novels, films, visual arts, dance, music, and other cultural projects as part of what may be called an Asian American arts movement. Unlike the BAM, little has been written about this political Asian American arts movement. Could it, like the BAM, be considered the cultural wing of the AAM? Ho offers: "The Asian Movement produced the greatest outpouring of expressive culture in all mediums, generated arts-specific organizations with a pan-Asian and political scope, organized its own presses and publications and united cultural production with community struggle."[34] Still, Ho notes that Asian arts was "not as politically affiliated [with] the Asian Movement as the Black Arts Movement was consciously the 'cultural wing' of the Black Liberation Movement."[35] Certainly, one would not call the AAM the political wing of an Asian arts movement, as Smethurst suggested about the close relationship between Black arts and Black Power. Ho presents an interesting argument: The lesser unity between Asian arts and the AAM rests on the more limited development of cultural nationalism in the AAM, at least compared to the well-developed and often anti-imperialist cultural nationalism of the BAM.[36] He offers nuanced analysis of, including critical support for, cultural nationalism—a position unusual among Marxist-Leninists, though in line with his views on national liberation.[37]

The linkage between Black art and social change is contained in legendary jazz drummer Max Roach's statement: "I will never again play anything that does not have social significance. We American jazz musicians of African descent have proven beyond all doubt that we're master musicians of our instruments. Now what we have to do is employ our skill to tell the dramatic story of our people and what we've been through."[38] Beyond their artistic contributions, Black artists were often political organizers. When artist-activists were on a performance tour, they would attend political meetings in various cities. Conversely, when in town for a political event, they would put on readings, concerts, plays, and so forth. Most famously, poet, playwright, music critic, and writer Amiri Baraka founded or cofounded important cultural and political organizations, including the Black Arts Repertory Theater and School in Harlem and the nationwide Congress of Afrikan Peoples. This lead Smethurst to comment: "Black Power and Black Arts circuits were often the same, not just ideologically, but practically."[39] By contrast, Asian cultural productions appear to be more ideologically heterogeneous than Black arts, and, even more revealing, there has been little advocacy for an entity called an Asian American arts movement of the 1960s–70s.

Still, there is no doubt that Asian arts flourished alongside the AAM.[40] In the late 1970s and 1980s, Ho was among those working as AAM "cultural workers," that is, professionals or amateurs who produce music, dance, literature, film, and so forth with the goal of advancing social-justice goals.[41] Because several of Ho's close musical collaborators were fellow activists in the IWK/LRS, and/or had radical politics, there was a greater ideological unity between politics and cultural production in the Asian American free jazz movement. Ho distinguishes this movement from two other Asian American jazz scenes. One was "a mainstream straight-ahead 'jazz' group, mostly older generation players such as Filipino pianist Bobby Enriquez, pianist Toshiko Akiyoshi, alto saxophonoist Gabe Balthazar (of the Stan Kenton Big Band fame), and the younger drummer Akira Tana," and the second was "a 'jazz fusion' scene with its most prominent Los Angeles–based band, Hiroshima, along with Deems Tatsukawa in Seattle, and others."[42] With the exception of the straight-ahead musicians, most Asian American jazz musicians were closely associated with the AAM.

For Ho and his fellow artist-activists, the development of the Asian American jazz movement contained two significant ideas, both promoted by IWK/LRS. The first theme directed the music to primarily, though not exclusively, reflect the experiences of working-class Asian American communities. Amilcar Cabral's return to the source is relevant here. Cabral observed that the petite bourgeoisie, including intellectuals like himself who had studied abroad, are most susceptible to assimilating the colonizer's mentality, resulting in the negation of their indigenous culture. But frustration sets in when they find themselves structurally blocked from full assimilation or when they are conscienitized by the surrounding national liberation movement. To participate in the liberation struggle, it is then necessary to decolonize one's mind. "A reconversion of minds," asserted Cabral, "is completed only during the course of the struggle, through daily contact with the popular masses in the communion of sacrifice required by the struggle."[43] The masses were seen as representatives of African culture. So in the mid-1960s, the artist-activists at Baraka's Black Arts Repertory Theater and School in Harlem, including prominent cultural workers like Harold Cruse, Sonia Sanchez, Larry Neal, Askia Touré, and Archie Shepp, came to see Black arts as "mass art" that reflected the experiences of ordinary people and as "revolutionary" in its radical vision of justice.[44] These ideas, carried forward in the movement, were already percolating within IWK and LRS when Ho joined these organizations. As a student alienated from the elite views surrounding him at Harvard University in the mid-1970s, Ho began to spend more time in

Boston's Chinatown. Working with the IWK/LRS, he helped to organize the Asian American Resource Workshop in Chinatown, which promoted community art by bringing art to the community and involving the community in creating art. The group organized monthly coffeehouses featuring local musicians, dancers, and artists in both Chinese and English; set up Asian American poetry readings in the community; offered Chinese folk-singing ensembles; and provided music, silk screening, and photography classes, among other activities.[45] Building on ideas by Cabral and Black arts and his own experiences with the Asian American Resource Workshop, Ho's concept of revolutionary music connects the art to the experiences of ordinary people, particularly the working-class community. Ho contends that revolutionary music must accomplish the following: "speak to the people . . . either explicitly (in the form of lyrics and/or song titles) or implicitly (in the sound and in its spirit)"; "go to the people," rather than expecting people to come to the music; "involve the people" ("The essence of cultural democracy is true popular culture—culture and the arts created by and for the common people and not by and for an elite"); and "change the people . . . [it] must revolutionize the consciousness, values, aesthetics, and actions of the people."[46] Ho's ideas echo Cabral's emphasis on developing political struggles in "complete absolute identification with the hopes of" and "through daily contact with" the masses of ordinary people.[47]

The second major theme was to create a new hybrid musical form. In the late 1970s, around the time Ho joined, IWK took the position that "Asian American art and culture necessitates a link to traditional Asian cultural forms."[48] This directive, combined with his experiences in Boston's Chinatown, motivated Ho to begin an intensive study of the folk traditions of Asian American culture. He notes:

> It became clear to me that a working class, even revolutionary, tradition exists in APA [Asian Pacific American] cultures. Such a tradition includes the first immigrant cultural forms: Cantonese opera, the woodfishhead chants, the talk-story traditions, the folk ballads and syllabic verses of the Chinese immigrant laborers, the Japanese American female plantation labor songs (*hole hole bushi*), the Angel Island poetry, the Filipino randalia and folk ballads of the manongs (Filipino immigrant bachelor workers), Japanese American *tanka* (syllabic verse) poetry, etc.[49]

Russel Baba, Anthony Brown, Fred Ho, Glenn Horiuchi, Mark Izu, Jon Jang, Gerald Oshita, Francis Wong, and Paul Yamazaki were instrumental in developing an Asian American free-jazz movement, as it emerged in the late 1970s, primarily in the San Francisco Bay area. All of them were committed to Asian American activism, collaborated with African American jazz musicians, and recorded with independent labels working to give power to Asian American artists and expression to Asian American arts.[50] They individually and collectively worked to create "a distinctive Asian American Music" by "combin[ing] actual Asian traditional instrumentation and Asian-inspired or influenced stylistic elements with predominantly 'free' or modal improvisation in the African American avant-garde 'jazz' context."[51] In this way, they were "returning to the source" of traditional Asian musical forms. Moreover, Ho views jazz as "revolutionary music," because the "entire history" of the music "has been the freeing of time, pitch, and harmony from fixed, regulated, predictable standards."[52] The improvisational form of jazz thus provides an opportunity for artists to think and play imaginatively and significantly, outside the confines of dominant culture.[53] Ho traces his musical genealogy to the politically radical Black free jazz movement embodied by Archie Shepp and Max Roach.

Jazz pianist Jon Jang, then a close collaborator of Ho's, conveys the difficulties of trying to create an Asian American musical aesthetic in the 1970s and '80s: "Although the Black liberation and third world movements and the power of African American music through John Coltrane liberated me on a humanistic, spiritual, and political level, I could only *imagine* the possibilities of my liberation through an Asian American music because I was unaware of any existing models."[54] Through a combination of activist practice, deliberate study of Asian folk traditions, and trial-and-error experimentation, Ho developed his own unique and evolving style. Ho's fascination with Japanese tanka poetry is an example. This three-thousand-year-old art form, initially enjoyed by the elite in Japan, became popular among ordinary Japanese Americans. Ho sees Cabral's "return to the source" in the efforts to keep tanka "an active spiritual and cultural force" among Japanese Americans during World War II and today.[55]

Similarly, in the Cantonese opera, Ho sees Chinese tradition, working-class culture, and resistance. Chinese opera was enormously popular among Chinese immigrant laborers from the mid-19th century until the 1930s, when motion pictures and television replaced performing arts. Because most Chinese immigrants emigrated from the Canton region, Cantonese opera was most popular. Compared to the more sophisticated Peking opera that was performed for the royal court, Cantonese opera was characterized by "its grander visual effects, its ample use of Cantonese vernacular, its inclusion of Cantonese folk songs, its use of spirited percussion, and its practice of secondary scenes. The plots typically included occasions for acrobatic displays, comic relief, and lyrical singing."[56] Ho explains: "Unlike bourgeois European opera in the U.S., Chinese opera in U.S. Chinatowns is a mass popular cultural form . . . typically performed in a makeshift theater where patrons go to eat and sip tea, chatter loudly until their favorite scenes appear on stage, then shout their praise or criticize the performance."[57] Jack Chen expressed that the Chinese opera "sustained the spirits of the beleaguered Chinatown dwellers" by providing Chinese immigrant workers with heroes, warriors, and great leaders who triumphed over wrongdoers and by preserving Chinese culture in the face of severe anti-Chinese hostility and violence.[58] To Jon Jang, the Cantonese opera provided a way to blend traditional Chinese form with African American blues. After reading about "the importance of spirituals and sorrow songs as the foundation of African American culture" in W. E. B. DuBois's masterpiece, *The Souls of Black Folks*, Jang wondered if Chinese immigrant laborers, strenuously building the transcontinental railroad, also sang work or sorrow songs. If so, what did they sound like? Jang discovered such "Cantonese blues" in the operas performed in Chinatowns in San Francisco and New York.[59]

The influences of Cantonese opera as well as Cal Massey's large-scale extended suites and Archie Shepp's "stunning and powerful combination of poetry and music" are evident in Ho's own works. Ho's compositions, such as "Once upon a Time in Chinese America . . . A Ballet and Music/Theater Epic" (1995), combine sweeping epic stories, radical political themes, physically powerful actors, and multimedia poetry, text, and graphics.[60] In interpreting Ho's *Journey beyond the West: The New Adventures of Monkey* (1995), musicologist Wei-hua Zhang observes that Ho "borrows devices from Chinese opera and uses linguistic referents for musical patterns." As one example, "the percussionist employs the Peking Opera percussion pattern *liu-shui* (running water) to accompany a folksong-like melody when Monkey feels happy . . . and the second, *ji-ji-feng* (swift wind) when Monkey wrecks the Peach Banquet." Zhang further notes: "[An] example of the fusion of Chinese and Western musical elements is to be found in the vocal part: Chinese lyrics sung in Mandarin, juxtaposed Western and quasi-Chinese melodies, and blended Chinese and Western vocal style. The vocalist also functions as narrator, comparable to the *daobai* (narration) in Chinese opera. The melodies are original. Ho does not employ traditional Chinese melodies or folksongs."[61]

Conclusion

During his time in LRS, through the late 1980s, Ho strove to create a revolutionary music and a collective way of working that required activist-artists to "put self-interest secondary to the goals of the movement."[62] As challenging and selfless as this effort was, it also produced mechanical and polemical boundaries to the creative process. In his 1983 review of five Asian American poets in the LRS publication *East Wind: Politics and Culture of Asians in the U.S.*, Ho was critical of works that were more personal than political, arguing that they become "individualistic musings." His assertion that "Asian American writers should draw more from the Asian American communities and working people's lives and struggles as sources for new, creative works [and] to inherit the progressive traditions of Asian and Asian American culture" sounds reasonable as a criteria for political art.[63] But he seemed to judge all art primarily on these political criteria: Does it focus on working-class communities? Does it resist oppression? Does it return to the source? Richard Oyama, in a later issue of *East Wind*, criticized what he saw as the narrowness of Ho's criteria, particularly for "ignor[ing] the *imaginative* aspects of writing." In response to Ho's rejection of the overly personal, Oyama wrote: "The women's movement has been credited with the phrase, 'the personal is political,' meaning that the seemingly trivial details of daily life, the single acts and choices we make and do during the day, are imbued with a political dimension."[64] Similarly, Robin Kelley argues in *Race Rebels* is that we need to look beyond formal organizations and institutions to discover the multitude of ways that ordinary people resist oppression.[65]

In the midst of intensive struggles for justice and while trying to figure out how to be revolutionary artists, particularly in the conservative period of the late 1970s and '80s, activists in LRS and elsewhere tended toward more perfunctory political messages. In the late 1990s, a decade after his departure from LRS, Ho himself offers this candid criticism of the movement, and ostensibly of himself:

> By and large, these attempts at a revolutionary theory of APA art and culture simply reiterated standard M-L [Marxism-Leninism] views (mostly from Mao's Yenan talks on art, literature and revolution) on the political and class nature of art, the propaganda value of folk and popular forms, the question of aesthetic form and its dialectical, yet subordinate, relationship to revolutionary proletarian content. This theoretical shallowness was reflected in an equally shallow early Asian American Movement music—a derivative of

> both white folk and leftist styles à la Bob Dylan and Pete Seeger or African American gospel, soul and rhythm and blues idioms. The major limitation of the American Left's theory and practice in cultural work has stemmed from the influence of socialist-realism (the Zhdanov policies of the Soviet Union), commonly regarded as "agit-prop." This theory regards art solely for its utilitarian value as a vehicle for propaganda.[66]

The growth of Ho's views on politics and culture, reflecting political and ideological changes in the social movements and larger society, is evident in his music as well as his writings. His writings in the past decade are clearer, more creative, more confident, and less mechanical (as in his rejection of all poetry other than the overtly political in his 1983 *East Wind* article), though still bold, still provocative, and still polemical in advocating for revolutionary change.[67] His music, while retaining explicitly radical political themes, is more imaginative and playful and places greater emphasis on form (hybrid synthesis of traditional Asian music and African American jazz and unconventional, even disturbing harmonies, as already discussed). Consider the way he described his work by the late 1990s: "While much of the twentieth-century Left's artistic tradition is heavily dominated by 'socialist' or 'critical' realism (the common working man or peasant as hero/protagonist), my work is revolutionary fantasy or vision-quests." He even goes so far as to say: "I reject socialist heroes, but I do populate my theatrical landscapes with tricksters, womyn warrior sheroes and supernatural beings. I draw from tall-tale trickster and martial Chinese opera stories to create a neo-mythology of a world beyond this one that unleashes the imagination enough for a two-year-old child (my biggest critic) to be both spellbound and revolutionized."[68] These themes can be seen in much of Ho's work in the past dozen years. His multimedia musical, *The Journey beyond the West: The New Adventures of Monkey!* (1995, 1997), and accompanying CDs feature the many adventures of Monkey ("China's most popular trickster character"), Buddhist Priest, Pig, Ogre, and White Stallion. Ho writes in the liner notes: "The entire work contains many radical allegorical themes . . . Monkey as an androgynous entity . . . Monkey's complete disregard and distain for private ownership of property . . . Monkey's communistic sensibility for equality." Ho's characters now reflect a more complex and nuanced humanity: "Monkey is also a contradictory creature: powerful and egalitarian, yet highly conceited, arrogant, violent-prone and with egotistical desires for recognition, comforts, and rewards."[69] Certainly, Ho has developed far beyond any mechanical application of "agit-prop" art.

Figure 9. Fred Ho in Boston Chinatown, tabling support for Chol Soo Lee case (a Korean American man wrongfully imprisoned in California), 1979. Credit: Iyanna Jones

While still identifying as a revolutionary activist-artist, Ho has made many changes in his political, cultural, and personal life. His battle against cancer, for example, further intensified his efforts to unify the personal and the political. He proclaimed, while undergoing chemotherapy: "The point of setting standards and striving for integrity and excellence is to evoke the transformation and transcendence of those around you, to inspire one another as part of the enhancing of all our contributions to transform society and the world to be free of exploitation, injustice, inequality, and oppression."[70] After thirty years as a Marxist-Leninist, Ho maintains the need for revolutionary socialism, national liberation, and internationalism, and for the centrality of culture in liberation struggles. Cabral's "return to the source," still relevant, advocates for the return to the progressive aspects of one's culture such that one rejects the allure of assimilationism into the dominant neoliberal or neocolonial capitalist culture. Cabral observed that "independence movements are generally marked, even in their early stages, by an upsurge of cultural activity."[71] Certainly, creative works, because they are seen as fiction, offer an ostensibly safer medium for expressing transgressive ideas. More so, creative expression unleashes the imagination and sparks "dreams of freedom." However far-fetched, the very act of freedom dreaming creates "poetic knowledge," or Robin Kelley's reference for the ability to "imagine a new society," to "transport us to another place," and to "see the future in the present."[72] It is hard to imagine a new society or a liberation movement not carried by freedom dreams. To Ho, such freedom dreams, such poetic knowledge, such cultural expressions insist on a "return to the source." This does not necessitate an uncritical return to tradition because, as Cabral noted, "no culture is perfect, finished whole."[73] But it does require a critical analysis of society, especially of colonial or dominating structures that foster inequality, and a decolonizing or reconversion of one's mind so as to reject the trappings of the ideology of power. Despite the difficulties of striving to remain a revolutionary artist-activist, Ho is invigorated by life and by "the music's 'spiritualizing' quality: to fortify and prepare us to continue the struggle until liberation."[74]

Notes

1. Diane C. Fujino, *Heartbeat of Struggle: The Revolutionary Life of Yuri Kochiyama* (Minneapolis: University of Minnesota Press, 2005).

2. Fred Ho, ed., with Carolyn Antonio, Diane Fujino, and Steve Yip, *Legacy to Liberation: Politics and Culture of Revolutionary Asian Pacific America* (San Francisco: AK Press, 2000).

3. For a discussion of the dawns that follow the darkness of the Ho's midnight hours, see my introduction to Fred Ho, *Wicked Theory, Naked Practice: A Fred Ho Reader*, ed. Diane Fujino (Minneapolis: University of Minnesota Press, 2009).

4. Amilcar Cabral, "National Liberation and Culture," in *Return to the Source: Selected Speeches by Amilcar Cabral*, ed. Africa Information Service (New York: Monthly Review Press, 1973), 39–56.

5. Fred Ho, "Fists for Revolution: The Revolutionary History of I Wor Kuen/League of Revolutionary Struggle," in Ho, *Legacy to Liberation*, 9.

6. Cabral, *Return to the Source*, 63, 45.

7. James Edward Smethurst, *The Black Arts Movement: Literary Nationalism in the 1960s and 1970s* (Chapel Hill: University of North Carolina Press, 2005), 14.

8. William L. Van Deburg, *New Day in Babylon: The Black Power Movement and American Culture, 1965–1975* (Chicago: University of Chicago Press, 1992), 9, 17. While Van Deburg also noted the intertwining of culture and politics—"Black Power was both a cultural and a political revolt, each thrust reinforcing the other" (189)—this does not negate his major emphasis on cultural resistance.

9. Michael Omi and Howard Winant, *Racial Formation in the United States* (New York: Routledge, 1994); Robin D. G. Kelley, *Freedom Dreams: The Black Radical Imagination* (Boston: Beacon, 2002).

10. Amiri Baraka and Larry Neal, ed., *Black Fire* (New York: William Morrow, 1968), 656.

11. Fred Ho, "Asian American Tribute to the Black Arts Movement," in *Wicked Theory, Naked Practice*, 172.

12. LeRoi Jones, *Black Music* (New York: Morrow, 1967), 145.

13. Frank Kofsky, *Black Nationalism and the Revolution in Music* (New York: Pathfinder Press, 1970), 9.

14. This research conducted in the early 1980s, a decade after Massey's death, and included interviews with Massey's wife, children, and fellow musicians; see Ho, "The Damned Don't Cry: The Life and Music of Calvin Massey," *Wicked Theory, Naked Practice*, 129–50.

15. Fred Ho, "Beyond Asian American Jazz: Musical and Political Changes in the Asian American Movement," *Leonardo Music Journal* 9 (1999): 45.

16. Max Elbaum, *Revolution in the Air: Radicals Turn to Lenin, Mao, and Che* (London: Verso, 2002), 291–94.

17. "Best-known figure" in ibid., 84.

18. Amiri Baraka, "The Congress of Afrikan People: A Position Paper," *Black Scholar* 6 (1975): 2–15; League of Revolutionary Struggle, "'Unity and Struggle'—History of the Revolutionary Communist League (M-L-M)," *Forward: Journal of Marxism-Leninism-Mao Zedong Thought*, no. 3 (January 1980): 55–97; Phil Hutchings, "Report on the ALCS National Conference," *Black Scholar* 5 (1974): 48–53; Amiri Baraka, *The Autobiography of LeRoi Jones* (Chicago: Lawrence Hill Books, 1984/1997), 426–41.

19. Among the many articles on the debate on Marxism and nationalism in *Black Scholar*, the following are the most cogent articulation of major ideas: Haki R. Madhubuti, "The Latest Purge: The Attack on Black Nationalism and Pan-Afrikanism by the New Left, the Sons and Daughters of the Old Left," 6 (1974): 43–56; Kalamu ya Salaam, "A Response to Haki Madhubuti," 6 (1975): 40–43; Mark Smith, "A Response to Haki Madhubuti," 6 (1975): 44–53; Hutchings, "Report on the ALCS National Conference"; Baraka, "Congress of Afrikan People."

20. Elbaum, *Revolution in the Air*, 113.

21. I Wor Kuen, "12 Point Platform and Program," in Ho, *Legacy to Liberation*, 405–7.

22. It is often difficult to pinpoint the precise dates of one's organizational membership. By his self-report, Ho joined IWK either in late 1976 or early 1977 ("Asian American Tribute to the Black Arts Movement," 190), in late 1977 (Ho, *Legacy to Liberation*, 5), or in early 1978 (Fred Wei-han Ho, "Marxism and Asian Americans: The Struggle Continues!," *Forward Motion* 11 [1992]: 66–71).

23. Ho states LRS was "never more than 20% white" and was "the largest M-L organization in the U.S." ("Fists for Revolution," 11); Elbaum asserts that LRS was 75 to 80 percent oppressed nationality (*Revolution in the Air*, 272). Elbaum notes that only one other New Communist group had majority women leadership: the predominantly White Democratic Workers Party (272, also 246). On merging into the

LRS, see League of Revolutionary Struggle, *Forward*, no. 1 (July 1978): "Statement by Seize the Time on United with the League," 105–8; "Statement by East Wind on Its Unity with the League," 109–15; and "Statement by the New York Collective on Uniting with the League," 117–18.

24. The CPUSA's influential Black Belt thesis, adopted in 1928, argued that African Americans in the rural South constituted an oppressed nation and in the northern ghettos, a national minority suffering special discrimination, both with the rights to self-determination and political and economic autonomy. The Communist top leadership, however, only gave lip service to Black self-determination. Nonetheless, this thesis not only enabled the CPUSA to establish itself "for the first time as the leading advocate of equal rights for black people," it had enormous influence on the ideological development of U.S. revolutionary movements in the decades to follow. By contrast, the Trotskyite position that the world revolution must be led by the working-class in the most advanced industrialized nations, rendered them less relevant to the struggles of U.S. Third World peoples. See Harold Cruse, "Revolutionary Nationalism and the Afro-American," *Studies on the Left* 2 (1962), reprinted in *Rebellion or Revolution?* (New York: William Morrow, 1968), 78; Robert L. Allen, *Black Awakening in Capitalist America: An Analytic History* (New York: Anchor Books, 1969); William Z. Foster, *History of the Communist Party of the United States* (New York: Greenwood Press, 1968).

25. Mao Tsetung, "On Practice," *Selected Readings from the Works of Mao Tsetung* (Peking: Foreign Language Press, 1971), 65, 71.

26. Fred Ho, "Notes on the National Question," in Ho, *Wicked Theory, Naked Practice*, 299.

27. Land is so crucial to Indigenous life that the Zapatistas rose up in 1994, in large part, to protest the revision of article 27 of the 1917 Mexican Constitution, permitting the privatization of indigenous communal lands and peasant *ejidos*. See James D. Cockcroft, *Mexico's Hope: An Encounter with Politics and History* (New York: Monthly Review, 1998), 302–7; George A. Collier, with Elizabeth Lowery Quaratiello, *Basta! Land and the Zapatista Rebellion in Chiapas* (Oakland, Calif.: Institute for Food and Development Policy, 1994); Malcolm X, "The Black Revolution," in *Malcolm X Speaks*, ed. George Breitman (New York: Grove Press, 1965), 50; also "Message to the Grass Roots" in same volume; Mo Nishida, interview by Fred Ho, in *Legacy to Liberation*, 313.

28. Stokely Carmichael and Charles V. Hamilton, *Black Power: The Politics of Liberation in America* (New York: Vintage, 1967), 54–55.

29. Richard Levins and Richard Lewontin, *The Dialectical Biologist* (Cambridge, Mass.: Harvard University Press, 1985), 287; quoted in Ho, "Marxism and Asian Americans," 71.

30. Vijay Prashad, foreword to *AfroAsian Encounters: Culture, History, Politics*, ed. Heike Raphael-Hernandez and Shannon Steen (New York: New York University

Press, 2006), xvi; Fred Ho, lecture, Asian American Movement course, University of California Santa Barbara, May 18, 1999.

31. Amiri Baraka, "Nationalism, Self-Determination, and Socialism," *Black Nation: Journal of Afro-American Thought* 2 (fall/winter 1982): 5.

32. Ho, "Notes on the National Question," 9.

33. Baraka, "Nationalism, Self-Determination, and Socialism," 10.

34. Ho, "Bamboo That Snaps Back! Resistance and Revolution in Asian Pacific American Working Class and Left-Wing Expressive Culture," in *Left of the Color Line: Race, Radicalism, and Twentieth-century Literature of the United States*, ed. Bill V. Mullen and James Smethurst (Chapel Hill: University of North Carolina Press, 2003), 253–54.

35. Ho, "Asian American Tribute to the Black Arts Movement," 170.

36. Ho contends that while Asian American literary scholars use the moniker "cultural nationalism" to disparage Frank Chin and others as narrow and essentialist, these writers did not self-identify as cultural nationalists, nor did the Asian American Movement of that day apply that term to them (Ho, "Asian American Tribute to the Black Arts Movement," 169–70).

37. Ho, "Notes on the National Question," 304–6.

38. Max Roach, interview for *DownBeat* magazine, circa 1960, cited in "Max Roach 1924–2007: Thousands Pay Tribute to the Legendary Jazz Drummer, Educator, Activist," Amy Goodman, *Democracy Now*, August 27, 2007, www.democracynow.org, accessed March 10, 2008.

39. Smethurst, *Black Arts Movement*, 14–15.

40. Amy Ling brings together brief biographies and sample works in *Yellow Light: The Flowering of Asian American Arts* (Philadelphia: Temple University Press, 1999). Two recent dissertations focus extensively on cultural production in the AAM: Gisele L. Fong, "The People United: Cultural Work and the Making of Asian America, 1968–1985," PhD dissertation, University of California, Los Angeles, 2003; Daryl J. Maeda, "Forging Asian American Identity: Race, Culture, and the Asian American Movement, 1968–1975," PhD dissertation, University of Michigan, 2001, published as *Chains of Babylon: The Rise of Asian America* (Minneapolis: University of Minnesota Press, 2009).

41. By using the term *cultural worker*, Ho follows the movement's rearticulation of art to explicitly integrate political resistance and reject the elitism of "high art" (Fred Ho, "What Is a Revolutionary Artist?," unpublished speech, New School for Social Research, New York, 1995).

42. Ho, "Asian American Tribute to the Black Arts Movement," 198 ; also Brian Auerbach, "Asian-American Jazz: An Oral History with Paul Yamazaki," *Option*, March–April 1985: 37–38.

43. Cabral, *Return to the Source*, 45

44. Amiri Baraka, "The Black Arts Movement" (1994), in *The LeRoi Jones/Amiri*

Baraka Reader, ed. William J. Harris (New York: Thunder's Mouth Press, 1999), 502–503.

45. Peter Nien-chu Kiang, "Asian American Resource Workshop: Art and Culture for the Community," *East Wind* 2:1 (spring/summer 1983): 11–14.

46. Fred Ho, "What Makes 'Jazz' the Revolutionary Music of the 20th Century, and Will It Be Revolutionary for the 21st Century?," *African American Review* 29, no. 2 (1995): 289–90.

47. Cabral, *Return to the Source*, 45, 63.

48. Ho, "Beyond Asian American Jazz," 46; also Peter Kiang, "Transformation—The Challenge Facing the Asian American Artist in the '80s," *East Wind* 4 (winter/spring 1985): 31–33.

49. Ho, "Beyond Asian American Jazz," 46; also Fred Houn, "Revolutionary Asian American Art," in Ho, *Legacy to Liberation*, 383–88.

50. Deborah Wong, *Speaking It Louder: Asian Americans Making Music* (New York: Routledge, 2004), 172; Susan M. Asai, "Cultural Politics: The African American Connection in Asian American Jazz-based Music," *Asian Music* 36 (2005): 87–108.

51. Ho, "Beyond Asian American Jazz," 46.

52. Ho, "What Makes 'Jazz, the Revolutionary Music of the 20th Century?," 285.

53. I recognize that jazz, like any other music, can also be used to reproduce dominant culture and society. Ho criticized Ken Burns's super-touted, huge-budgeted documentary series, *Jazz*, for selecting artists and music that reinforced assimilation into dominant (oppressive) culture while neglecting those artists and songs that "sound the aspirations for freedom." As George Lipsitz observed: *Jazz* is "not just a film *about* history, this production *makes* history"—and a history that promotes the master narrative of heroic individualism and bureaucratic multiculturalism and limits critiques of U.S. democracy and racism (Fred Ho, "Highlights in the History of *Jazz* NOT Covered by Ken Burns"). George Lipsitz, "Jazz: The Hidden History of Nationalist Multiculturalism," *Footsteps in the Dark: Hidden Histories of Popular Music* (Minneapolis: University of Minnesota Press, 2007), 81, 79–106.

54. Jang, response, in Ling, *Yellow Light*, 340, original emphasis.

55. Fred Houn, "Tomoe Tana: Keeping Alive Japanese American Tanka," *Asian Week*, June 17, 1988.

56. Nancy Yunhaw Rao, "Racial Essences and Historical Invisibility: Chinese Opera in New York, 1930," *Cambridge Opera Journal* 12 (2000): 136–37.

57. Ho, "Bamboo That Snaps Back!," 244.

58. Jack Chen, "American Chinese Opera, Chinese American Reality," *East Wind* 5:1 (spring/summer 1986): 16.

59. Jon Jang, response, *Yellow Light*, 340–44; W. E. B. DuBois, "Of the Sorrow Songs," in *The Souls of Black Folk* (New York: Bantam Books, 1989/1903), 177–87.

60. Ho, "Beyond Asian American Jazz," 45.

61. Wei-hua Zhang, "Fred Wei-han Ho: Case Study of a Chinese-American Creative Musician," *Asian Music* 25 (1993–94): 101, 103.

62. Ho, "Asian American Tribute to the Black Arts Movement," 201.

63. Fred Wei-han Houn, "Five Asian American Poets," *East Wind* 2 (fall/winter 1983): 65–67.

64. Richard Oyama, "Five Asian American Poets: A Response," *East Wind* 4 (winter/spring 1985): 44–45, original emphasis.

65. Robin D. G. Kelley, *Race Rebels: Culture, Politics, and the Black Working Class* (New York: Free Press, 1994).

66. Ho, "Beyond Asian American Jazz," 46.

67. Peter Kiang seems to be commenting about Ho's aggressively political reviews, many of which were published *East Wind*, when he writes: "Similarly, musician/writer/activist Fred Houn deserves credit for establishing, at the very least, an unequivocal viewpoint in his reviews of Asian American poetry and music" ("Transformation—The Challenge Facing the Asian American Artist in the '80s," *East Wind* 4 (winter/spring 1985): 32–33.

68. Ho, "Beyond Asian American Jazz," 46.

69. Liner notes, *Monkey*, part 1, composed by Fred Ho, performed by the Monkey Orchestra (KOCH International, 1996).

70. These words were drawn from his artistic collaborator Magdalena Gómez; Fred Ho, *Diary of a Radical Cancer Warrior: Fighting Cancer and Capitalism at the Cellular Level* (New York: Skyhorse Publishing, 2011), 72–73.

71. Cabral, *Return to the Source*, 59.

72. Kelley, *Freedom Dreams*, 9.

73. Cabral, *Return to the Source*, 50, 60.

74. Ho, "What Makes 'Jazz' the Revolutionary Music of the 20th Century?" 290.

5

Red Dragon, Blue Warrior

Fred Ho's Ethical Aesthetic

SALIM WASHINGTON

I think of Fred Ho as a red dragon, signifying upon his Chinese ancestry and his commitment to socialism. Indeed, he has named his media company Big Red in part in honor to Mao Tse-tung. For Fred, "Red" also refers to his intellectual and cultural indebtedness to Malcolm X, known in his hustling days as Detroit Red—(light skinned blacks frequently being referred to as being "red [boned]"). I call him a blue warrior, because he has infused his work with the African American blues-jazz aesthetic, and has been a steadfast warrior against capitalism and national and gender oppression. Fred Ho is a fearless revolutionary who early in life found out that capitalism—based not only on the exploitation of workers, but also slavery, genocide, imperialism, patriarchy, misogyny, and the rape of the earth itself—must be resisted.

Ho strives for consistency and truly models the notion that resistance must come in all forms. He is willing and able to take the fight against various forms of oppression to many levels, but ultimately has chosen consciousness as his domain of battle. The compendium of black thought that operates through love, openness, and acceptance in part, and resistance, critical thinking, and irony as well, is the matrix within which he has staged his most heroic battles.

I first met Fred Ho in 1976. I was an incoming freshman and he a sophomore at Harvard College. We were both profoundly alienated in the Ivy League setting, despite what on paper would have seemed like more than ample preparation for each of us. I was a graduate of an elite prep school and Fred the son of an academic. The truth was, however, that in addition to our pedigrees, we were possessors of complex and sometimes contradictory self-identities, and frequently at odds within the social world of our would-be peers. For my part, I was cautious after the battles won and lost in high school and weary from the social dislocation I felt while being inducted from the working class into the U.S. educational elite. But mostly I was dismayed at the class and cultural differences between the scholarship kids I associated with in high school and expected to find in college and the shameless bourgeois wannabe children of the black nouveau riche I so frequently encountered at Harvard. As the younger brothers of the first generation of "oppressed minorities" to invade the halls of the nation's elite educational institutions in large numbers, in response to the freedom movement of the 1960s and 1970s, we were betwixt and between our aspirations for high achievement in that setting and our revulsion at the decadent excesses and shallowness of many of the privileged class of which we were (however reluctantly) a part.

The Fred Ho I met in the late 1970s was an intense young man, dedicated to revolution, and ready to teach and enlist me—and others—in the cause. We began by mobilizing protests against the upcoming Bakke decision, one of the early lynchpins in the dismantling of affirmative action. Soon we were working in a cultural organization based in Boston's Chinatown, participating in Marxist study groups, and staging protests, among other things. Aside from Fred's undeniable intensity and tenacity (once, after a lengthy conversation, I remember him reaching under his bed, with the eye gleam worn by proselytizers reeling in the fish for Christ, for a stash of—you guessed it—political newspapers and pamphlets), he had well-researched and articulate positions on everything from the role of the petty bourgeoisie in capitalist economy to the failures of the Cuban revolution to the abandonment of socialism by the Soviet Union. And while he supported student activism, such as struggles to induce Harvard to divest from apartheid South Africa and resisting the university's attempts to strip the Afro American studies department of its political content and structures, it was always clear that his political focus was wider and deeper. My own political leanings at the time were toward Black Nationalism. I had joined the AAPRP (All African Peoples Revolutionary Party) and the RNA (Republic of New Africa), found the white socialist would-be organizers trying to sell newspapers in Roxbury's black ghetto not only ridiculous but offensive, and saw the "loonies on the left" (trust-fund socialists) in Harvard Square as maybe a step or two below the *Harvard Lampoon* in their theatrical value and a flat zero for political value.

But Fred and his activist cohorts were serious and thoughtful, if a little insensitive to some of my specific political concerns. I was dismayed, for example, when a friend and I were politely but unequivocally pushed out of a study group, of which Fred was a member, for questioning whether a socialist United States would solve the social and political problems that black people faced. We were working to ensure the health of the Asian American Cultural Workshop in Boston's Chinatown and organizing against the Bakke case. So an African American friend of mine and I were thus included in a socialist study group run by Chinese American activists associated with the organizations selling the newspaper *Unity*. I was not amused that our concerns over the "race issue" raised doubts about our commitment to socialism. Fred was hard-core in those days (in *those* days?), but thankfully he did not condone the rest of the group's foolishness. At that time, many socialists were evangelical in nature and temperament, with all the internecine squabbles that are so frequent in Christendom. Fred was always quick to point out theoretical correctness and demanded a strict ethical code, but as an organizer he was also able to tolerate people of all stripes.

The thing that initially attracted me most indelibly to Fred, however, was his relationship to the music. More than the "correctness" of his political "line," it was his understanding of music that marked him as hip in my eyes, and which initially secured our friendship. Fred had studied with legendary icons such as Sonia Sanchez, Archie Shepp, and Max Roach in his hometown of Amherst. Other than a brief set of encounters with Dizzy Gillespie, who was an artist-in-residence at Harvard that year, I had not yet had the privilege of meeting jazz giants, let alone studying with them. But I *had* been turned out by a John Coltrane record (which single-handedly converted me from an R&B trumpeter to a jazz saxophonist) and at the time could not start my day without listening to Charles Mingus. Fred and I were both saxophonists and flutists, and we were both serious about being composers. I admired his ability to write long forms, and he admired my ability to write good bass lines. But while my compositions had been about my love affairs and other adolescent longings, Fred's were about political struggle and dismantling the capitalist system. I was intrigued.

We began performing together, mostly playing Fred's compositions and reciting his poetry. His aesthetic was closer to DuBois's notion of art as Truth and Propaganda than the Ellisonian ideal of symbolic heroism. We chanted for the death of multinational corporations, decried the greed of capitalists and landlords, and championed the oppressed nationalities and the working class in our shows. My love of the Last Poets, Gil Scott-Heron, and Rahsaan Roland Kirk had prepared me for these experiences of meshing political vision with jazz technique. How thrilling it was to collaborate with a like-minded person. While most of our musical peers down the street at the Berklee College of Music were staking their lives on being "discovered" and becoming famous as the baddest cats on their instruments, Fred was already demonstrating that an artist could be dedicated and sincere without being careerist *and* without living in an artistic ivory tower.

Our music wasn't all politics, however, and we put a lot of store in building our technique and understanding how the masters built their art. Fred encouraged me to memorize études from Yusef Lateef's *Flute Book of the Blues* and to transpose them in all keys, a text and practice that I use with my students to this day. One day he gave joyful notice to the fact that I had circled the upper tensions in the chords to one of his compositions to help me include less obvious and more interesting note choices in my improvisations. Despite what I thought at the time were rather pedantic leanings, Fred could also recognize and rely upon more intuitive approaches to the music.

There were moments of tenderness as well. We performed together in 1979, shortly after the death of my mother, when Fred quietly omitted "Sometimes I Feel Like a Motherless Child" from the program. I also remember some slight improvisations I used in the poetry recital that night to add a more vernacular phrasing and greater urgency. He responded by sending a letter thanking me for playing and reciting beautifully. This was a cherished letter coming from a young man who seemed long on criticism and short on praise. Shortly after, we went our separate ways. Fred moved to New York and I went south on the road with a band of jazz spiritualists. It wasn't long before I got a letter from Fred chronicling his musical growth and success. He had carved out a space for himself in the Big Apple. In between, he sent me a letter about the jazz luminaries that he was meeting and playing with after joining drummer Charlie Persip's band. He was now going through a box of reeds every week, he wrote. Fred's exuberance was just the beginning. He would soon become a big name in the Asian American jazz community on both the East and West Coasts and recognized as a composer.

By the late 1980s and 1990s I had begun to think that my music was best used for fomenting greater connection to spiritual consciousness and became less involved in organized politics. Meanwhile, I went to a Boston performance of Fred's (featuring the soulful, incendiary saxophone stylings of the late Sam Furnace) that included a polemic against Trey Ellis's recently published essay about the "New Negro."[1] As we were catching up, Fred informed me that he was trying to rebuild the socialist movement in the United States. I got the feeling that he was fully prepared to do so single-handedly, if necessary. But despite these differences, Fred and I would frequently cross paths and always dealt with each other in pleasant and mutually beneficial ways. When I moved to New York briefly as a young man (the epitome of the starving artist), Fred hooked me up with a gig with Makanda Ken McIntyre.

Later, when I moved to New York, I wrote musical arrangements for Fred and performed with him. He has always shared his expertise and information with me and has donated his time to speak with my students. Fred has been especially encouraging with respect to my writing about music, and we have supported each other's performances and projects. Most importantly, we have continued our conversations about music, art, politics, and the human condition.

While Fred is nothing if not consistent and persistent, I am struck by his personal growth. A staunch individualist, he has taken to wearing his hair shaven save a small triangle in the front to, as he says, ensure that his hairstyle won't allow him to capitulate and get a job working for someone else. He wears only clothes of his own design; beautiful, flowing robe-like articles that he says "helps me be in touch with my feminine side." But what surprised me most was when he gave my daughter an eagle feather, telling her that the Native people say that it contains great spiritual power. As we see below, Fred doesn't like the term *spiritual*. But I was impressed that he gave voice to this dimension of the human experience, which he had never emphasized in our youth. A self-described devout atheist, Fred has developed as stringent an ethical system as any religionist, while simultaneously allowing for what he calls transcendence to take precedence in his yearnings and actions.

The transcendence that Fred Ho seeks is not predicated upon some Judeo-Christian notion of the holy residing in an outside force. There is no striving to be humble or self-deprecating. When we were warming up to do a performance commemorating the 40th anniversary of the Attica prison uprising, he showed me his command of the altissimo register, proclaiming it superior to all other baritone saxophonists, including that of technical whiz James Carter. Later, when addressing a group of Columbia students, he lamented the lack of a viable revolutionary vanguard among the youth, declaring, "you guys should be breathing down my back. You should be kicking my ass mentally and physically, but most of you can't." As he told me in the interview that constitutes most of the rest of this chapter, "[there will be no] mice in my life!" Fred is not squeamish and will tell you what he thinks you should be doing. He has no problem explaining how his music is better and more interesting than the usual fare of the industry's stars, how his projects have more integrity and vision than those of celebrated mavericks and iconoclasts, and in general what a bad motherfucker he is. As he says, "the militant, *not* the meek, shall inherit the earth."

For Fred, because people judge our "ethics and integrity" directly by our actions, they "are very materialist propositions." For example, he brings his

Marxist understanding to his struggle with cancer, as we see in the interview later in this chapter. Perhaps he is right to construct his moral concerns as ethical rather than spiritual, as he remains very much a materialist and is quite fond of the pleasures of the flesh. But let me emphasize that, while Ho is a materialist, he is *not* materialistic. He has downsized his life to make it manageable without working or hustling gigs, living in a tastefully appointed co-op with mostly second-hand furniture and a few items that he has had since his college days. He makes his own clothes, making a fashion statement while refusing to endorse clothing magnates. His search for fresh, healthy, tasty food is tireless, and has resulted in an insider's knowledge of the best mom-and-pop-type restaurants in New York and other cities throughout the country. And, while he appreciates art, he is not a collector ("I don't have the space"). Rather, Fred has spent his considerable energy and talents writing and performing operas, traveling with his Afro Asian Music Ensemble and the Brooklyn Sax Quartet, organizing, and writing about the movement and the music.

I spoke with Fred Ho as part of my ongoing project, interviewing New York–based musicians who are important to the art form of jazz but who have not been lionized within the jazz industry. As the interview progressed, I became aware that I was hearing a major political and aesthetic statement by one of our most interesting and important artists.

SALIM: Just say "my name is Fred Ho and today is August . . ." What is the date today?

FRED: 23rd. Fred Ho, August 23rd, 2007. My house in Greenpoint, Brooklyn, New York.

SALIM: All right. Fred, I'm glad that you consented to do this.

FRED: Well, we go back a long ways.

SALIM: Yeah, we do.

FRED: I mean, we're college buddies.

SALIM: Right, right. So, I want to begin with that if I can. Actually, I was reading the Harvard magazine, the one that had the spread on you, and I found out some things I didn't know about you prior to you coming to Harvard. And I think that part of your history is very interesting too. You have some military experience right? And how did that come about?

FRED: I don't really want to talk about that.

SALIM: Okay.

FRED: All I want to say is that a very close friend of mine who was African American, his name was Kenneth Noel. We grew up together as teenagers. He went into the military and I went with him. We were working out together, he was into martial arts and weight training and I was just wanting to hang out with him because I really enjoyed our friendship. He later committed suicide as a result of being unable to reconcile the fact that he was working . . . he was stationed in the very northernmost part of Alaska, at a Soviet listening-post monitoring the then–Soviet Union. And then when he was discharged he went back home and lived with his father in Connecticut and committed suicide because all he could do was find a job driving a car delivering pizzas.

And I didn't commit suicide because I found politics, you know? And before I went into college I would describe myself as a yellow revolutionary nationalist. I was a nationalist in the sense that I really believed that white people and white culture and white society were the source of the oppression of oppressed nationalities. I wasn't narrow in the sense that it was only just Asian people and that was it. I didn't have an Asian supremacist position. Some people I know still do and it feeds into antiblack hostility when they hear about Chinese deliverymen being assaulted or even killed in black/Latino neighborhoods.

I was never narrow; I was an anti-imperialist. But I believed that imperialism . . . the source of imperialism was Europe, were Europeans, European culture, European society, European people. But I was really committed to understanding how to end that oppression. And what was going on in the Left in the United States was a big transition in the '70s—mid-70s—and a lot of the people and organizations that came out of the national movements were looking seriously into Marxism. That had a big impact on me and I think that gave me [an] understanding of how to deepen my commitment to revolution. [That] was my salvation.

My friend Kenny; for example, he was very smart, he had gotten a scholarship to Williams College and he went there, and all the well-known black studies professors, who I won't name publicly, were smoking dope all the time because of their alienation. So, there's a lot of alienation amongst our generation who were kind of the firsts. The first to get into higher education, elite higher education. But because we were the first, there was extreme alienation. The whole life . . .

social life, dormitories, curriculum, everything else was so foreign, alien to us, but also hostile in many ways.

Going to Harvard was really an irony for me because it was the only school that accepted me. I had applied to two others. I applied to Amherst College, which is in my hometown; didn't get accepted. And then I applied to Yale and was wait-listed. Eventually I got accepted to Yale, which really was my first choice, but I couldn't wait so I just went to Harvard. I learned a year later, my sophomore year, from an activist who was working in the Yale admissions office who had read my file, that the admissions people conspired to send me only to Harvard because . . . on the application you listed the books you read and all my list . . . my list consisted of Karl Marx's *Das Kapital*, selected works of Mao Tse-tung, all of Franz Fanon's books. That was my reading and essentially they decided that only a school like Harvard would cool me out.

In fact there was a major exposé on that in the mid-80s among Ivy League admissions people that it was not based on merit but it was almost like trading horses. And it was quieted down because there was an out-of-court settlement that was finally made to stop that practice. But that was the kind of insider trading that was going on among the elite schools.

SALIM: And this was targeted at minorities?

FRED: Everybody, everybody, but I learned of it early on because somebody found my file at Yale and read the minutes and told me about it. But it almost worked, I was fairly alienated my first year but my first year you hadn't arrived yet. I think we met . . .

SALIM: The second year.

FRED: Yeah, right. But my first year the saving thing were the activists . . . and the remnants of the Marxist-Leninist movement. There were many groups and organizations there from the early '70s. But when I arrived in '75, it was diminishing, but the few remaining ones did a lot to help ground me and give me a sense of community, sense of understanding and perspective of what I was doing there. Then a good friend of mine, Gwen Mok, convinced me not to drop out of school because I was really thinking seriously about doing that. She said, "just get through it as quickly as possible." And that was my intention.

I really was very disgusted with my whole Ivy League experience and, in fact, don't mention it at all. In fact, in doing music, very few musicians knew that about me and certainly when I went to work in construction after Harvard I never brought it up. Because people would just look at you strangely, "Why are you doing manual labor? You graduated from Harvard." I also had the very disgusting experience of applying to graduate school my senior year, getting accepted, ironically, into every school I applied to. All the big-name schools: Columbia University Graduate School of Sociology, the University of Chicago, which is a premier one, and one other one I can't remember, maybe it was Northwestern or something. It was a big sociology school or maybe the University of Michigan; I can't remember what the third one was.

I got into them even though my GRE scores were miserably bad, because I was so conflicted about taking the GRE in the first place and the whole notion of going to grad school that I stayed up all night the night before. And I fell asleep in the middle of the GRE. I couldn't even complete them. So, I had something like less than 100, I mean it was abysmally bad. [Though my scores were] abysmally bad . . . the privilege of [having graduated from] Harvard got me into every single graduate school, the top sociology graduate schools, because I was a sociology major. And I knew there was something wrong. I knew that in my gut because I had planned to self-destruct on the GRE, so I knew my heart wasn't into going but I did it. And then to get accepted everywhere when I deliberately self-destructed showed me that the ruling class was not what I wanted to join, or to be an ideologue of the ruling class.

And so I turned my back on it all, washed my hands of it all, and have never gone back to higher education. I perform once in a while at colleges and I give lectures or very short artist-in-residencies. The longest one I'm going to do is next year; for five months I'm going to be an artist-in-residence at the University of Wisconsin in Madison. But I don't stay very long and I guess it's because I've always believed that there's a lot in terms of posturing, appearance, and fakery in academia and I've always respected direct production. What you can make with your hands, your creativity, and I enjoyed that the most, and felt that would be the basis for my evaluation and not how much I could spin on paper.

So, my years at Harvard were extremely alienating but it was the activists, the Left activism, that kept me challenged and going. And I lived off-campus for most of my time there and I became very involved in the Chinatown community. I joined at that time, I Wor Kuen, that later merged [with the predominantly Chicano organization August 29th Movement] and became the League of Revolutionary Struggle. I was trying to recruit you and a number of other people on campus as just part of the requirements of being in organizations. Every movement has to recruit so I had some success. I think in most cases you mostly have very few successes and most times you're not able to recruit people.

SALIM: Success doesn't have to only mean success for recruitment.

FRED: No, no, sure.

SALIM: You were very influential in a lot of people's thinking, my own included, who may not have signed up, so to speak. I remember one day in a study group where we were talking about the need for socialism. And I remember asking the question, "What guarantee do we have in a socialist revolution that there won't be antiblack racism?" And then I remember that was almost like throwing a wrench into the discussion. It got to the point where I was being questioned about whether or not I believed that socialism was better than capitalism, which had nothing to do with the question I was asking. And then I remember being kind of engineered out of that particular discussion group into another one and I thought . . .

FRED: Yeah, that's still a general problem . . .

SALIM: The role of doctrine . . .

FRED: The general problem of raising contrary . . . to being contrary to the status quo of thought and practice in organizations is a conundrum that will continue to confront us. My answer in general to all of these things when people ask for guarantees is that there are no guarantees. You only make what you can make from struggle; however, structural change facilitates a different situation, it doesn't guarantee it, but it facilitates it. Just as capitalist society is structured in such a way to be competitive, dog-eat-dog, to be ruthless and exploitative. It structures us that way.

A more cooperative society will promulgate different values and different modes of behavior. Doesn't guarantee it because it's still an ongoing struggle. But at least structurally it bans the rapacious, wanton exploitation that goes on. And that's why I believe that the movement . . . that it was a correct situation for the movement to implode and to fail. Because it did not offer a better "basis" for human relations because there's still a lot of control going on. What you would call doctrine, I would also describe as . . . a lot of problems [of] overcentralism, cult of personality, in-group/out-group, the worst of politics, which is the jockeying and maneuvering and positioning, currying favors, being part of the favored versus the disfavored or the un-favored. And I think that's a challenge that we're still struggling with.

I'm still struggling with that theoretically, ideologically, but I think that, for example, Richard Wright, in his writings about all the problems of CPUSA, the Communist Party USA, does us a favor because I think that one of the things I've learned is that we need to boldly air dirty laundry. Boldly air it and find the truth in it; find the lessons in it no matter how excoriating it can be or who the messenger is. Just take it and learn from it. The worst of it we should just take and learn from.

SALIM: It doesn't matter the spirit, or to what end?

FRED: No, I think that we can learn even from our enemies railing against us, you know? I think we're better for it if we can take it.

SALIM: It seems to me some of that would depend upon how you erect a response. Richard Wright, for all of his criticism of CPUSA, was also very guilty of some of the same type of actions towards other people. Junior writers who looked up to him.

FRED: That's right, that's why I say you take it from whoever the messenger is. That you don't get defensive, you don't add a "but" to it. "Yes, but . . ." You just take it. "Yes, this is true and thank you, thank you for the lesson." I think that the ethics and integrity of revolutionaries is a frontier that we have only touched on the surface in terms of trying to really understand it and internalize.

SALIM: I'm glad that you mentioned that because I think that may give me language for the questions I'm trying to formulate. [. . .] You're not a pacifist. I don't think humility is a favored virtue that you would extol above others in the way that the Judeo-Christian . . .

FRED: Right, I subscribe to Mother Jones' statement, "the militant, not the meek, shall inherit the earth." And I have a new thing in my life, "no mice in my life."

(*Both laugh.*)

SALIM: Okay, so when you talk about the ethical dimension of being a revolutionary, and when you think about the points of implosion of the movement and how some of them center around these kind of questions, I wonder do you have any kind of generalized thoughts or any specific thoughts about spiritual development as it relates to the revolutionary project?

FRED: I have always shied away from or shunned the word *spiritual* because it's been so prostituted from the new ageism to a complete idealism, which is contrary to materialism. I've always been a devout atheist, as I describe myself; in the sense that I believe ethics and integrity are very materialist propositions because it's not judged by your words or what you espouse. They're judged immediately, fundamentally, by your actions, what you do. And that's very materialist. And what I'm struggling with now in my war against cancer is how to deepen my Marxism down to the molecular and cellular level. And to really understand dialectical materialism from the point of view that quantitative changes lead to qualitative changes.

Those quantitative changes happen at the molecular and cellular level and they lead . . . they may take a long time in terms of even geophysical change. Continent shifting, that sort of thing. But they change at that minor, minor, minor level and that's how I understand "the personal is the political." Because it's through our behavior that we impact upon those quantitative changes that lead to qualitative transformation. Qualitative transformation would be for better or for worse, and that's how I understand the "spiritual." That's how I feel; in fact, indigenous peoples, when they talk about the spiritual, they're not just simply talking about chanting and wishing. They're talking about a behavior change through rituals, actions. For example, if you kill an animal, then you have to replace it with something. That's the idea of replenishment, recycling—it's very materialist. It's just it may be expressed in nonmaterialist terms.

I don't see a distinction between "spirit" and matter and science. I think that . . . what I disagreed with is this idea of the separation of spirit from matter and practice. I feel that spirit can only be manifested and understood and revealed by practice. I guess what my opposition to how spirituality [is commonly understood is that it] has been prostituted. [The mechanism that makes this distortion possible] is the separation of the two. I believe in the integration of matter and spirit. Spirit matters because of what it does to matter and it's based upon your actions.

So, one of the things early on as a youth I had to struggle with—and why I joined the Nation of Islam—was hypocrisy and inconsistency. Nationalists who were very antiwhite but they had white wives. I'm talking about the men for instance. Or they took paychecks from big white institutions. They espoused one thing but their behavior was contrary. At that time, the way I understood it, [it] was hypocrisy, inconsistency, in those kinds of terms . . . I wasn't a Marxist yet so I didn't understand in terms of contradictions. And that those contradictions led me . . . because I didn't have the materialist grasp, I went to the Nation of Islam because my perception of them was that they were more morally consistent and less hypocritical. But then I saw the hypocrisy and inconsistency and the contradictions within the Nation of Islam.

There were both negative, but also very positive examples. I would credit Sonia Sanchez; my experience with her when I was a teenager. Another person, Marilyn Lewis, versus some others, particularly the men, who were outright hustlers and con artists. So, I've always struggled with this question in the movement and that is . . . one of this relation between the personal and the political. And for me I can accept spirituality, spiritualism, as long as it's not in contradiction with materialism in the sense that if we both agree that people's actions or practice is the sole criterion of truth, that's fine. And that we understand the interconnection, reciprocity, and mutual effect of people's contradictory aspects.

So, many people have contradictions [. . .] we all have contradictions but it's more like what is the trajectory of what we're doing? Do our so-called personal failings and flaws and bad karma accumulate quantitatively to a point where it's going to quantitatively mean we go down a path of either self-destruction or toxicity to others?

SALIM: One can imagine a person believing that their materialist conditions and actions can be consistent in one direction and have personal habits or actions that somehow they separate from . . .

FRED: That separation is what I reject. That's undialectical—the two can't be separated. It's a matter of how you "manage" them. I've seen this with comrades who have passed away and I get to learn about their personal lives that I didn't know when I was active with them. Their personal lives were a mess. One comrade had many mistresses and that's what I think killed him. Just that kind of managing your life when you have all these secrets and escapades and . . . it creates a lot of stress on every level just to conceal things. It's very burdensome, very stressful.

There's an explanation for everything. I don't think that there are these mysteries that will never be understood because it's simply a design of divinity. I'm of the belief it's just our theoretical and practical framework hasn't developed to the point where we fully understand it. Like, for example, we don't really understand how our actions influence ourselves. We know it to some degree. So, certainly if you stand in front of radiation all the time . . . but we don't understand on the day-to-day level that if we're not doing the worst things how we can be still exposing ourselves to toxicity all the time.

I think that the great gaps in Marxism, Marxist thought, and thinking and theory are several things, but they're all connected. One is the tipping point, which is related to the productivist or Prometheus view of Marxism that all we need to do is make progress, technological progress. That we can all somehow live in this technological utopia and not understand that the technology itself could be extremely toxic to us. And that it could actually affect the tipping point where the world's resources and its ecology would be so degraded or consumed—eliminated—that it can't be repaired.

SALIM: That's related to how you use technology, too.

FRED: It's how you use it, but more than that it's whether it should be created. That we have to reach a point of wisdom where we're going to say certain technology would be more harmful than helpful. Or we need to take a Luddite position so that we reduce its impact, lessen it, and somewhere political decision making [and] will needs to be exerted in saying that do we need 2,000 different forms of cell phones, for instance. Or can we design a cell phone that would at least reduce the amount of electromagnetic radiation exposure? Instead of the capitalist free market where everybody has the right to manufacture and design a cell phone, put [the less toxic version] out on the market and market and sell it and promote it. And then have people buy and consume it.

I think that these are the challenges for revolutionaries. For revolutionary thinking and for revolutionary practice [and] organization, because materialism will teach us that everything is finite.

SALIM: Would it be fair to say you're striving for perfection?

FRED: . . . I don't think that it's an absolute or stationary thing. I think that the struggle for excellence is a process. I disagree with the notion of perfection as a static thing. I think that what I would say

I'm struggling for is transcendence. I'm trying to understand the proposition that Sun Ra posed to us when he talked about equations. When someone asked Sun Ra, "Are you ever bothered by or do you ponder the fact that you perhaps, being black, face racism and discrimination?" And his answer was quite [typical of] Sun Ra but I think very profound, and that's, "I can't be bothered with that. I'm too busy thinking about equations."

That's not just kind of like a humorous type of thing. I think it's actually true. I think that the challenge is to not be confined to a linear conception of possibility. To think that one plus one doesn't have to equal two, it can equal something greater than two. That would be revolutionary to figure out [that] one plus one can be greater than two. And that's how it should be with all relationships. I won't get "married" or set myself with a single person until I believe that that partnership will be greater than the sum of our individual parts. Otherwise it's a compromise. I don't want one plus one equals two. I want one plus one equals ten.

SALIM: Your striving for transcendence and excellence is not towards some stationary notion of perfection.

FRED: Nothing finite.

SALIM: But it is contrary to compromise.

FRED: Right, completely contrary to compromise. I guess I like what Bruce Lee said: "The point of technique is to have no technique." To play the saxophone completely intuitively but as a force, what the Chinese call . . . or Asians in general describe as *chi*. Now in the West it's been described as spirit, energy, that sort of thing. But that's how art, music, imagination becomes a material force. It's *chi*. When unleashed it allows us to transcend realism, to think of possibilities, or to feel possibilities beyond what we have, to inspire us to feel that we're not just hammered down or kept where we're at. And that's the evocative proposition of art, imagination, inspiration. It's catalytic energy and that's what I'm striving for.

I'm striving for . . . when I lost a lot of my manual dexterity through the side effect of one of the chemo drugs—it's a condition called peripheral neuropathy. And it was also painful to touch metal and glass. And saxophone keys, it was painful, I had to wear gloves and then take them off and play and put on gloves again. That's diminished now, but it's still there, but I have to learn that velocity, technique were both things to be transcended. That it came to a question of just pure sound. If you go and play one note, that note had to be a great, powerful force. Say everything and say everything that hadn't been said.

And I guess I've never looked at that as spiritualism because the way spiritualism has been so prostituted it actually cheapens the catalytic force that this energy can become. Because it's not about you finding contentment with the status quo as the way things are, learning to adjust or just letting it roll off your shoulders or avoid it, evade it, disregard it, learn how to zone it out. It's just the opposite. It's really learning how to confront it full force and with such transformative power that you actually *eliminate* it.

I've always said this, "I'm trying to find a sound that will bring down the walls of Jericho." Find a sound of biblical proportions. And I think that the music of Trane was that, you know? It was an energy beyond this planet. Or Sun Ra, I think that Sun Ra got it right, that the earth is finite, it's limited, and if we ever got our act together and learned how to venture out into the cosmos it will transform us and there would be discoveries way beyond what we could even fathom today on this earth. That's why I have a problem with so much of popular culture's [treatment] of the genre of science fiction. It's all hierarchical, it's militaristic. Admiral, captain, lieutenant, ensign, you know? It's a culture still with extreme stratification. In the *Serenity/ Firefly* series you have the core planets that live in utopia and then you have the periphery which is like today. You have the First World and the Third World.

There's no transcendence. For example, the assumption is in Gene Rodenberry's future in *Star Trek* that somehow we Earth people have figured out how to eliminate class. In fact, they talk about how there's no more money. I think in one episode of *Star Trek: The Next Generation* the character Jean-Luc Picard says, "We don't strive for gain or profit—we simply want to better ourselves."

SALIM: But "better" is according to a Pax Americana.

FRED: Right. So, there is no transcendence or transformation. It's kind of just assumed, but I think the real . . . that's why I've actually moved considerably . . . I used to be a *Star Trek* fan and now I've kind of like turned my back on it in a lot of ways because I think that the greatness of *Star Trek* was never achieved in the sense of really confronting how they got to the [24th] century, and eliminated racism, sexism, stratification, money. They don't talk really about what kind of economy [there would be], although there are capitalist species like the Ferengi, who have these rules of acquisition, and [are] simply about making profit. And [they have a] completely sexist society, because the women are all subservient and don't wear clothes. And they're just sexual objects for the males.

That, I don't think is what we're going to find in advanced species in the cosmos. We're going to find beings that we can't even fathom, understand.

SALIM: Science fiction, including the *Star Trek* series, is not about the future of the world. It's about now, it's about us. And so the political dichotomy is assumed, and really the frontier of the morality plays is around psychological interiority; what does it mean to be human, what are the gradations between [humanity and] being an automaton, being an android?

FRED: Yeah, those big moral issues are Shakespearian in the sense that they still represent the values and questions of bourgeois society, [such as] the question of individualism, individuality. Those issues are what Shakespeare wrestled with as England was making the transition from feudalism to capitalism, modern capitalism. So, those issues still remain in science fiction. So they're basically questions of bourgeois morality, and not really questions of social change, which I think really has to be the basis of science fiction.

SALIM: Are there any science fiction writers that you feel are moving in that direction?

FRED: I don't follow the genre in terms of literature. Mostly I watch the movies. [. . .] I used to read a lot of Isaac Asimov, but my problem with Isaac Asimov is that he's a technologist. And as a kid growing up, I used to for science class take independent study and try to draw pictures of future machines and that sort of thing. But he doesn't really wrestle with the profound questions of social change.

SALIM: He's not a humanist.

FRED: Right.

SALIM: Maybe you might enjoy somebody like Octavia Butler.

FRED: I read some of her stuff.

SALIM: Sam Delany maybe.

FRED: Yeah, I've read some of them. I'm still not blown away by them in terms of revolutionary thinking. I like some of the stuff that has elements of social criticism like technology gone rampant, technology's destructiveness, genetic engineering, and the potential disasters from that. I think those are all warnings. They're social criticism but I don't really see futurism.

SALIM: The future is now. Well, like I said, I don't think science fiction has ever really been about the future.

FRED: Well, that's what we're wrestling with in the Sun Ra opera. I'm having big discussions with Quincy Troupe about that, because we had to move away from our characters being humans into hybrid extraterrestrials; extraterrestrials who had spent time on earth. And we didn't want to get into this thing of trying to explain how do you travel through space. We're not trying to explain warp drive. What we're trying to say is that basically this community operates on consensus and that the collective and consensual operations are the energy that empowers their journey. Without that they can't go anywhere together.

SALIM: So, it's almost like a fictive metaphor of what you were talking about—the molecular level of Marxism and struggle. That's very interesting.

FRED: And we're looking at music as a vibrational force for social change, which was always Sun Ra's premise. We wanted to eliminate ranks in this, though there is leadership. But that leadership is questioned and criticized and challenged.

SALIM: Not militaristic.

FRED: Right. And they don't pull rank in order to make a decision. They have to argue and debate and reach agreement in order to move forward. So, that's the propulsion of the spacecraft.

SALIM: When you talk about the musical vibration as a force, I'm interested because one of the things that has always impressed me was the degree to which your musical and political visions were intertwined. You as a person, in your music, in your words, your poetry, and I'm wondering, where does this come from? Is this from the very beginning of your consciousness as a musician or is this something that was fashioned differently?

FRED: Well, it began at the same time I reached consciousness being Chinese American, Asian American, at around age 14. That consciousness was catalyzed by the ideas of Malcolm X. And then music . . . at that time, music to me was a pretty perfunctory activity. I enjoyed it; it was recreational playing in the school band. But once my consciousness changed and I became much more interested in social change and revolution, revolutionary activity, music and writing and just about everything, including cooking and designing my own clothes, became part of my energy.

Everything I did had to be devoted to furthering revolutionary change. So even my identity, everything, how I cut my hair, all became part of developing philosophy. It's still developing. So, that's why I checked out the Black Arts Movement so intensely because to me that was the most revolutionary cultural activity happening. And I was living at the tail end of it. I became conscious in the early '70s. But I immersed myself in it and my understanding of integrating politics and music developed. At first it was somewhat mechanical, it was much more of music could be a statement; it could be propaganda, ideological.

And then I understood the aesthetic dimension that music could create new values, new identities, and even now I would say I'm kind of beyond the question of content and form. And looking at process in the sense that I think it's still important that we create something whether it be a performance or recording or a show. But the journey to make it has to be a precursor or a template for a social process for a new society. The challenge with that is that most of the people who are working with those artists don't necessarily think in that way. But it's how to make the work in such a way that, at least for you and hopefully for the others who want to be part of that journey, that we begin to delineate how it's going to happen.

For example, there's been this struggle I've been going through in terms of how making music, particularly revolutionary music in the tradition of African American music, which I believe was the revolutionary music of the 20th century. What the 21st century holds, I don't know yet. But for the 20th century, I think the revolutionary music of the 20th century was black American music. That it be a template for political organization. For example, yes, there's a leader, but the role of "side people" is extremely important. The interplay, the dynamic is very, very important. The need for everyone to know the tune but it doesn't have to always go in the same direction. The whole call-and-response aesthetic, or what I would call social process, is one of exchange. [It's] dialectical; it can be quite frictional. But that's the energy that propels this forward.

I'm really wrestling with that, how the music and its process can be a metaphor for, and even instructional to, political organizing. So that all the things we talked about—problem of command as in overcentralism, manipulation, cult of personality—how those are all struggled out in a positive, better, more progressive way in the context of an ensemble. The real question of ensemble is how does the whole become greater than the sum of its parts? That everybody has different roles to play but those roles are critical to understanding where you want to go and . . .

SALIM: What do you do with an extremely charismatic player or prodigious talents? What if a person is like Sonny Rollins?

FRED: That person has to learn transcendence. Simply that. Otherwise it is egotism . . . the iniquity of individualism becomes dominant and not the ingeniousness of individuality. It's a distinction: the iniquity of individualism is the egomaniac in which the whole is not greater than the sum of its part because the ego won't allow it. So in some ways it's a curtailment, it's a brake, it's a restriction to transformation. However, the ingeniousness of individuality [is in] that leader who knows how to make all the players better.

In the words of Phil Jackson, for the Los Angeles Lakers or the Chicago Bulls, yes you have a Michael Jordan, but you don't win a championship with Michael Jordan alone. You need 11 others. And the genius of Michael Jordan is how to make all 11 better. And then the possibilities are limitless. So, that's the problem with Kobe [Bryant]. He has the iniquity of individualism; he does not know how to create transcendence. How to make the people around him better, transform them. That's true leadership.

SALIM: He has to be on the bench for others to shine.

FRED: Right, so, these are very powerful lessons. They can be applied in a capitalist, competitive way of earning championships. I think it can be applied in an anticapitalist way of inspiring . . .

SALIM: Artistry of the game.

FRED: Yeah, artistry, excellence, transcendence, new possibilities. I guess what I react to is a lot of this new age marketing that is designed to promote individualism for profitability. Increasing profitability, increasing material wealth, those things. The irony of it all is that you can do that, but it's harmful for the commonality.

SALIM: The art suffers.

FRED: Everything suffers. Ecology suffers, environment suffers, other people suffer. So, I think that the wisdom of communism, or the wisdom of matriarchy—which I believe is the first and final form of communism—is to understand that productivity isn't a quantitative thing but a qualitative thing. You don't need more to be better. Better is not stronger, faster, more powerful. I think better is transcendence. Better is being able to have a lot with less. Better is to be . . . I think I discovered that in fighting the cancer war. I think it illuminated for me a lot more, but I was on the route to it in the last few years when I downsized my life.

I went counter to the American way. I have a term called counter-Western. It's like counterpoint. Instead of more, instead of . . . when I sold my duplex loft buying a smaller place, taking out another mortgage, I downsized considerably. That alone solved my future. Two thirds of the money I made on the sale of the duplex loft I put away for the future. One third I kept for a new place, to help fund my business, which always has been working at a loss, and to really embark upon this thing of living in New York City debt-free, completely secure, and with an allowance of no more than $15,000 a year.

But you can only do that if you don't do it the American way. Have dependents, children, family, more debt, accumulate, have to have a bigger house because you've got more. You've got more kids and more things. I sold 70 percent of my material belongings. I only took three pieces of furniture here. This cabinet, that file cabinet, and this bed. This cost me $250, that cost me—when I bought it my freshman year at Harvard—$30, and this cost me $100. That's what I kept. Everything else . . . well, I kept my books, and my LPs and my saxophone, and my clothes and some kitchenware. That's it. Everything else, I built from scratch. Started anew. And [. . .] a concept of the potlatch of Native Americans was [that] you give away. You bring your stuff and you give it away. It's always a rebirth, cleansing, a purification.

SALIM: What about child-rearing, Fred? Is that something that's anathema to your notion of transcendence?

FRED: I don't think I could live the life I've led if I had kids. First of all, I couldn't afford them. I think there was a statistic that came out that for a child in America, the average child in America between day one of their birth to 21 years of age, the average cost is about $290,000.

SALIM: I believe it, as the father of four.

FRED: (*Laughter.*) Right, so you've got to pay over a million! Right, so I couldn't do what I did. It's just impossible. I'm not against children per se, but I do have a viewpoint that someone shared with me in that in the First World, bringing in children adds to . . . unless you can guarantee they'll be revolutionaries . . . adds to the exploitation of the earth. Americans are 5 to 6 percent of the world's population but we consume over half the world's resources. We consume and waste. What we need is not just zero population; we need a minus population. "Minus" in terms of our waste and consumption. We need to do reparations for the world. [. . .] I guess for me personally, I don't either have an interest in wanting to have children and I can't afford them and I also think that it would be irresponsible, particularly as we are nearing the tipping point.

How can I give to a child the consequences that we still yet can't even imagine of new diseases, natural disasters, greater drought, calamity . . .

SALIM: You can give life. Life is a great gift, though.

FRED: It is, but you have to use it wisely. As I get older I become more draconic about my one-time nonchildren, but now it's become more antichildren, position. Particularly for myself, I hold to myself. And, knock on wood, in all my years of sexual activity, only one woman has gotten pregnant, and we both agreed she would have an abortion early on. But as far as I know, I have no offspring and . . .

SALIM: And surely you would know if you did.

FRED: Don't know—sometimes you wouldn't. But, as far as I know. So I think it's important to turn kids into revolutionaries.

SALIM: If you can.

FRED: If you can.

SALIM: But kids have a funny way of doing what they want to do.

FRED: Yes, especially with the parents. But I think as a nonparent I have a better chance of working with your kids than you would with your kids.

SALIM: You know, that's so true. I've raised more kids than my biological kids. And it seemed that they listened to me more.

FRED: Exactly. So I think being uncles and aunties is better. And I create all that work, every single show is aimed at my harshest critic which is the two-year-old. That's my harshest critic. If I can't hold their attention through my entire show then I've failed. No matter what, whether it be a solo saxophone concert, to my band, to one of my big shows. That's my criteria. A two-year-old has to. And they don't have to understand it, they don't even have to like it. They just cannot be bored by it.

I reject a lot of these things like [when] this director said to me, "Your Sun Ra opera can't work in my black theatre because most of my audience doesn't have a clue about the character or what the character is talking about." Most people on earth when Sun Ra was around didn't have a clue about what he was saying. But they need to be exposed.

SALIM: And he had sold out audiences wherever he went.

FRED: But you know, that's always a problem, even if you're an artist but you have a gatekeeper roll. Like if you're a curator or just a director of an institution, the institution itself is a problematic situation. I believe if we could dismantle them and redistribute the resources to empower artists to be self-producers, that would be a better situation than the structure that's been set up and that's these institutions. The certification of 501(c)3 nonprofits, it creates institutions which are inherently conservative because institutions have become self-perpetuating. So, their missions have to always . . . even though they may have really visionary or idealistic missions, the practicality of running those institutions always makes the mission, no matter how idealistic, secondary.

SALIM: In the best of all possible worlds, where would you produce your works?

FRED: Anywhere.

SALIM: Just on the streets?

FRED: Anywhere, anywhere, anywhere.

SALIM: Do you perform on the streets?

FRED: In terms of just like busking?

SALIM: Just in any way? Just like, do your opera in the park or something? You know, like . . . who used to do that . . . from L.A.? Horace Tapscott.

FRED: I believe we could do that if the conditions were right. Horace Tapscott had the benefit of being . . . of doing that in a period of time when social consciousness was quite high. And he had a lot of organizational support from activists. He rehearsed in the Black Panther Party office, and a lot of community activists supported him. I wish we had more of that symbiotic relationship today where the activists and the cultural people were more united, more collaborative. So, if the conditions were right.

Otherwise I think sometimes it's like handing out fliers. You can do it but its impact will be very mitigated if you don't have the proper context and situation set up for it to be maximum. For example, when Strata-East Records was around, their biggest selling record was Gil Scott-Heron's *In the Bottle*. We know that because we were of that age and we partied to that song, but they sold a lot of records from the back of a truck at black Left events. For example, African Liberation Support Day events in Washington, D.C., in the park, Strata-East would be selling records right there, and people would buy these LPs and carry them with them all day as they're doing their demonstration marches and so forth. But they would sell a truckload of records that way.

Or Kalamu Ya Salaam was telling me how films like *A Luta Continua*—these things that came from the liberation struggles in Africa—they had no distribution here. And the movement would set up distribution showings in the park and that sort of thing. Community centers, we did that with films from the People's Republic of China in Chinatown. We would just set up in a parking lot or in a storefront space and show them. But we had a lot more of what I would call social momentum. It's hard to do that sort of thing because there isn't the social momentum. Plus you're competing with the nonprofits. You're competing with Jazzmobile. Jazzmobile was set up out of the Black Arts Movement of the '60s. That's what they did; they had people like Milford Graves playing on flatbed trucks in the middle of Harlem.

Now there are different accounts . . . some people said that Harlem residents had no clue and didn't like it but they had crowds.

SALIM: People also say that they were enthusiastic.

FRED: Yeah, I wasn't there, I can't say from firsthand account. But you look at pictures—like Valerie Wilmer has done a great service for documentation. She documents that with photographs. So, you look at the pictures and there were thousands of people around. There's a picture in her book *As Serious as Your Life*. So, Jazzmobile is the nonprofit answer to those self-determined projects. So we're competing with those and they have a lot of funding. They have much more marketing so we're competing with the very things that were . . . this is the whole lesson, the cultural pimps and the policy pimps, because the revolutionaries created the first social services programs, first TB testing, first free breakfast programs, first free health clinics, first free legal aid, first free transportation for elders, all of that. And then the state comes in and creates those in order to thwart the popularity of the revolutionaries.

In the cultural front all of this was created, and then some of these became nonprofits and they had to become conservative and palatable to the system that was funding them. The ones that didn't couldn't compete with them.

SALIM: But as a practical matter, do you want your government to have these types of programs?

FRED: Yes, but they should be run by revolutionaries so that we have experimental art widely available and popularized, and that's taught in the school curriculum. And young people are given a background and a framework to appreciate and understand and participate in that work. One of the things that even a conservative composer like Charles Wuorinen, who ironically—I'm happy to say that he's a friend of mine as well—has gotten me to understand: it's not enough to teach music appreciation, you have to teach actual music lessons.

For people to really understand music, they need to be playing. And that's popular cultural democracy. People are creating themselves. They're not passive anymore, accepting what's coming out from either the art anointers or the commercial realm. They're making their own stuff, and they are better able to assess and judge what's being marketed to them.

SALIM: They will then make the artist better.

FRED: Right, and that's popular cultural democracy. That was the greatness of the Black Arts Movement; it allowed that proliferation. Sure, there were a lot of bad saxophone players and poets that came out of that movement. That's cultural democracy! So, Skippy Gates and Stanley Crouch condemn those poorer . . . the poor version of what they call the "poorer performers and poets." But then there were great ones too. And the great ones they would never have celebrated.

SALIM: As well as some of the great ones who would not have survived artistically without the Black Arts Movement.

FRED: Cal Massey being one example. The explosion of cultural democracy offers you genius, and offers you massive mediocrity as well. But what it does is allow the determination of what happens much more on a popular level—not by anointers. Not by the establishment. And that's why the Black Arts Movement was such a threat. It continues to be a threat to the establishment because it's set its own criteria. It set its own determination of who was legitimate and qualified, and not institutional arbiters. Not institutional valorizers or gatekeepers. So, that's why it was revolutionary. The most revolutionary thing is to exert independence.

Figure 10. Fred Ho, performing at Harvard Asian American freshman orientation, 1979. Credit: Iyanna Jones

SALIM: Which can then be used towards this project of transcendence.

FRED: Right, because you are no longer looking for acceptance, legitimating approval, [receiving] subsidy from anyone. The problem is, unfortunately, narrowness that was a byproduct of certain nationalist projects. Transcendence is anathema to narrowness. Because transcendence means you have to accept and learn from everything.

SALIM: And be beholden to nothing.

FRED: Right, right. Transcendence can't happen with dogma, with doctrinarism. Transcendence can only happen if you allow the truth to come and hit you and change you. You have to embrace that. When you exclude stuff, you can't transcend.

Notes

1. Trey Ellis, "The New Black Aesthetic," *Callaloo* 12 (winter 1989): 233–43. Ellis's piece posits a postintegration black aesthetic that was removed from issues of authenticity and blackness per se. Not simply a clearing of space for new black artists who freely mined their "white" influences, it was also a generational and cultural distancing from the political content of the Black Arts Movement.

6

In Fred Ho's Body of Work

BILL V. MULLEN

> The life of the species, which applies to both humans and animals, consists in the physical, in which humans, just as animals, derive their life from inorganic nature, and the more universal man is in comparison to animals, the more universal is the sphere of inorganic nature, on which he lives [. . .] Physically, human beings live only on the products of nature, whether they might appear in the form of food, heating, clothing, dwellings, etc. The universality of humanity manifests itself practically even in this universality, in which the whole of nature becomes the *inorganic* body of human beings, both inasmuch as 1) it is a direct means for life, and 2) the material, the object and the instrument of humanity's life-activity. Nature is the inorganic body of humanity insofar as it is not a human body. Humanity lives on nature, which means that nature is humanity's *body* with which it must remain in objective dialogue with or else perish. That the physical and mental life of human beings depends on nature has another sense: nature depends on itself since human beings are part of nature.
>
> —KARL MARX, *Economic and Philosophical Manuscripts* (1844)

Fred Live

A live Fred Ho performance begins with the swagger of physical form in motion. Fred emerges from the wings of the stage clad in bright orange, or purple, or green textiles resplendent with African or Asian motifs. The clothes are designed, and handmade, by Fred. They feature brocade dragons breathing fire, mad geometric patterns, ornamental flourishes of flora, fauna, and telltale beauty from the physical world. His suits are broad and loose-fitting, hence ungendered: the body within might take any form. The colors run outside the palette of commercial convention, bending toward a tableau rather found in nature. Fred's signature Mohawk is a vivid slash visible from the highest reaches of the theater. His boots are alligator skin, custom designed by Noel Escobar Jr. in Austin, Texas, who Fred visits once a year to renew their relationship and dedication to the handicraft of form. Fred's body is thus *martialed* and designed to resist mass consumerism, mass production, and capitalist exchange, as well as the dominant performative wardrobe of male/female difference. Once Fred lifts his massive baritone sax to his lips, the body is again made new, original, improvised: deep sonic blasts tremor through the feet, arms and legs of his audience. We are reminded that sound is *physical*, that we experience it from our synaptic nerves down to our feet and toes. We are moved and moving with the music just as the stage production deepens: now lithe, cat-quick martial artists emerge from the wings, warrior artists gesticulating the concepts flowing through Fred's horn, literally sketching in the air movements conceived by Fred and his company. The entirety of the performance is an organic, dialectical whole: the players, the dancers, the audience are of one mind and one body.

This dialectic references both the aesthetic and political resolution of historical antimonies animating Fred's corpus of work, a process he calls "true kreolization, the free and voluntary intermingling, cultural synthesis and crossfertilization, occur(ing) at the bottom of society, among the varying oppressed peoples" (Ho, "Kreolization"). Against the backdrop of my epigraph from Marx, we might also understand Fred Ho's struggle to represent the body as a struggle against the body's history under capitalism in totality. Marx suggests that humanity's alienation from "nature" is itself a social construction of historical forces: the division of labor, the division of races, the division of genders, Marx suggests, all constitute a diminution of human freedom away from an organic sense of the human as inseparable from itself, what Marx calls the universality of humanity. Restoring the human to itself, and to nature, thus means repairing the body's physical relationship to the world. This is especially true under colonial and imperial capitalism, which ravages the bodies of women in general, and women of color in particular. Fred's stage work is especially dedicated to performing the history of these processes: his corpus of music, lyrics, and performance encapsulates and renders violence and resistance to violence as one of the body's primary struggles.

In this essay, I examine ways in which Fred Ho's *body* of work is about the body: the body as a lived political location, as a tool for revolutionary change, as a site of attack by capitalism, racism, and sexism, as an instrument for cultural and political transformation. I write this essay in homage to the real body of Fred Ho, which is currently beset by cancer, against which he struggles every day. In August 2006, at the age of 49, and in the benign midst of a beautiful, well-lived life—suffused with healthy foods and mineral water swims, long hiking and diving in the world's most beautiful regions, from the Corn Islands of Nicaragua to the rocky beaches at Kauai—Fred was diagnosed with colon cancer. He has undergone two radical surgeries to remove tumors; endured two protracted rounds of chemotherapy and radiation treatment; suffered the excruciating agony of life lived largely at home, in bed; and been forced to cancel most of his performance schedule up until the time of this writing. Fred has typically, however, used his cancer as a key to deepening his understanding not just of the meaning of his own life, but the lives of others. Through the course of his illness, he posted online his "Cancer Diary," a brilliant, jagged, painfully honest account of his illness, still available at his Myspace page and his homepage; it was the basis of his *Diary of a Radical Cancer Warrior: Fighting Cancer and Capitalism at the Cellular Level* (published in 2011). The journal and book are Fred live: writing from the front line of his war with cancer. The cancer diary and the resulting book represent the continuing creative, intellectual, and political vitality of his *body* of work, a body that shows no signs of quitting in the face of extraordinary physical and emotional attack. In this essay, I want to show how Fred Ho's life and art remind us that indeed we are *not* necessarily estranged from ourselves or the natural world. Though capitalism, sexism, and racism try to mark and delimit the body, separate it from its mental and physical potential, and segregate it from other bodily forms, music, dance, clothing, and ideas bring us back to the fighting idea that what does not kill us only makes us stronger. Finally, the essay contends with Fred's efforts to overcome the contradictions of working as a male performer and performance artist on the margins of the cultural scene attempting to negotiate from that position a sustainable critique of patriarchal capitalism.

Male and Female Bodies in Struggle

Fred's 2000 album *Yes Means Yes, No Means No, Whatever She Wears, Wherever She Goes!* is dedicated to the struggle of women to assert control over their own bodies in the face of a violent, sexist, capitalist culture. Fred appears naked in profile on the cover, swinging his saxophone through the air like a weapon. The photo is the corporeal icon of "S(w)ingin' with a Sword in My Hand," the album's fifth track. The substitution of the horn for the phallus as a "sword" connotes Fred's effort to reimagine even the privileged male nude form as a tool in the liberation of both men and women from sexism. Put another way, Fred rewrites phallocentric history as the struggle to undue phallocentrism itself. This is signaled by the backdrop in the photograph: a wall with a gaping opening onto a blue sky. The wall stands outside of contemporary temporality, perhaps prehistoric, perhaps apocalyptic, representing a utopian (or nowhere) space for reimagining gender norms. The human body is not fallen in its nakedness in the image, rather it stands sturdily, an epic historical struggle for sexual and gender equality as old as civilization itself. "Fuck Patriarchy" and "Sexism Is a Fatherfucker," blistering tracks from the record, do for our ears what the photograph does for our eyes: remind us that there is no rest or relief from the battle for a just world.

Indeed, Fred has always foregrounded powerful female bodies and voices in his antisexist corpus of work. His female collaborators include Ruth Margraff, librettist for *Once upon a Time in Chinese America*; Alma Villegas, Puerto Rican spoken-word performer and one-time member of the Afro Asian Music Ensemble; Esther Iverem, also an Ensemble member; the renowned Japanese American poet Janice Mirikitani; and the Puertoriqueña performance poet Magdalena Gómez. Fred describes his own gender politics as "matriarchal socialist," and has written in detail about prepatriarchal societies as the radical foundation of modern-day antisexist practices. In his 2002 essay "Matriarchy: The First and Final Communism," Ho argues that precapitalist society was matriarchal, female centered, and nonexploitative. Ho argues that feminism can thus turn both capitalism and patriarchy on their heads, providing an alternative politics and epistemology. Doing so will disclose and center a "plethora of goddesses across cultural groups who were associated with nature, creation, and life" (Ho, "Matriarchy," 9). Fred's epic masterpiece *Warrior Sister: The New Adventures of African and Asian Womyn Warriors* is an extended, two-disk performance in collaboration with librettist Ann T. Greene that puts this theoretical history into cultural practice. The work is the imaginary meeting of four historical revolutionaries: Fa Mu Lan, the Chinese Boxer; Nana Yaa Asantewa, Queen Mother of the Ashanti Nation; Assata Shakur, leader of the Black Liberation Army; and Sieh King King, the Chinese feminist. Each of the women bears the historical stigmata of sexism and oppression: Sieh King King sings of justice with "unbound" feet; Nana Yaa Asantewa is chained, "covered with blood, dirt and gunpowder"; and Assata Shakur is kept pregnant in prison while awaiting trial. Fa Mu Lan leads the rebellion of Boxers who are "unarmed except for martial arts weapons and their boxing abilities." Stage directions for the libretto set the woman warrior against a tradition of masculine physical domination and brutality in which the woman's body becomes the first line of defense. Nana Yaa Asantewa sings of "Men who watch and quiver / As womyn's breasts are girded / to fight a war!" The action of the opera literally culminates in a pitched physical battle led by Fa Mu Lan—on a thundering white horse—who rides through a multinational demonstration of women in New York City bearing banners that read:

> VIOLENCE AGAINST WOMYN WILL ONLY END WHEN WOMYN DEFEND THEMSELVES! WOMYN CONTROL OUR BODIES! FUCK PATRIARCHY! END SEXUAL EXPLOITATION AND CAPITALISM!

Warrior Womyn is a drama in which humanity, led by women, recapture their essential relationship to nature as one not based on oppression but on growth and love. In the last scene of the opera, Assata Shakur nurses a newborn daughter while the Womyn's Chorus sings:

> Oh Earth Mother
> We fight to heal you
> To kill the parasite,
> capitalism.

Capitalism is the world's cancer. "Womyn warriors" purge the world's body of the diseases of sexism, racism, colonialism, imperialism. Or, as Fred as put it elsewhere, "for indigenous peoples, a 'feminine' nature is to be loved and venerated. For the predator cultures, a 'feminine nature' is to be dominated, controlled and conquered. Thus, the interconnected triple struggle to save the planet's indigenous peoples and womyn is the struggle to stop ecocide, genocide and matricide" ("Matriarchy," 22–23). *Warrior Sisters* suggests two necessary stages in this social shift: revaluing gender ideology, and foregrounding the struggles of women whose physical and political commitments are to ending both exploitation and oppression, including gender oppression.

Fred Ho and the Body at Work

> Estranged labor estranges human beings from 1) nature and 2) from themselves in their own active function, their life-activity, and from this, it estranges human beings from their *species;* estranged labor makes the *species being* only the means for the individual life. First, it estranges the species life from the individual life, and second, it makes the individual life in its abstraction the purpose of the species life, even in its abstracted and estranged form.
>
> —KARL MARX, *Economic and Philosophical Manuscripts*

Marx's words here extend his meditation on human alienation from both "nature" and the human to the realm of labor. Work itself, writes Marx, undoes our relationship to the natural world; the body, which our species being inhabits, is the site of that alienation. Fred's work pays constant heed to the role of work in capitalism, particularly the physical work done by women as a means of measuring what might be called alienation, its discontents and resistance to it. Fred Ho's repertoire includes the work song "Hole Hole Bushi," a folk tune sung by Japanese women impressed into labor as sugar cane workers in Hawai'i. Like most work songs, the rhythms of the song mime the physical act and process of labor: swinging a scythe, stacking cane. Just as Fred's live performances iterate the physical and political potential of the body to fight back, songs and their material references in the world remind us of the physical processes in the world that gird our bodies to battle back against the brutal physicality of capitalist exploitation. On *The Underground Railroad to My Heart*, Fred's 1994 Soul Note release, the title track recalls the long journey out of slavery; the physical migration of black bodies out of subjugation, and the trail of tears north that freed slaves broke with their own feet and hands as they reached for the physical freedom of the North. On *Turn Pain into Power!*, Fred's 1997 release, Alma Villegas's lyrics for "A Song to My Liberation" provide a corporeal account of body in revolution:

> After more than ten years
> today I can raise my visage
> today I can face you
> and feel that I have triumphed
> That the strength of my race was more
> than your colonizing claws
> That the struggle has made me strong.
> That I grew in the battle
> That within your entrails
> I feel that day by day
> I retake what you have taken from my people
> That I learned your tongue
> And I made it my Sword.

This is not the colonized Caliban-body of postcolonial theory but the dialectical transformation of oppression into revolution. Villegas imagines inhabiting the "body" of capitalist imperialism—"That within your entrails / I feel that day by day / I retake what you have taken from my people"—in order to destroy it from within. Thus nowhere in Fred Ho's corpus of work does the body lie down. It cannot afford to: "We carry this country like a hole in our heart," writes Esther Iverem in "Essay to Us." Iverem suggests that the body, like the mind, can be interpolated by capitalism, forced to bear the stigmata of oppression and exploitation, hence the body must always be alert to the struggle to fight back. What does not kill us only makes us stronger. This is as true for the women on the front lines of the garment industry as it is for Fred's stage performers. Work, and cultural work, are symbiotic processes of actual and physical "representation" of human being reclaiming bodily labor for growth of both individual and collective survival and health.

Indeed, for Fred, the essence of Afro Asian solidarity and exchange lies in working-class African American and Asian American expressive culture as the process of physical making and becoming, the disalienation of human work. The labor of African American slaves in brickwork, agriculture, architecture, sowing, planting; the handwork of Asian Americans in laundry work, railroad construction, food preparation, cane cutting, harvesting. These expressions of the body inform the centrality of the working body in Fred Ho's stage presentations and choreography. The martial-arts aesthetic of the body as self-defense weapon embodies what Fred refers to as "bamboo that snaps back," the dialectic response of the human form to racism, sexism, or the physical abuses of extractive capitalist process. Fred's own work process and collaborations seek to overcome the manual/mental divide of bourgeois stratification criticized by Marx: the singers, songwriters, musicians, dancers who work with Fred do so in total relation to each other and part of an independent form of guerilla cultural work that doggedly seeks to stand outside of the standard mechanisms of capitalist and cultural exchange. This "standing outside" is figured by the strong, positive agitprop quality of Fred's work, which embraces the polemical as the latent form of resistance consciousness.

Put another way, Fred's persistent attention to exploitation and oppression in his artistic representations also stand as figures for the problematic of "creativity" and creative labor endured by writers and musicians seeking to tell stories in a highly commodified cultural world. For Fred, "selling out" means putting up for sale the thoughts and ideas and physical gifts of artists who, like his revolutionary hero Monkey, struggle against the confines of institutionalized and oppressive capitalist structures in part by representing those structures within the creative work itself. "Estranged labor makes the *species being* only the means for the individual life. First, it estranges the species life from the individual life, and second, it makes the individual life in its abstraction the purpose of the species life, even in its abstracted and estranged form" writes Marx. In Fred's creative work, labor is culture turned back into the very art of being human and connecting to other humans via culture and performance.

The finished "work" organically remains the work of those who produce it in part because it refuses to concede itself to an easily commodifiable form.

The Cancer Artist

> We cannot cure or get rid of cancer until we "cure" capitalism. The two are mutually enhancing as long as you can sell these new drugs that cost about $250,000 to take. If that is still profitable, then eliminating things like processed foods, pesticides, the industrial manufacturing of food, the drowning of electromagnetic radiation we are saturated with, the dependency on the treadmill, all those things that set the conditions for the growth of the cancer, unless we deal with those sorts of things, there will not be a cure.
>
> —FRED HO, "Cancer Diary," quoted on *Health Watch*, WBAI, August 6, 2007

Fred was diagnosed with colon cancer in August 2006. On August 25, 2006, he underwent surgery to remove a cancerous tumor and began the first of two rounds of strenuous, life-draining chemotherapy and radiation treatments. From the beginning, Fred's plan was to make his cancer a transparent allegory, or X-ray, of life under capitalism. His vehicle for doing so was the "Cancer Diary," blog postings at his Web site. Fred's electronic cancer diary is a self-described Luddite attack on the biotechnological fetishism of a privatized society that funds killing machines for war but leaves the human body uninsured, vulnerable, and at the front line of toxic capitalism. Like Malcolm X, or a prison poet such as Fred's deceased comrade and collaborator Raul Salinas, Fred writes out of the "incarceration" of his body to reach beyond the biological "cell" of cancer in order to shake up and wake up the world. In a May 2007 entry titled "Cancer Diary #12: The Cells of One's Sounds," Fred writes:

> in accepting Ludditism (Contrary to popular mythology, the Luddites did not oppose machines per se, but "machinery hurtful to Commonality."—Mitchel Cohen) I have come to reject Technological-Industrial Fetishism (both meanings of fetish—the traditional meaning of conferring power to something and the Freudian concept of obsession with something). Industrial organization and the over-reliance of technology as a fix-it-all solution intrinsically contains the destructive and exploitative content of the capitalist system that engendered and shaped its development and character. Therefore, that which is bigger, faster, more efficient, more powerful is NOT necessarily better and in the terms and manifestations of capitalism, often toxic, destructive and inimical to Commonality (the well being of the ecological systems and organisms of

> the planet, including the social ones necessary to humanity). Cancer cannot and will not be cured as long as there is more profit (money to be made) in "managing" it, in coming up with newer and more expensive "power drugs and treatments" rather than eliminating pesticides, environmental toxicity, greatly reducing processed foods and chemical additives, prepared food businesses that rely upon deep fried, high tempered/burned cooking, the cigarette industry, a privatized profiteering insurance-company multi-payer industry instead of a single-payer national health insurance system, etc.

Fred's public rumination on the decaying state of the ecotechnosystem is the backdrop in his Cancer Diary for an affirmation of what might be called holistic anticapitalist living. Fred reports selling off almost all of his material possessions, including his "yuppie" Brooklyn apartment, in 2000 and dedicating himself to living on a $15,000 annual budget in New York. In other cancer blogs he renounces what he calls the treadmill of accumulation, otherwise known as careerism. He has stripped down to a primordial self, a negation of individualism, in order to become the battle against the disease. He has, for example, taking up organic farming, trying to produce as much of his own food as possible and to reduce his interaction with mass-produced foods and pesticides. He has assumed an even more rigorous program of exercise and rest, drawing back on his performance schedule when his body dictates. At a 2008 concert at Purdue University, this was made dramatically manifest when Fred cut short the end of a performance due to exhaustion. He used the moment to speak to the audience about his cancer struggle, thus making it part of the performance.

By staying within the physical limits imposed by the disease, Fred both embodies and confronts the challenge of permanent recovery. At times, this can require a refusal or negation of the body and performing itself. It is for Fred a question of living strategy and a strategy of living: he compares the "breathing" of his invigorated saxophone playing to the drawing of the breath of life. To play well is to have no technique, he writes, just as to live well is to consider nothing beyond what is necessary to sound the depths of one's existence. Fred Ho is now the cancer artist. His body is a *performance* of how one lives a life of radical utopian possibility in the face of war and carnage against the self. Also in "Cancer Diary #12," Fred writes:

> I believe my saxophone playing and my musical consciousness have attained a level of transcendence I could not previously expect nor imagine. I wrote this to composer-friend Stefan Hakenberg when he asked me via email how has my saxophone playing been in this cancer war:

> "My sax playing is very strong, even stronger than before I entered surgery. After surgery, my diaphragm had to heal before I could play again. But now I play with a lot more power and control. This stems from the breathing exercises I've been doing, but also from the development of my CHI energy. I basically have out grown everything made for the bari sax. There isn't a big enough mouthpiece commercially made for me. I need reeds harder/stronger than the #5, the hardest commercially made. I play the horn now like a double reed instrument, barely touching the reed with my embouchure. From the power of my breath alone, I can make it vibrate without touching it. My fingers have molded the ivory and brass to fit my hands. I have actually altered metal from years of my touch. It is truly man over metal."

Fred's rumination on the body's relationship to its "tools" recalls the struggle even the cultural worker faces to remain unalienated from the means of her or his own production. Put another way, Fred reminds us that music and the body exist in a relationship of mutual dependency and interrelation, and that balance and symbiosis, or what one might call a nonexploitative equilibrium, is the objective at the very point of musical production: "While my philosophical-political-world view remains what it was prior to getting cancer, the war has taught me important lessons and changed me in profound ways that may never have happened if I didn't have to face it myself. It is the experience of fighting cancer that has instilled a new imagination in me about how to fight to detoxify and liberate ourselves and the world" (Cancer Diary #12). This short quotation contains for me a resolution of what might be called the problem of the body's alienation from nature with which I began this essay. Cancer has had the ironic effect of returning the artist to the world with a heightened understanding that mutual healing is the only healing possible. In this, he stands nearer the position of ecological subalterns in his work: women, particularly women of color, who have experienced the violence of racism, sexism, and capitalism on the body. Hence Fred's most recent political work has made the destruction of the environment tantamount to an attack on the human. Around 2009 he began working with the organization M.O.T.H.E.R.S., whose acronym signifies Matriarchal Organization and Tribes of Honorable Eco-centric Revolutionary Socialists. The group's ten-point program, modeled on and revising those of early nationalist (and male-centered) organizations like the Black Panther Party and Red Guard, reads as follows:

PRINCIPLES FOR THE MATRIARCHY SOCIETY (M.O.T.H.E.R.S. = MATRIARCHAL ORGANIZATION AND TRIBES OF HONORABLE ECO-CENTRIC REVOLUTIONARY SOCIALISTS)

1. We are for matriarchy, the rule of mothers ("matri" = mothers; "archy" = rule) and by the majority of producers of all use-values. Therefore we seek to end patriarchy (class society in all of its forms and divisions), especially the capitalist system. We reject patriarchal socialism as well.

2. Our values are nurturance, independence, self-reliance, self-sufficiency, compassion, generosity, and creativity.

3. We are fighters for a matriarchal future and believe that we should fight by any means necessary. We believe that necessity is the mother of invention! As well as "from each according to how they can fight, to each according to how much they can fight!" . . .

4. We are eco-centric, including all aspirations for common-ing (and the end to the enclosures in all manifestations), ludditism (opposing all technology that is harmful to the planet or to people); eco-socialist (rational planning of production, including zero growth, zero waste, etc.).

5. We are indigenous-centric and do not subscribe to the nation-state borders, but to communities that are freely associated and cooperatively self-sufficient.

6. We are future forward-oriented. Our deepest concern is for the future, a world of peace, health, creativity and ecological responsibility to reign supreme. This is a Love Supreme.

7. We do not subscribe to any social constructions of gender and believe all beings should freely create their identities and sexualities.

8. We seek to eliminate ego and to generate a "7 generations consciousness" in all of us, to consider our impact for seven generations in the future before we act.

9. We meet as often as necessary and in a way to best meet what needs to get done.

10. We accept anyone and everyone who wants to be a MOTHER . . .

(http://www.scientificsoul.org/Education%20pages/Matriarchy.htm)

Numbers 6 and 7 point especially to what might be called a utopian dialectic of the body in Fred's work. The elimination of national, personal, and temporal boundaries around the self reconstitute the self and its body as a self-defining agent of world-historical change. MOTHERS represents a radical revision and self-critique of Fred's earlier "matriarchal socialism" by delineating the destruction of gendered identity and sexual prescription as

Figure 11. Fred Ho, 1997. Credit: Jason Jem

a template for radical social transformation. This includes a redefinition of the historical "maternal" not as biological but social. The body itself comes unmoored from its oppressive origins of a patriarchal past. MOTHERS is thus Fred's conceptual answer to Marx's problematic of the human divide from nature under capitalism. The divisions of race, labor, and gender that constitute capitalist, colonialist, and imperialist exploitation are dialectically refuted by a reimagining of social relations through a reimagined body in nature.

Of course, like much of Fred's work, MOTHERS exists in a utopian continuum of revolutionary thought still delimited by the world as it is. A cure for cancer and a cure for capitalism both await. That Fred has now wedded these two struggles speaks to a new phase of his ever-evolving artistic and political growth. That the body has become more central to this struggle speaks not only to Fred's personal circumstances but to the pedagogical and political value of the problems faced by women of color in particular, women everywhere, and men who seek to join their struggle.

Works Cited

Burns, Emile, ed. *A Handbook of Marxism.* New York: Random House, 1935.

Ho, Fred. "Cancer Diary." http://www.myspace.com/fredhomusic and http://www.bigredmediainc.com/brmflash/, accessed July 1, 2012.

———. "Kreolization, Cross-Fertilization, or Cultural Imperialism." Box 19, folder "Drafts 1999–1993." In Fred Ho Papers, Archives and Special Collections at the Thomas J. Dodd Research Center, University of Connecticut Libraries.

———. "Matriarchy: The First and Final Communism." Box 19, folder "Drafts: 1992–1998." In Fred Ho Papers, Archives and Special Collections at the Thomas J. Dodd Research Center, University of Connecticut Libraries.

———. *Turn Pain into Power!* O.O. Discs, 1997.

———, and the Afro Asian Music Ensemble. *Warrior Sister: The New Adventures of African and Asian Womyn Warriors (A New American Opera).* Avatar Studios, 1999.

Marx, Karl. *Economic and Philosophical Manuscripts of 1844.* http://www.marxists.org/archive/marx/works/1844/manuscripts/preface.htm, accessed 1 July 2012.

PART III

A Life in Community

THIS EVENING

(For Fred Ho)

This evening
I'm thinking of
the revolutionary content
contained in your personal behavior
The independent flashes on
revolutionary edges of consciousness used to
transform the private situation of the heart
& transitional movements of spirit
into a deeper analysis between desire & struggle
between political thought & artistic freedom
between internal emancipation & external reality
& how the invisibility of evolution mixed with activism &
the rough entry into revolutionary moments can
open the door for the inflamed sky of sunsets
& the upside down saxophone in fuchsia pants

—Jayne Cortez

7

Machete and Chopsticks

MAGDALENA GÓMEZ

Here's to the was you been, to the is you in.

—SEKOU SUNDIATA, "Shout Out," *The Blue Oneness of Dreams* (1997)

As I look up the meaning of *ibid.*, I am reminded to advise you that I am not an academic. This will be less of an essay and more of a glimpse into my personal diary that is riveted with anecdotes of Fred Ho. I could have chosen the word *laced*, but *rivets*, where Fred Ho is concerned, are much more to the point.

On December 19, 2002, the New York air was still acrid with the horrors of the previous year. Suspicion, paranoia, uncertainty, fears shuttled across the faces of the masses as a face here and there unconsciously glanced upward at rooftops and skyscrapers. It was all in the eyes; the posttraumatic stress of a wounded country collapsed into the clammy arms of a vile and imbecilic leadership. A toxic silence arose from the ashes of September 11 muffling howls of protest and the wailing of mournful lamentations. The rhetoric of freedom was sharpened to a point and used to lobotomize otherwise savvy Americans into flag-waving, emotionally distended, couch potato soldiers. French fries were rechristened Freedom Fries, and road rage had found its justification. Bumper stickers and car magnet sales skyrocketed as hunger in America continued unnoticed. Revenge was the order of the day as the dissimulated face of the true enemy stalked our lives with impunity. Deep in the belly of our nation we could feel the absence of truth, but it is not easy to make a fist with broken fingers. On December 19, 2002, I met a man who could: Fred Ho.

An old and dear friend of mine, the poet and visual artist Sandra María Esteves, had told my partner Jim Lescault and me that she was reading at

Revolution Books in Manhattan that evening at the invitation of Fred Ho. We were grateful to be visiting the city at that time. What good luck: a chance to hear the Madrina of the Nuyorican Literary movement at a live reading with baritone sax monster Fred Ho. I had moved out of my beloved city years earlier and was happy to know that the bookstore had survived our national dementia and passivity. Immediately on entering the building and breathing in the pungent fragrance of rebellious memory, I was struck by the sight of a handsome, muscular Asian man with a triangular haircut reminiscent of a woman's perfectly formed pubis. He was sitting in the audience, so I assumed that like us, he was waiting for the performers. He smiled, and within moments my partner and I were fully engaged with this affable stranger who we later learned was the legendary Fred Ho. Waiting for Sandra María to arrive, I scanned the shelves as Fred scanned the landscape of my body. I'd be a liar if I said I didn't like it. This was clearly a man with a lust for life and a ravenous, unapologetic desire for sex. By the time I had flipped through a book on the essays of Don Pedro Albizu Campos, I was in need of a cigarette in the absence of a cold shower. Fred will hate to read this because he has never approved of smoking even when the desire is provoked by the ferocity of his sexual vibration. Okay, I had a stick of gum instead. Big Red.

The evening was a celebration of Fred's most recent edition of the *Sheroes Calendar*, which highlights 365 unsung women who as Fred writes on the back cover are: "womyn who have challenged their societies and have advanced the struggle of the oppressed and exploited. For being sheroes, many of these womyn have decidedly not been celebrated by patriarchal or Eurocentric, bourgeois establishment. Indeed, for their defiance and independence many of these womyn have been attacked, denounced, imprisoned, even assassinated or executed. History has maligned, distorted obscured and disappeared many as well."[1] To date, Fred continues his commitment to this worthy project that brings him little monetary reward.

Among the books and electrically charged air, pulsing with Fred's sax and Sandra María's poems, I prophesied to Fred that we would become artistic collaborators, he agreed, and we've been working together ever since. At our first rehearsal in Brooklyn, it was as if we had always been performing together. No clashing of egos, no discomfort; his unrelenting baritone saxophone jamming up against my unrelenting poetry. Bam! Bam! Bam! Raw, animal sex without physical contact. Fred played without backing down, I read over his monstrous sound without the need for a microphone. A match made in a Brooklyn church basement: atheist and believer both in love with the power of art to snap awake the sleeping mind. We share an equal disdain for those who knowingly choose to remain asleep because it is easier to gossip about oppression than to wield your machete and dismember it.

There are many who consider Fred an irritant, a royal pain in the ass. In fleeting moments, I have been among them. Fred Ho is idiosyncratic, complex, unyielding in debate, transparently manipulative (I'm happy to say he's terrible at it, unless you're a moron), paradoxical, and has on occasion committed acts of deception he refers to as "passive aggressive" that are a source of great personal regret. He is opinionated in the way that Changó relates to thunder: it is woven into the fabric of his being. He is a magnet of controversy and defiant even with fashion choices of self-designed clothing in an eclectic mix of Afro Asian textiles. Fred believes that everything in one's life must be intentional, aesthetically pleasing, and utilitarian, even to the detail of how long and wide you want your belt loops. Nothing is left to chance. Some would call Fred an Alpha dog; I call him an A-riginal.

Tyrannical and Merciful, Judgmental and Embracing, Cosmic Bully and Great Nurturing Mother, Machete and Chopsticks, Choke Hold and Tender Embrace, Hay Mattress and Feather Blanket, Raw Meat and Sizzling Fish, Creator and Destroyer. Yes, Fred Ho is my own personal Kali. I have never met anyone who is indifferent or wishy-washy about Fred Ho. If only we could harness the magic of that penetrative Fred Ho force and apply it to our passive society, rendering docility and shoulder-shrugging to the domain of past tense.

Despite these lofty descriptors, I must anecdotally confirm that Fred Ho is a mere mortal like the rest of us yearning, huddled masses. He is neither saint nor hero but one who nonetheless lives a heroic life.

Fred has access to more gray matter than most of us. His ability to see beyond the earthbound horizon keeps him in a state of constant negotiations between the essence of his prophetic vision and the here and now. Fred doesn't just look at people, he looks into them. He sees not only who you are in that moment, but also who you are capable of being. He does not only relate to the person in front of him, but to their potential. As he moves into seeing the fullness of who you might be if you dared, he becomes impatient with the lesser you. If you are willing and open, Fred will tutor you, challenge you, provoke you, incite your dormant dragons, direct you on a path of personal and professional opportunities (his roster of friends and colleagues is staggering), cook your dinner, *and* do the dishes. However, you'd better show up with the sharp side of the blade glistening. Fred Ho does not waste time. (In fact, he doesn't waste anything; he'll make a palate-tingling sauce from the juices in a pickle jar.) Fred is equally impatient with himself. He voraciously seeks out the next challenge, the new book, the undiscovered artist he will encourage and tutor, the woman he will arouse, the institution he will take on, the audience he will inspire, or the rugged landscape he will traverse to swim among his beloved dolphins and whales. During his battle with stage 3B colon cancer, Fred also proved to be a formidable opponent; cancer is an enemy he has, to date, successfully and miraculously defeated.

Fred Ho does not smell the roses; he grabs them by the thorns and eats them. One of the weapons in this warrior's arsenal is an enduring sense of humor that thrives even in life's darkest moments. I can relay many comedic Fred moments. One that comes to mind is the image of Fred playing a washboard with a güiro pick, at an arts salon in my home, where musicians and nonmusicians created a celebratory musical cacophony. Fred left his saxophone untouched, modeling the joy of improvisation, and shameless, creative risk-taking, defeating the potential intimidation factor for all the nonmusicians in the room. Fred often shows his generosity and love in understated, surprising ways, putting others at ease with humor and grace.

Standing in Fred's sagacious presence elicits and magnifies one's predominating character traits. His laser-like gaze makes it nearly impossible to hide. Fred's provocative manner is motivated by the desire to know who you are at your core. If you are on the emotional-weakling side, chances are a relationship with Fred Ho will be perpetually rocky or finite. The atheistic awareness of his mortality urges him to make the most of every moment on this earthly plane. It takes a great deal more faith and strength to live as an atheist than as a believer without the afterlife promise of paradise. Fred has no penchant for the seesaw. You either want to fuck (allegorically speaking) or you don't.

The finely constructed and tuned aesthetic of his life makes him highly organized, fanatically clean, and constantly recycling what is no longer useful, intellectually stimulating, or emotionally engaging. Fred enters every relationship front and center, smack in the eyes, squared off, and ready to dance with whatever monsters or mutants deem to show up. Fred is as well-equipped for battle as he is for fun. He has traveled the globe in search of places where he can swim in the company of dolphins and whales. He does this at every opportunity. A formidable swimmer, I once watched him do endless butterfly laps in an Olympic-sized pool in Costa Rica, mesmerizing the many families who watched in delight from the sidelines. After a while, we agreed that we didn't see a man—we saw a dolphin.

Fred loves to laugh. He is however, no easy laugh. I have added many Fred moments to my inner treasure trove of memories that I want panoramically displayed when, in the end, my whole life flashes before me. One such recollection was when I spontaneously launched into a character named Mabel and became Fred's imaginary complaining wife for the evening. Given Fred's distaste for conventional marriage, chauvinism, and the heterosexist nuclear family model, the idea of a Mrs. Mabel Ho was funny enough. Fred laughed with such gusto that he lost his appetite. Soon after the cancer operation I played ventriloquist with a fish head, and he popped his surgery stitches, prompting my desperate call to his physician sister, Florence. She assured me that the medical benefits of laughter were worth the price. Fred reinvented the belly laugh that day. It was his first outing since the cancer tumor was removed, and his close friend, Jennifer Feil, had taken us to a riverside park and then for lunch at Fred's favorite fish place in Astoria, Queens. The simple acts of taking a walk in the sun and sharing a meal had grown in meaning to Fred. There would be no fast walking, fast talking, and rushed eating on the way to rehearsal that day. Fred's sense of urgency had been put on hold. Death had blown in his ear, but Fred decided to pass; the Grim Reaper was not his type. Since the cancer war, the scales have tipped dramatically to the fun side of things, like two-and-a-half-hour dinners with friends at a "bohemian" (as he calls it) five-table restaurant where an Egyptian man in his 60s named Ali is "the chef, busboy, waiter and dishwasher," as Fred describes. "You can't go there if you're in a hurry. And there's no refrigerator. Have you ever been to a restaurant without a refrigerator? Ali buys and prepares the food all in the same day. It's fresh. No processed foods. All preserved by marinating, like the old days. The whole operation is a one-man show."

In some ways, Fred was describing himself. A self-proclaimed matriarchal socialist, who defines the C in cancer as the same C in capitalism, he has been creating art like Ali prepares food: all fresh ingredients, nothing processed. He does so with limited outside financing and without the imprimatur of the mainstream. While it is true that Fred is an internationally acclaimed and respected artist, as of this writing, you won't find him on the cover of *People* or *American Theatre* magazines, despite the fact that he has self-produced and coproduced over fifteen grand-scale, cutting-edge, martial-arts dance-theater operas and an even greater number of recordings.

Fred is a regular collaborator with one of the most brilliantly innovative voices of contemporary North American theater, Ruth Margraff; fellow visionaries such as Thaddeus Squire of Peregrine Arts in Philadelphia; the socially committed and controversial Wisconsin-based choreographer, Peggy Choy; and the underexposed and highly talented performer, dancer, and martial artist, Marina Celander. He has collaborated with exciting fellow composers and musicians such as David Bindman (with whom he cofounded the Brooklyn Sax Quartet), the late Sam Furnace, Haleh Abghari, Aib Gomez-Delgado, Taylor Ho Bynum, Art Hirahara, and countless others. Fred has been favorably reviewed by the *New York Times*, has been written about in most major jazz magazines, the Harvard alumni magazine, referenced in countless periodicals, journals, articles, papers, and books, and is known in radical circles as someone who has never sold out, a fact espoused even among his detractors. Fred's anticapitalist stance and outspoken radical politics have kept his work off the main stages of a dummified, Disney-fied, sanitized, pull-plays-out-of-your-ass-in-a-day-and stage them, acultural, pro-commodity North America that has committed genre-cide. The exponential rise of national reverie of mediocrity hasn't stopped Fred Ho from creating and staging new work, even after the onslaught of cancer and ten months of energy-zapping chemotherapy. As of this writing, we have learned that Fred will be the 16th recipient of the Harvard Arts Medal, previously bestowed on artists with more mainstream acceptance, such as Yo-Yo Ma and Joshua Redman. It will be interesting to see who among the previously absent will now deem to dial his number.

Combining elements of "jazz" (a term Fred qualifies by instructing us on its racist origins), Chinese opera, experimental, global working-class and oppressed-class musical traditions, various dance and martial-arts traditions, comic book–genre aesthetic, science fiction and poetry, Fred's theatrical works cannot be classified; no one box can be checked. This inability to fit in the crayon box and his revolutionary politics (rooted in self-defense, not violence) render Fred's work a threat to the unimaginative and the purveyors of bottom-line, crowd-pleasing mediocrity.

Thankfully, Fred's work has been embraced by alternative venues with mainstream clout, such as New York City's Brooklyn Academy of Music, the Apollo, and new works presenters such as the Whitney and Guggenheim Museums. Smaller venues such Philadelphia's Peregrine Arts, have also given Fred the heartfelt financial and moral support that encourages him to move forward despite the odds and scattered recognition. His work with Thaddeus Squire, Ruth Margraff, and others pushes and challenges Fred into new and perhaps, at times, unfamiliar territory. This was evident at a staged reading of Ruth Margraff and Fred's collaboration, *Dragon vs. Eagle: Enter the White Barbarians*, which Thaddeus directed. It was clear to me that being part of this triumvirate had enhanced Fred's work. I find it admirable that Fred seeks out artists who will pull him out of the temptation to remain in his comfort zone. I'd bet the farm that rehearsals are no picnic, but I am equally certain of the high esteem in which he holds his fellow collaborators, a fact he has heartily admitted on more than one occasion. It is my hope that this trend of artistic and personal expansion will send a message about the intrinsic artistry of Fred's work, politics aside. Poised with guerilla fervor and discipline, an army of talented and committed supporters (individuals and institutions) too numerous to mention here, keep the Fred Ho comet in orbit.

While Fred was recovering from cancer surgery, I stayed with him for three weeks. During this time I witnessed the profound and unconditional love Fred received from countless friends, colleagues, and family members. Even friends he has at times offended appeared at his door ready to vacuum the rugs, scrub the toilet, cook, or grocery shop. They all came bearing gifts, giving love, comfort, and practical support. I will never forget Thaddeus Squire of Peregrine Arts offering to drive from Philadelphia to take Fred to a doctor's appointment if no one else was available. Or the weekly trips to Chinatown for dinner with Abraham Gómez-Delgado, Ayesha Saini, and Taylor Ho Bynum. Or Ayesha's cooking, in which Fred admitted to tasting love. Or Paget Walker appearing at the hospital, her little Emma in tow with snacks for me—a total stranger to her at the time—to ensure that as I took care of Fred I was also taking care of myself. Paget's partner, Peter Adelman, showing up at Fred's door with two gallons of exquisite homemade chicken soup. Derek Bermel taking time out of his strenuous schedule to stay with Fred so I could take a break. David Bindman vacuuming the rugs, cleaning the apartment. Art Hirahara and Joseph Yoon always poised for a grocery run to Trader Joe's or a ride to an appointment. Marina Celander with her bouquets of stargazers and life-giving smile; a battalion of artists and people from all walks of life. It was at that level that Fred's tribe responded to this life-threatening health crisis. Nurse's aide Richard Miller at the hospital (studying for his RN degree at the time) a genius and fan of complexity, stepped up from stranger to friend within days of knowing Fred, providing comfort and intelligent, thorough, health advice. Poet and librettist Ann T. Greene organized the troops daily; she and her husband Mark, on call, 24/7 and ready for any toxic missile the cancer conspired to deploy. Volumes could be written on the acts of kindness and friendship that I have witnessed not only during Fred's illness and recovery, but also throughout our friendship.

On the generous invitation of Limor Tomer, former curator of the BAMcafé (Brooklyn Academy of Music), I was able to organize a surprise tribute to Fred on January 6, 2007. The planning took several months and in all that time, no one had a slip of the tongue. There are no snitches in Fred's life, either. The room was filled beyond capacity with friends coming to perform and offer support from as far away as California. Joe Melillo, executive artistic director of BAM, greeted Fred and escorted him to his table, front and center. The artists donated their fee to Fred, and the BAM staff matched it. The tech crew juggled the 30-plus artists in 10 acts without a hitch. They worked with the fervor and accuracy of the Secret Service guarding a president. The entire staff at both BAM and the Apollo leave me breathless with their hospitality at every visit.

It is impossible to write about Fred and not write about the loyalty and compassion of the people in his life. Forgive me, dear ones, you are too numerous to mention all here, but I could readily sing all of your names, alphabetically, if needed. Any story about Fred Ho is incomplete without them, since ultimately they are the sanctuary in which Fred takes his deepest breaths as he struggles against the odds in life, in art, in health, in politics and daily survival as a creative anomaly. They, whether Fred knows it or not, are the manifestation of the utopian dream Fred has pursued throughout his life. They are his generosity returning to him tenfold.

While it is true that Fred launches multidisciplinary extravaganzas and collaborates constantly with distinguished artists, he is the centrifugal force that separates the milk from the cream on any project. If you're going to collaborate with Fred, wear a seat belt, be punctual, and bring your best game. Whether in relationship with living beings or his physical space, Fred demands clarity, punctuality, and excellence. His war with cancer since August of 2006 has softened his edges a bit and some roses now linger by his bed, but Fred is still sharpened to a point by an inner grindstone, an arrow aimed at the existential question of what it means to be fully alive and committed to social change through excellence in art. Fred will not settle for social "chump change." Fred wants complete social transformation and revolution. As I have heard him put it, he does not want a slice of the pie, he wants "a whole new pie" and he is relentless in his revolutionary creative pursuit of this vision.

Some of us who know and love Fred believe he at times exhibits a personality disorder. He may well have several. I have yet to meet anyone who doesn't have a glitch or two; some simply move among the undetected with the skill of Claude Raines. How does one live in a sick society and remain unscathed? I've heard stories about Fred's raging temper and belittling commentary in rehearsals when he perceives sloppiness or compromised professionalism. I have never personally experienced this side of Fred. But I have, however, witnessed his impatience, bossy sense of entitlement, and verbal bullying as he fought to take back the steering wheel from the sense of lost control provoked by cancer. Fred, healthy or not, also has the ability to lie with impunity, slick as a coyote, when he deems it as humorous (as in aging himself by more than a decade, rendering his muscular physique even more impressive), necessary (as an artist who will not be erased from the annals of history and mythologizes elements of his life by air brushing the hyperbolic portraiture), and justified (when he feels a colleague is not living up to his demands of business acumen and ambition). Fred approaches life and artistic collaboration with the urgency of guerilla warfare; the pitch heightens if he doesn't feel a singular purpose among the comrades or supported in battle. Fred's battlefield is the stage, and, just as a soldier would not forget to load his gun or put on his boots, Fred will not go on stage unless he feels armed to the teeth. These so-called personality disorders are the same attributes that helped him defeat the physical invasion of a tumor the size of a golf ball that had festered undetected for ten years and had broken through his perineum. These are the traits that actuate his exciting new music in unexpected meter and highly imaginative theatrical spectacles that audiences love or hate, fear or embrace.

The number of family, friends, colleagues, and strangers who mobilized to support Fred as he battled cancer is a testament to the quality of his life, his generosity, his capacity for love, and the profound impact he has on one's life, whether you like his delivery methods or not. It is impossible to remain indifferent to Fred Ho. We remain indifferent to and detached from so many social evils, including our tacit consent to war crimes by the Bush regime; we remain ungrateful to Nature and her bounty; we ignore and/or allow racism, bigotry of all forms, violence against women, child pornography, human trafficking, worker exploitation, government crimes, and brutality against the undocumented, but I'll be damned if I've ever met anyone indifferent to Fred Ho. Societal passivity and collective amnesia are exactly what Fred feels he is fighting against. We are in a state of siege and Fred knows it. Worse, we are in a national coma and Fred knows that, too. My question is, why aren't more of us as agitated and ferocious as Fred?

I once heard a rather mediocre performance artist euphemistically intone that Fred was "quite a philosopher." The difference between them is that this person is a celebrated dilettante embraced by audiences who seek to be coddled and only peripherally challenged (just enough to assuage their liberal guilt), and Fred is an artist who cannonballs into the pool and gets you wet.

Fred the child and Fred the man are fully aware that the world is not a safe place. A difficult childhood as the son of emotionally oppressed parents in a troubled marriage, Fred grew a layer of self-protective armadillo casing at an early age. He sought his refuge among elder revolutionary artists such as Sonia Sanchez, whom he has often mentioned as always available to him during those confusing adolescent years in the predominantly white and affluent Amherst, Massachusetts.

His adolescent rebellion and search for identity led him to become a Muslim. An intellectual outcast among his peers, Fred cut his first fangs of self-defense in the warm embrace of the Black Nationalist Movement, which for him represented personal liberation and what became the catalyst for a lifelong identification and solidarity with all oppressed peoples, regardless of gender, orientation, race, or ethnicity. An idealist at heart, Fred has been destined to a life of constant disappointments. I've often heard him say that "The difference between the Master and the Slave is that the Master has all the guns." Fred has dedicated his life to disarming the Master; but when the Master's lackeys are Fred's fellow field-workers, he masks devastation with rage. Fred is intolerant of weak links and sycophants, as he calls them. I cannot deny that I have similar traits and intolerance, however I have honed my skills of diplomacy and expanded my capacity for compassion. Ironically, I have learned this from Fred. He is the widescreen, high-definition image of why I must not just write someone off because they do not meet my expectations of who they should be, how they should live, or how they should behave.

I could have walked out on our friendship the first time I watched him eat: voraciously and with vacuum suction. I had written off many for less grave offenses, but in our first encounter I had seen his fingers travel the body of his saxophone. No, the sounds he played were not what moved me, but the way his fingers danced on the pads. The way he moved his hands when he spoke, the generous way he extended his hand gifting us with one of his books: "To Jim and Magdalena—What new super friends and comrades you are! Love, Justice and a Better World for All! Fred Ho, 2002." A better world is all that Fred Ho really wants and works for; it's just that sometimes his dragon tail whips about uncontrollably among glass figurines.

The day after Jim and I met Fred, he sent an email to let us know how pleased he was to meet us, how happy he was for us that we had found each other, and how much he wished he could be in Jim's shoes. He sent it to us both. He had seen Jim clearly: noncovetous or jealous. Fred was unafraid of exposing his heart, stating his desires, nothing underhanded or secretly seductive. Vulnerable and to the point. He has since let us both in beneath his skin.

I can truly say that Fred Ho has always evinced the best in me. I arrived in his life already a strong and defiant woman; I am now a ferocious and more compassionate one. He has also raised the bar for my creative work by his constant encouragement and clear, honest feedback, and I am the better for it. Shortly after we met he advised me of the Julia and David White Artists'

Colony in Costa Rica and urged me to apply. We conspired to apply for the same time period so we could travel and work together. We were accepted for residency in November 2003. While in Costa Rica I got to see many sides of Fred Ho that are not immediately apparent, even to the most stealthy and acute voyeur.

First and foremost, was Fred the Socialite. Upon arriving, Fred made sure to connect with everyone who might advance his career, offer intellectual stimulation, or provide something otherwise useful to enhance his residency and experience of Costa Rica. I was more interested in the cook, housekeepers, and grounds caretakers. Clearly, we had a lot to learn from each other about balance.

We took frequent trips down the hill into Ciudad Colón and bus rides to San José. Fred often walked blocks ahead of me; I strolled, he marched. Given his penchant for loud colors and floral summer patterns, I never lost sight of him. Not that it mattered; I never feel lost anywhere, whether I speak the language or not. It's another trait we share in common: home is wherever we happen to alight. From time to time I would ask him to hold my hand just to keep pace. Fred the Old School Gentleman emerged. Sensing my exhaustion in the dense humidity of rainy season, he would kindly comply, doing his best to disguise any form of begrudging, and always offered to carry my packages. Holding hands with me would surely impede his chances with the local women, but he did it without complaint. I always got first dibs on any available seat or the window. I provided the advantage of Spanish as my first language, but Fred had made it his business to learn enough travelers' vocabulary to fend for himself without me.

Next came Fred the Clown. When he ran out of words, he delighted the Ticos (as the Costa Ricans call themselves) with his physical antics, such as playing the part of a chicken and pointing to his preferred dark meat parts when ordering dinner. Fred the Philanthropist, handing over $5,000 to the now-deceased director of the artists' colony, Bill White, as his show of support for Bill's dream to create a monument on his property to those who had died in the struggle for peace and justice in a country without a military.

Fred The Benefactor, providing networking opportunities, free CDs, books, and picking up the check when meeting with struggling Tico artists who showed promise. Fred the Lothario, who could not resist staring at beautiful women or flirting with his eyes, or making the direct and unabashed approach: "Why are you working as a prostitute?" as he asked matter-of-factly of a woman who had previously waited on tables at our favorite restaurant. When she responded she made more money this way to feed her children,

Fred responded with compassion and nonjudgment, letting her know he understood her predicament and choice, aware that, at that moment in her life, it may have been her only choice. Fred Ho believes that being a sex worker or a porn actor are a person's prerogative and as viable a profession as being a dentist. He also admires and congratulates anyone who does their job in an impeccable and professional manner, whether they are conducting a symphony or performing fellatio. What is important to Fred is that they take their work seriously and preside over business with integrity. Fred once told me that if he had life to do over again, he would spend some time developing a career as a porn star. With a look I assured him it isn't too late. We are both of the mind that if one acts with conviction and incorruptibility any profession can be righteously subversive and revolutionary for the benefit of humanity.

Fred moves with ease anywhere and connects with total strangers as if he were at home among friends. He is the Perfect Traveling Companion, as happy to be in company as to be alone.

The Sensual Fred Ho spends hours generating music notation by hand, foregoing the timesaving advantages of computer programs. He prefers the feel of the sharpened pencil in his hand, the brush of paper against the fleshy parts of his hand, the heft of the old-school pink eraser, the visual art of drawing each note. I have seen him sit naked at his kitchen table, with a temporary colostomy bag as his annoying companion, finishing a suite by hand, defying all threats of death, in the act of creation, note by note, determined, willful and completely at ease with his nudity, scars, ostomy bags, and precarious health. The sun streamed over him, as time stopped and any thought of despair was transformed into the creation of art. Fred loves extra pillows on the bed and soft, light comforters on his skin. He surrounds himself with political art, bright colors, and natural light. Thanks to the insistence of his friend Michael Surdej, Fred has also developed a love of plants and their healing, oxygenating properties. The Fatherly Fred Ho who doesn't ascribe to the nuclear family and deems it irresponsible to have biological children, burdening an already overexploited planet and ignoring the needs of orphans, delights in the company of children who are alert, well-mannered, and precocious.

Fred loves and appreciates all forms of beauty and is constantly making himself available to a broader definition of beauty and its relationship to what it means to live a revolutionary life. It all comes back to living with intention and clarity of purpose. Nothing is left to chance, not even the pattern on the dinner dishes. If we live with intention, then we are awake. If we are awake, then we not only see injustice but must also take responsibility for our own complicity in it, as well as dismantling it.

It is clear from his ever-increasing time spent with friends rather than in aggressive and insatiable pursuit of work, that Fred is increasingly resisting the allure of what I coin accomplishment-holism, which in and of itself is a toxic by-product of capitalism's viselike grip on the human psyche that tells us we are only as worthy as our bank account and the notches on our résumé. The latter is so much more insidious and pernicious, masquerading as the price one must pay in social struggle for change. It is basic human truths that if we are incapable of self-nurturing, reflection, achieving balance and transformation, how can we think that we have the skills to enduringly bring these attributes to our society? If I pollute and exploit my own body with stress, poor eating habits, and excess, how will I model for others a path of justice and healing? All the rhetoric on the planet cannot replace one single act of truthful, intentional positive action. In the end, it is not what we say that matters, but who we are. It is not what we accomplish that changes the world, but whom we touch, motivate, and inspire.

Fred Ho has motivated and inspired countless people throughout his lifetime to examine and reexamine their thinking, their habits, their art, their politics, and the lens through which they view themselves and the world at large. Although a Harvard graduate, most of Fred's learning has been autodidactic. He is the eternal student, always longing to be challenged, to have his mind blown open and his ass kicked. Before he met his collaborator, Ruth Margraff, he went to his friend, playwright Aishah Rahman, and asked her "Whom do you know as a writer who can kick my ass?" Ms. Rahman directed him to Ruth. Fred wants to be challenged, and although an exceptional and inspiring teacher, he is also equally fervent as a student. It is beyond my comprehension why Fred still has not been offered an endowed chair. Don't we as a society want to cultivate free and expansive thinkers? Do our institutions wish to be challenged? Don't we want students who will excel their teachers, challenge their views and question their authority? Or are we flailing blindly in the shadow of McCarthyism where the purpose of education became to create a compliant, submissive workforce? It appears we have succeeded in this goal, as evidenced by the majority of the earth's resources, hoarded and exploited by a privileged minority. Greater power looms in fewer and incapable hands. This equation for self-demise in formulaic, capitalistic, amoral avarice rules our day. We are a society that blames the victim and criminalizes the poor. If students had professors like Fred, perhaps they would understand the simple fact that humanity and the planet are not threatened by the lack of resources, but by their brutal exploitation.

It seems so obvious, so simple, but all we have to do is listen to the silence that drones over our once-vibrant cities where we marched and enacted the howls of self-defense. A pestilence of silence covers the United States like the fog of foul breath; no one wants to admit it or call it out so as not to cause a disturbance, embarrassment, or discomfort. We want to be liked, to be accepted, to stay out of Guantanamo. It is the silence that lives between the truth and a lie. The silence beneath incessant public alerts that urge us to report suspicious packages, suspicious neighbors, and suspicious behavior, as long as we are not seeing and naming these same suspicious behaviors in our government.

For me, Fred Ho is representative of the social discomfort I crave: the high-wire tension of true debate. The high-stakes risks of what we as a nation must do to take back our country, transform our leadership, and make reparation to the nations and people we have defiled. The trickster who is not afraid to blow his nose or fart in the midst of prayer, who reminds us that to be fully human and awake is the prayer itself.

Speaking for myself, I assure you that I am more of who I am by witnessing Fred in his struggle to constantly be more of who he is; who he authentically is. Like it or not, in your face, and fully Fred.

Do we as individuals and as a nation dare to be fully who we are without fear of retribution? If it's personal it is political. The political is inescapable. One cannot marry without a license. You go out to dinner and you pay tax on your meal. Since 9/11 your phone calls can be monitored, your taste in reading materials investigated at the library without your knowing or consent; when you travel by air, terrorist activity is assumed to be hidden in your toiletries, and they will be confiscated if you don't follow the packaging rules. You can't carry your own bottle of water past the gate and instead are forced to buy water inside at jacked-up prices. You shit in the woods? Guess who ultimately owns and controls the woods? Privately owned? Government owned? Eminent domain. It takes guts to speak, be, and live as the essential self if one is a nonconformist, nonassimilationist, or as Fred Ho refers to himself, a "matriarchal socialist." Nuff said.

Ché Guevara might agree that every individual act of unconditional love is the foundation for every act of resistance. Every belly laugh is fuel to build and the soul food for courage to go on. There is no leftward movement without humor, and there will be nothing Left without struggle. Personal struggle that reaches across the dinner table, that spirals out the door and into the streets.

Figure 12. Fred Ho with Magdalena Gómez and Raúl Salinas, *Caliente! Circle around the Sun*, Hampshire College, Amherst, Massachusetts, 2006. Credit: Jim Lescault

A struggle dressed in loud, vibrating prints. The noise of Fred Ho and his off-meter music; the noise of the friends who love him even when he stings, who show up when it's inconvenient. A personal journey that mobilizes action and love among strangers.

Now that's what I call revolution.

Notes

1. *Sheroes Womyn Warriors Wall Calendar*, created by Fred Ho and Big Red Media Inc. Published by the Gustavus Myers Center for the Study of Bigotry and Human Rights, 2007.

8

Somewhere between Ideology, Practice, and the Cellular War . . . the Dolphins Sing

An Improv on the Fake Book of a Revolutionary Artist

PEGGY MYO-YOUNG CHOY

Let me say, at the risk of seeming ridiculous, that the true Revolutionary is guided by great feelings of love.

—CHE GUEVARA

Real revolutionaries are not measured by words, just as real love evades avowals.

—UNKNOWN

I know that Fred loves dolphins. He doesn't talk about this part of himself too much—the part that loves to swim in the ocean with the dolphins, in the ocean where he himself can become a dolphin. His love of the ocean and the life that it supports is something he experiences nonverbally, communicating this experience nonverbally, even nonmusically.

These observations contrast markedly with my many interactions with Fred over the past 16 years that I have known him. We have often dropped into intense conversations ranging from the state of Asian American studies vis-à-vis radical politics, to how to wage effective battles in the belly of the performing-arts world. These conversations are punctuated with ideological commentary, personal critique, and hard dares. Conversations can get heated. He can be as ferocious as he is wildly imaginative.

But there is a very quiet and inwardly aware side of Fred Ho. He can sit back, observe, and wait. Just as Fred enjoys swimming vigorously, I imagine that he can also enjoy floating and feeling the nuances of the ocean when it is quiet. We have not had lengthy conversations about the ocean. He would simply say that he had traveled to some place on the globe to snorkel, and had loved it. I accepted this silence about his aquatic life as part of our conversations that include improvised gaps. I have learned to feel as comfortable in these spaces, just as much as I have come to feel all right with arguing about an issue—personal or political. Some time ago, when I suggested to Fred that he compose an opera in dolphin language, he said that he didn't "reveal that side of himself." I accepted his statement without explanation, taking it as his prerogative to protect a more vulnerable, softer side. Eventually, however, Fred came around and expressed the desire to collaborate on a new work that will take place "completely underwater." There is no boundary to the ebb and flow of creative vision. Fred now wants to plunge into the watery world through performance. He is embarking upon a creative project inspired by his nonverbal, deeply organic passion for life. If the ocean, with its strong and unpredictable currents, can be a metaphor for life in a difficult world, Fred consistently dives into its depths, headfirst, with an intensity that comes from merged energies as both artist and cultural worker. This combination guides his artistic boldness, his political and cultural fearlessness. His "rad" artistic sensibilities feed his "rad" political views and vice versa, a synergy that drives his creativity. Reflecting on the lessons learned from his 11 years in the radical Asian American organization I Wor Kuen/League of Revolutionary Struggle,[1] Fred concludes that dissention, debate, and creativity are essential to a vital movement:

> I was kicked out of IWK/LRS because I didn't play by the rules to dissolve socialism, because I knew that it was a set-up to eliminate socialism and revolution. I opposed this vigorously. They were trying to control debate and process. . . . After 11 years in IWK/LRS, I was criticized for being "individualistic." An artist should be individualistic, which is different from "individualism," which is self-interest. The final lesson [is]—the authoritarian, "commandist" cannot handle independence . . . independence and dissent was suppressed and banished. A movement that suppresses dissent, debate and creativity is doomed to failure and deserves to fail.[2]

I interpret Fred's words to also mean that you need to dissent and debate in order to create. Whether the focus is a political or cultural movement, or a performance, Fred would say the same thing—that in his creative process, his goal is "a radical unity of form and content."[3] He looks to create new forms that confront and challenge the dominant culture, beyond artificial, apolitical, and superficial fusion of multiculturally inspired performance—what he calls "multicultural fusion confusion."[4] The radical unity of form and content is necessarily organic and taps into the source of our identity. Ultimately, this makes for a strong culture of resistance. We know this from Amilcar Cabral:

> To take up arms to dominate a people is, above all, to take up arms to destroy, or at least to neutralize, to paralyze, its cultural life. For, with a strong indigenous cultural life, foreign domination cannot be sure of its perpetuation. [. . .] The value of culture as an element of resistance to foreign domination lies in the fact that culture is the vigorous manifestation on the ideological or idealist plane of the physical and historical reality of the society that is dominated [. . .] Whatever may be the conditions of a people's political and social factors in practicing this domination, it is generally within the culture that we find the seed of opposition, which leads to the structuring and development of the liberation movement.[5]

Although Cabral was writing in the context of the anti-imperialist struggles in Africa, before his assassination by Portuguese agents in 1973, it is clear that his ideas are relevant here since Fred is producing music and performance in a capitalist-imperialist country that engages in war not only abroad, but wages war on its own workers and oppressed peoples. In merging form and content with revolutionary consciousness, there lies the hope of liberation from within the belly of the beast.

This radical form and content that Fred espouses is necessarily linked to the creation of a cultural identity that is women-centered. Again there are clues in the oceanic world. The word *dolphin* comes from the Greek words *delphin* and *delphis*, which are linked to *delphys* or "womb."[6] A creature of the ocean is just a few letters away from the woman's amniotic sea. The womb is where radical creation takes place; each creation—the baby that emerges—is unique, not known in the world before. The act of birth can be violent as it is transformational, the ultimate, transgressive struggle of the Terminator woman warrior.[7] She is forever undefeated, even when flat on her back, sometimes cut open, sometimes with drugs injected into her spine, sometimes at the edge of death. *Delphys creation* encapsulates the notion of creation of a unique form with unique content that takes on a life of its own, and that emerges from a process of complete engagement in transformation. There is no room for self-doubt, hesitation, or losing one's nerve.

Delphys creation as a woman-centered birthing metaphor assists in articulating the importance of form and content in a liberation struggle. Without form and content that is visionary—not seen or heard of before, and rooted in woman-centered intention—the struggle to transform the world around us will not lead to the future but back to a point from which we were trying to emerge. Whether consciously or not, Fred understands *delphys creation*. His work is formed as if in an extravagant womb. *Voice of the Dragon: Once upon a Time in Chinese America . . . The Martial Arts Epic* is one example of Ho's productions that create an explosion between his music, martial arts, legends, and radical political ideology, one that shoots him into a universe with few peers and far beyond the mainstream. Mainstream critics acknowledge his creative impact and skillful fusion. For example, Jennifer Dunning writes in the *New York Times* that *Once upon a Time in Chinese America* is "one of the best dance scores to be heard in these parts in recent times."[8] The *New York Times* music critic Jon Pareles writes: "[Ho] achieves his cross-cultural goals with skill, grace and humor. The music merges Duke Ellington and Charles Mingus with Chinese instruments and vocal styles from Western opera, Chinese opera, and jazz; for a fusion that never seems forced."[9] Larry Birnbaum confirms both Pareles's view of Ho's unforced "fusion," and my own view about the organic nature of his compositions. In *DownBeat*, Birnbaum says: "Ho's style is a genre unto itself, a pioneering fusion of free-jazz and traditional Chinese music that manages to combine truculence and delicacy with such natural ease that it sounds positively organic."[10]

These critics fail to see, if not ignore, Fred's *delphys* vision, that is actually key to understanding his artistic and political vision. With his *Warrior Sisters: The New Adventures of African and Asian American Womyn Warriors* (1998), Ho brings to life the meeting of four legendary female revolutionaries from China, Africa, and America—Fa Mu Lan, Nana Yaa Asantewa, Sieh King King, and Assata Shakur.[11] In 1993, he composed the album *Yes Means Yes, No Means No, Whatever She Wears, Wherever She Goes!* for the Afro Asian Music Ensemble. The title of this work speaks for itself as feminist focused. We can also see this focus in Ho's cultural production innovations, such as his *Sheroes Womyn Warriors Calendar*, first published in 1998 and still published annually. The calendar—full of photos and researched captions—celebrates and honors some 400 womyn (including my grandaunt and my mother) who have fought for and inspired new social formations. He writes in the calendar's introduction:

> We walk in the footprints of phenomenal women, and we do so sometime knowingly, but more often not knowing of their efforts, both their achievements and the cost they paid for them [. . .] we celebrate and honor womyn of the past who have been rebels and fighters against patriarchy, who opposed and fought invaders and aggressors to their homelands, and who represent radicals and revolutionaries of their times and societies. [. . .] We take out

> the "men" in "women" in recognition that women are not a subset of men. We use the words "sheroes" and "womyn" and "warriors" intentionally to convey women's agency and women's power.[12]

I drew direct inspiration from the *Sheroes* calendar's description of Sarraounia, the Aznas queen who lived during the late 19th century: "Warrior queen of the Aznas, [Sarraounia], who in early 1899, through brilliant tactical maneuvering and creative promulgation of her reputation as a 'witch-demoness,' successfully defended her African kingdom from the advancing forces of French colonialism."[13] I choreographed a dance, "Sarraounia," that was performed by Dyane Harvey, as part of a full-evening work, "Ki-Aché: Stories from the Belly," with live music directed by Fred, and played by Fred on baritone sax, royal hartigan on drums, and Sam Furnace on soprano sax. The work was commissioned and presented by Danspace Project in New York, premiering in 1997. What inspired me about Sarraounia was her tactical prowess in the art of war fueled by her indigenous Aznas cultural-spiritual knowledge and unrelenting anticolonial stance. The calendar includes words from a Griot song that highlights Sarraounia's qualities that made her legendary: "Gentle Sarraounia with iron hands, you break your enemies as sure as the panther crushes the bones of its prey."[14]

Since the early 1990s, Ho has made a point of sniffing out women artists with something strong to say, honoring and encouraging these artist-performers to be heard and seen in their own right—those crying out against domestic violence, prostitution, and sexual slavery. Like the dolphin who swims in a pod (group) to hunt and play, he seeks out collaborations with women and creates music about women, a path not often tread by other Asian American male artists:

> I have been one of the few Asian American male artists to deal with the oppression of Asian and Asian American women; e.g., "Home Is Where the Violence Is" (1992), an anti-domestic violence performance art work; "Song of the Slave Girl" (1989), the extended aria of a Chinese prostitute circa west coast/19th century; "Picture Bride" (1992), collaboration with Korean American dancer/choreographer Peggy Choy about Japanese and Korean arranged marriage in Hawaii's sugar plantation experience; "Bound Feet" (1985), Jodi Long's text/dance work, about the oppressive feudal Chinese feminine beauty practice; "Lan Hua Hua" (1990), a reworking of a traditional folk song that was a protest of arranged marriages; "What's a Girl to Do?" and "Rockin' in Revolution/Drowning in the Yellow River" (1984) based on Janice Mirikitani's poetry. And of course, love songs about and for Asian Americans: "Shao

> Heh Bao" (Chinese language); "We'll Make Tomorrow!"; a self-criticism for womanizing, "I'm Sorry (For Kayo and Sayo)," A new work is "Yes Means Yes, No Means No, Whatever She Wears, Wherever She Goes!," a suite dedicated to WHAM! (Women's Health Action and Mobilization) and BWARE (Brooklyn Women's Anti-Rape Exchange). Such works are about women's oppression, creating revolutionary aesthetics and changing the relations of cultural production.[15]

The inclusion of pieces in one's own body of work that speak to "self-criticism for womanizing" is risky and decisively honest, like a promise, both public and personal, to crush the roots of one's own chauvinism. In working with Fred and other key people in my life, I have gone through my own transformation of acquiring the power to speak out clearly when I have felt put down, dismissed, or not respected. In keeping with his promise, on these occasions, Fred sincerely listened. I have noticed a continually developing consciousness between us that includes listening and humility. *Delphys creation* in continuum . . .

Fred's organic merging of theory and practice is based on ideological clarity. He writes: "Without revolutionary theory a movement is blind and groping, with no strategic vision or framework. We need to study and integrate the collective, shared and combined lessons and experiences from revolutionary struggle from around the world with our experiences in the U.S."[16] I experienced how Fred merged theory with practice when he invited me to be a part of his residency at the Atlantic Center for the Arts at New Smyrna Beach, Florida, in 1993. He gave me the gift of making my choreography the center of the residency. The specific work that took shape, "*Jongsindae*/Comfort Woman," expresses the torture and abuse of the 80,000 to 200,000 Korean girls and women who were abducted into sexual slavery for the Japanese soldiers during World War II.[17] Fred organized our "pod"—Fred, myself, and other artists including royal hartigan, Wei-hua Zhang, Janet Higgins, and Didi Dubelyew—as a mutually supportive collective, distinguished from the other groups who worked within a hierarchical master artist/emerging artist structure. We cooked and ate together and shared the responsibility of marketing and cleaning up. We debated the dialectics of women's oppression and patriarchy as seen in different historical and ethnic contexts. We discussed how the political is personal, and we shared information about social and political movements in Hawai'i, the continental United States, and internationally.

There was also time for fun and laughter; ours was not a morbid or rigid cadre. We went to the ocean, shopped for costume fabric, and looked for secondhand books. Even nature was a participant trickster. A hurricane hit the area, not unusual for Florida in March. While the wind whipped the rain against the windows, we had good food (my Korean chicken?) and great discussion late into the night, ending with talk about horror movies and Asian and Hawaiian ghost stories. I had admitted that I hated to hear ghost stories and to watch horror movies because my imagination would run wild afterward. During a lull from the heavy rains and strong wind, Janet and I headed back to our room, stepping over broken branches on the wet path. Out of the dark, a howl sounded in back of us. Turning around, a white ghostly figure approached; Janet and I screamed in terror. A laugh came from under the flapping white sheet. It was Fred.

Another memory is of being in the ocean. Fred and I went swimming off the coast of New Smyrna Beach trying to find manatees.[18] We were both smug as we entered the water. I had grown up swimming and surfing; Fred was an experienced swimmer. The tide was unexpectedly strong. I felt myself being pulled away from the shore. I turned around and struggled to swim back, but I was getting tired. Fred, who was already swimming into shore ahead of me, looked back and said, "Do you need help?" Even though I wondered if I really would make it without help, I said I could do it. I did. Later I was happy I could say that I got myself back to shore, and I would not have to say forever after that "Fred Ho saved my life." Fred and I did not talk a lot about this experience. I was surprised to learn of his own impressions about the occurrence years later: "After I heard about and saw dolphins swimming in the channels, I wanted to find them and swim with them. The current was very strong, if you didn't swim very hard, it would pull you very fast, and it wasn't towards shore. It was very dangerous, something dolphins could easily handle, but not humans."[19]

What emerged from living theory and practice in Florida? "*Jongsindae/* Comfort Woman" came together and was performed for all the artists at the end of the residency, and became the seed for my larger work, *"Seung Hwa": Rape/Race/Rage/Revolution*. I danced solo, and Fred directed the music with himself on baritone sax, royal hartigan on drums, and Allen Won on soprano saxophone, with costumes by Janet Higgins and artwork by Didi Dubelyew. The full-evening work was performed first at Cornell University for the Asian American Studies conference, and later premiered in New York at Dance Theater Workshop in 1994.

The Florida experience was not only about product. There were two lucky lessons. First, I learned that musicians, dancer, and fabric artist could grow creatively through fearless debate. This process continued even after Florida. The musicians, Janet Higgins, and I argued for an agonizing amount of time about whether or not the musicians were going to pull down their pants in the final part of their playing to reveal the red Japanese rising sun sewn onto the crotch of their white boxer shorts. In the end, my decision as director prevailed—the pants came down! Second, I learned that if the creative process is fearless, then the performance may itself be controversial or even cause unrest. At a performance of *"Seung Hwa"* at the University of Pennsylvania, three armed police sat in the front row throughout the piece because the university feared that because of the provocative title, the piece could incite a riot. Fred reflected that this incident serves as an example of the ways in which we become marked persons when we make our politics so explicit. On the other hand, this performance has had transformational effects. I have had women share with me how they were able to let go of their own personal horrors of rape after they saw my "Comfort Woman" piece. Ho has consistently sought and continues to seek challenging collaborations with outstanding women artists. For his opera *Warrior Sisters: The New Adventures of African and Asian Womyn Warriors*, Fred collaborated with deeply rooted writer and librettist, Ann T. Greene. The opera was performed at the Aaron Davis Hall at the City College of New York in 1998, a weeklong run at the Kitchen in New York City in 2000, and at Arizona State University–Tempe in 2001. In 2006, his Afro Asian Music Ensemble recorded a piece, "Blasé Redux" (2006), with text by Native American lesbian writer Christine Stark, about domestic violence. Stark's words—as performed with painful clarity by Jennifer Kidwell[20]—cut like knife on bone against a relentless almost haranguing, yet understated and chillingly gentle piano, drums, and bass.

The pod of women artists widens beyond Ho's own collaborations. He wanted me to meet the powerful writer and performer Magdalena Gómez, whom I asked to write a narrative and perform it for my full-evening work, *Gateless Gate: Women of the Scarred Earth*, which had its world premier at the Wisconsin Union Theater in 2007. Here is a taste of her incendiary narrative:

> Girl fetus
> violated by
> the barrel of a gun
> clings to the power
> of her mother's womb.
> Howls mingle with whimpers
> find each other,
> across centuries;

a letter written,
scroll hidden,
secrets strummed,
mysteries cured in brine
memories neatly folded
into the hidden drawer of time
strategies bound to unbound feet
Look! A pile of bloodied rags
our toes grow back!
21st Century.
25th Century.
From your broken mouth
we drink ancient wisdom.
From your slit throat
we devour
the woman warrior's cry;
her back will not break
from the weight
of fallen trees.
No.
She carries them,
they take root again.[21]

Her powerful poetic narrative charged both the audience and performers, exuding *delphys creativity*.

Dolphins and *delphys creators* are prepared to dig and defend. The dolphin's rostrum or snout is very hard and is used for digging and attacking enemies. Unafraid to wage his cellular war with cancer, Fred dug deep for answers for the best means of waging the war in partnership with his doctors. He continues to overturn the expected. In his daily life, Fred is trying to live more simply and more at peace in a world that is technologically enslaved. Fred's Luddite views articulate the nature of his battle and underscore what Amilcar Cabral means when he says, "You must consider the society in which you are fighting."[22] Fred explained to me:

> The U.S. makes up 5 to 6 percent of the world's population yet consumes and wastes 50 to 60 percent of the world's resources. We cannot continue to consume and waste at this rate. We must consume less. The Third World has the right to raise its standard of living. We have to lower ours.

> In *Harvard Magazine* about one and a half years ago, in my interview, I said I was not Luddite. . . . [M]y cancer changed me. There is no single cause for cancer, it is part of the very fabric of our modern existence. . . . that something bigger, faster, stronger, more powerful is not better. All the wrong standards on which to measure quality. Actually our standards are toxic, cancerous. [A friend of mine] . . . says cancer and capitalism is part of the same process—of over-consumption . . . resulting from over-accumulation. Cancer cells multiply eight to ten times faster than normal cells. This is how capitalism behaves—quickly, cheaply [through exploiting others].
>
> Capitalism has raised the standard of living, but the problem is overproductivity. The social consequences of that logic of overaccumulation, overconsumption, is that all is then measured in a perverted way with no response for quality but rather for the quick, immediate gratification and for profit, with no long-termed but rather unsustainable toxic, and ultimately self-destruction. I have written, "So many channels, so little choices . . . so much information so little wisdom."[23]

Fred's reflections since his battle with cancer reveal the transformation of both his ideology, and daily practice. I also see in his cancer diary reflections of what he has learned from the turquoise sea of love that has buoyed him during his fight:[24]

> I am someone who believes in the struggle to find answers [. . .] I don't believe in stasis: we are all constantly changing, even at the cellular level, the question is: how are we changing and is it for the better? [. . .] The war against cancer has brought about this transformation, revelation and application on my part. I have been tremendously humbled by this war and at the same time learned to fight on a cellular level and to apply a cellular approach to the technical, emotional, creative and spiritual challenges of making music. The cells of one's sound is what is supreme, infusing one's breath or CHI-energy to that cellular vibration of making one's sound a life-force. [. . .] probably the MOST important transformation for me: to never harbor envy, jealousy, competitiveness, to speak the truth (even if it is very critical of friends and loved ones, but to do so without comparison and always with compassion).[25]

Every dolphin has a signature whistle. Fred's signature sound is calling us together in an ever-broadening, fearless cohort. His call resonates with all who are unafraid to plunge into and cavort in the ocean of *delphys creation* with revolutionary energy. While dolphins inspire Fred's imagination, I want to mention a fish that inspires me. The *hīnālea luahine*, or the Old Woman

Figure 13. Fred Ho, in residence at the University of Wisconsin–Madison, 2008.
Credit: Bryce Richter/University of Wisconsin–Madison

Wrasse, swims nonchalantly in Hawaiian waters. Quite dull in color—as if grayed by the tides—it is ever curious. It is fearless even around humans. Not a picky eater, it ingests almost anything, even prickly sea urchins. If we listen carefully, to the ocean, we can hear the aquatic wisdom of *delphys creation*, not only from the dolphins but from the *hīnālea luahine* as well. I am inviting Fred to compose an opera in dolphin language, but challenge him to include improvisatory sounds of an ancient chorus of *hīnālea luahine*!

Notes

1. I Wor Kuen/League of Revolutionary Struggle (IWK/LRS) was a radical Asian American organization modeled after the Black Panthers. Fred was a member from 1978 to 1989.

2. Fred Ho, interview by the author, September 23, 2007.

3. Fred Ho, "'Jazz,' Kreolization and Revolutionary Music for the 21st Century," in *Sounding Off! Music as Subversion/Resistance/Revolution*, ed. Ron Sakolsky and F. W. Ho (Brooklyn: Autonomedia, 1995), 143.

4. See Fred's discussion of the exoticism that continues in the Euro-American performance world in "The Real Next Wave: Multicultural Artists and Empowerment

as Sources for New American Art," in *Reimaging America: The Arts of Social Change*, ed. Mark O'Brien and C. Little (Philadelphia: New Society Publishers, 1990), 124–27.

5. Amilcar Cabral, *Return to the Source: Selected Speeches of Amilcar Cabral*, ed. Africa Information Service (New York: Monthly Review Press, 1973), 39–40, 41, 43.

6. *Webster's 7th New Collegiate Dictionary* (Springfield, Mass.: G. & C. Merriam, 1965), 247.

7. On one of my visits with Fred, we watched the DVD of *Terminator 2* (1984) with Linda Hamilton as Sarah Connor, a character thrown into a life-and-death struggle with evil forces to protect her son. I mentioned to Fred that she was "the madonna of the dark side," not only because of her titanic physical and mental capacities as a warrior mother, but also because her son was born through "sci-fi miraculous conception."

8. Jennifer Dunning, "Next Wave Festival Review: Of Old-Time Treachery with Modern Precepts," *New York Times*, November 9, 2001.

9. Jon Pareles, "Next Wave Festival Review/Music: Chinese-Jazz Fusion in Monkey's Tale," *New York Times*, November 24, 1997, E31.

10. "Fred Ho," *DownBeat*, November 1994, 57.

11. Ho's opera with libretto by Ann Greene had its world premier at Aaron Davis Hall, City College of New York, in 1998.

12. Fred Ho, introduction, *Sheroes 2008 Womyn Warriors Wall Calendar* (Boston: Gustavus Myers Center for the Study of Bigotry and Human Rights, 2008).

13. Fred Ho, July, *Sheroes 2008 Womyn Warriors Wall Calendar*.

14. Ibid.

15. Ho, "'Jazz,' Kreolization and Revolutionary Music for the 21st Century," 142–43.

16. Fred Ho, "Fists for Revolution: The Revolutionary History of I Wor Kuen/League of Revolutionary Struggle," in *Legacy to Liberation: Politics and Culture of Revolutionary Asian Pacific America*, ed. Fred Ho with C. Antonio, D. Fujino, and S. Yip (San Francisco: AK Press, 2000), 10.

17. *Jongsindae* is the Korean term for the comfort women. The women were brutally raped, sometimes up to 200 times a day. Many died of venereal disease and were physically and psychologically scarred. I continue to perform this solo, but I now title the piece "Comfort Woman" without the Korean term because the comfort women included not only Korean women but many women from Singapore, Malaysia, the Philippines, and China.

18. The manatee are an endangered plant-eating mammal (genus *Trichechus*) that swim off the coast of Florida and in its fresh waters.

19. Fred Ho to author, email July 24, 2001.

20. "Blasé Redux" CD recording by Fred Ho. Original music and text by Archie Shepp (1969), arrangement by Fred Ho with new text by Christine Stark (2006).

21. Magdalena Gómez, *Gateless Gate: Women of the Scarred Earth*, 2006, 9–10, unpublished manuscript courtesy of Magdalena Gómez.

22. Cabral, *Return to the Source*, 77.

23. Ho, interview by the author.

24. Fred composed a piece with the gorgeous title, "Blazing on the Turquoise Sea" (2006)—a piece with a buoyant timbre, playfulness, and uplifting shape. While Fred denied the need to compose about his love of sea creatures and the ocean, I was surprised to see he had already composed this piece in 2006.

25. Fred Ho, "Cancer Diary #11," emailed to his Warriors for Fred Listserv recipients, March 9, 2007.

9

"That's Why the Work Is What It Is"

An Interview with Fred Ho

MIYOSHI SMITH

It had been some time since I had sat down and talked with Fred Ho. I conducted this interview one week after his first week of chemoradiation treatment. He was amazed at how much he had needed to sleep during this process: 10–16 hours a day after the treatments. This was the first day he said that he had enough energy to sit up for some time. He looked good: toned, wearing his confidence, and rather peaceful despite the week of intense dosing.

MIYOSHI: What are your first memories about yourself as a child, as it relates to music?

FRED: I don't have really any memories as it relates to music, because I never expected to become a musician. Probably about my teenage years, I thought I was going to become some type of radical activist. I was politicized by three different kinds of experiences growing up:

- Racism and racist violence,
- Domestic violence and the oppression of my mother, and
- The advantages my mother gave to me at a very young age, which in many ways prepared me to deal with the first two constant experiences.

One of the earliest experiences I can ever recall was racism. I was in preschool, either three or four years old—and I've told this story before—but my sandbox was segregated. I went to an all-white preschool; I was the only person who wasn't white. And I remember the teacher distinctly telling all of the other kids not to play with me because I am Chinese. And on one hand I felt the alienation of being estranged or singled out, on the other hand I enjoyed having my own sandbox and it became a metaphor for the rest of my life. The estrangement and the attempted marginalization of me only fueled my own efforts at self-reliance and self-determination.

And I grew up facing constant racism in the Amherst community. It was a community in transition from rural farming background of about 100 years in the Connecticut River Valley, into a major educational hub. In fact, by the late '60s, education became the principal industry of Amherst, Massachusetts. And there was a lot of liberalism, but it clashed with a lot of the old rural narrow backgrounds of the longtime residents. And I grew up with both kinds of kids. So there were a lot of racist insults and jeers and taunting, and a lot of racist violence when I played sports. Opposing teams would deliberately try to injure me. I would have sprained ankles every basketball season because they would consciously step on my feet as I was about to do a lay-up or jump shot.

I faced domestic violence constantly as well, from a very young age. My father inflicted terror upon all of us, not only my mother, but also my sisters and myself.

MIYOSHI: Excuse me. Just to interject here, I want to ask you about the memories of growing up with your father. Could you also include how you felt about him, as well?

FRED: Well, my father was a self-made man in the United States. And the story my mother tells is that he was raised very badly. His mother beat him and his sisters were prostitutes. He left home at a very young age and made himself. But he harbored a lot of patriarchal and oppressive ideas and behaviors towards women.

The dominating impact of my father was that he was someone to fear, someone who intimidated us considerably—and motivated us to do things out of fear of reprisal. Extremely authoritarian. Not generous at all. In fact my mother was arrested when I was very young for shoplifting, because he had her on allowance. I think it started at 75 cents per week and finally I think it increased to about $2 per week. So she couldn't even afford to buy her own sanitary napkins, and she stole them from a local department store and was arrested. And her name was in the local newspaper and it was a great embarrassment to her. Not so much to myself, because I understood the motivation of my mother. I never saw her as a criminal or anything like that. She would oftentimes steal presents for us because she couldn't afford them.

You know, I blame my father for that. He was a university professor, albeit somewhat low paid; he was discriminated against in his profession. But rather than fight that discrimination, he brought it home and took it out on us. That kind of bullying is something that I've always opposed: the infliction of suffering upon people who are weaker than you, just because you can't direct your anger and rage towards the more powerful—the true causes of your problems.

So he was a university professor, highly educated, but very schizophrenic. On one hand he was raised very feudalistic, in a very Chinese Confucian tradition. But on the other hand, here he was part of the intellectual elite. But I never took much intellectual example from him. In fact I think most of my life I was motivated to become contrary to him, to become something different. He was an example of someone I didn't want to be or emulate. And that brings us to really the third experience of my childhood: the advantages my mother gave me.

My mother in many ways was really the catalyst because in first or second grade, after I came home from school, she would create lessons for me, primarily math and reading, that were ahead of the curriculum and gave me that advantage. So when I went to school I was more prepared than the other students. And it gave me an awareness of the importance of preparation. Only later in life did I come to realize that when she was helping me learning how to read—very fundamental kinds of children's books like *[Fun with] Dick and Jane* and the *See Spot Run* books—that she was also using it as a way to teach herself English, since my father forbade her from going out, learning how to drive, speak English, from earning income. She was really a domestic slave. But those advantages she gave me early on made it possible for me to out-compete the other students. And also it gave me a sense of confidence that I transferred also physically in the sense that I was growing I think at a faster rate than other children my age. So I would out-compete them physically as well. So maybe it worked too well, because I think in fifth or sixth grade I was voted the most conceited kid in my class (*laughter*).

And I grew up in a context that was very white. And I also remember the first day of entering public school, first grade, in Amherst. My mother had made a Chinese lunch for me and the kids made fun of it, called it Play-Doh. These were steamed flour buns that my mother made, that looked like Play-Doh.

So I was made to feel ashamed of being Chinese, and I did a lot to try to eradicate my Chinese identity. But the racism would always seem to keep coming. So no matter how hard I tried to erase my Chinese identity, I couldn't. By the time of the late '60s, the explosion of the Black Power and Black Arts Movement, I was desperate and hungry to seize upon the explosion of pride and self-identity of that era. The Black experience of course became a way for me to conceptualize, synthesize, and analyze my experience as an Asian American.

MIYOSHI: And how does the music of that era fit into your life?

FRED: Well music doesn't come until much, much later—around age 14. Both the upsurge in American popular music as a whole, the rise of very accomplished bands that used horns like Blood, Sweat and Tears; Chicago; Bill Chase Band . . . popular music, movies, and television; Lalo Schifrin's *Mission: Impossible* scores, then coupled with the Black Arts Movement. Music along with writing became a way for me to express the transition I was going through—the self-awakening. I think for all young people, music becomes a form of individual expression and search for self-identity. And I think that was the same for me.

I wanted to play saxophone, but the only available free instrument from the public band was the big baritone, and nobody else wanted to play it. So it was a hand-me-down instrument and it became my voice, my identity. I worked for over a year and a half as a stock boy in a women's lingerie store; I saved my weekly earnings and stuffed over $1,000 in an envelope and put it in my shoe and went to Rayburn's in Boston and bought my Selmer low A baritone saxophone. But I wasn't very serious about music until after my college years. I mean, I loved music and I enjoyed it. I saw it as an important consciousness-raising tool. I was a cultural activist, cultural producer, putting on festivals and events and performances both in my high school, then later in my college years, but I primarily saw myself as some kind of activist fighting the incorrect establishment ideas, the false consciousness among Third World peoples. I was very nationalistic, very antiwhite, until my college years, when I was won over to Marxism. Not because I found "good White people," but I began to understand the class basis for the contradictions among Third World people: why certain Third World people sold out, others were hypocrites. I thought it was because of their adoption of white values or white identification. I didn't really begin to understand it was because of their beholdenness to the system. So that class analysis doesn't happen until I enter college and the caldron of political and ideological struggle sharpens and deepens my understanding.

So music . . . I was involved in Harvard University Big Band for about a year and a half but quickly left because I thought it was really just another version of the marching band, even though the director, Tom Everett, and I remain very good friends. The overwhelmingly white privileged composition of the students—even though Tom tried to introduce many far-more-creative artists and works—the nature of Harvard at that time didn't allow for a band that was going to be what I wanted it to be: some kind of expression of the Black Arts Movement. I became primarily an organizer: a Marxist-Leninist student activist, and community activist as well. I did things both in the Boston community as well as on campus.

But I don't start to really think about music as something I really want to make my life until I finish college. I'm a construction worker and starting to practice a lot more and realizing that there were two moments in my life that were significant for me as young musician. Around age 16, I spent a whole summer just really learning my scales and overcoming initial frustration where I could actually really develop some fluency on the instrument. The second period was during periods of unemployment as a construction worker; practicing long hours and feeling that I could make a leap. And just being young and somewhat naive and realizing I should just move to New York and give it a go.

MIYOSHI: Sorry, let's stop here for a moment. Just want to ask you a few questions about your parents. Are they still living?

FRED: My parents are both living; they divorced in the late 1980s. They are both alive. My mother is 80. My father is 83.

MIYOSHI: That was all pretty traumatic for your mother: her life, the divorce. What did your mother actually do after the divorce? Can I assume that all of the children were finished with college?

FRED: Well my mother was very inspiring to me because she fought my father, this very dominating, powerful, authoritarian figure for 10 years, unremittingly, in the courts. She went to about three dozen lawyers. She would have me type her briefs and just use other people's briefs as a template. And she was completely uncompromising. After

10 years she wore out my father and won everything she wanted. She's been an inspiration as far as someone who is uncompromising and completely resourceful. Luckily, I went to school at Harvard and lived in Cambridge, Massachusetts. Cambridge is a fairly liberal town. So she was able on her own to navigate and secure everything that she could get. To this day she lives on a combination of public assistance and alimony from my father, which is not a lot—I think it's $700 per month. But she persisted. *She persisted*, with no English ability, no marketable job skills, no resources whatsoever. *But she did it.* It is quite a testament to her will, her strength, her resourcefulness. She had no advantages herself, in any kind of way.

My father retired. He lives on his pension from his years as university professor. He has a small condo; I've never visited it. But I sided with my mother in the suit against my father. My father and I are not very close. But to me all of this is in the past and so many years went by where there was no closeness. So I don't actually feel very filial towards him; I'm much more filial to my mother. I see her quite frequently and speak to her as often as I can. But also she was not undamaged through this. She suffers from some mental illness. So it took its toll. But she relishes her freedom and her independence and will not trade it for anything, and in some ways I have that as well. You know I'm not interested in settling down: marriage, children, that sort of thing. Although she did all of that, she doesn't regret it. But she will not have that again. She doesn't even want to babysit my nieces and nephews (*laughter*). She wants to be free.

MIYOSHI: Good for her. So how many sisters do you have?

FRED: Florence, who is a year younger than I am, and Flora, who is about six or seven years younger than I.

MIYOSHI: Is your mom still in the Boston area?

FRED: Well she lives in Cambridge. She lives in a senior-citizen assisted-living facility.

MIYOSHI: I hear you talking about the influences of your family and school experiences in shaping whom you are. So how have your family dynamics, your school experiences, and politics influenced your independence in what you do professionally? It seems like all of those things were a catalyst in moving you to independence?

FRED: The big lesson for me, the overarching theme in my life is that when I tried my hardest to fit in, that I still couldn't be accepted. So why do you even try to fit in? Let's just reject that completely and be independent and self-reliant. So that was, I think, one key thing. And I think that my mother helped give me certain tools like discipline, the need for preparation. I also think that very early on I had a very overactive imagination. I work best in a very rigidless structure. Now that might seem to be a contradiction in terms. But Amherst public schools were a testing ground for a lot of new educational programs. So this idea of the open classroom, independent studies—I did well in those situations. I've come to learn that I teach myself the best when I'm most motivated. When it came to memorization, I did it by rote, it was mechanical, I had no passion for it, and I was mediocre. When I could come up with my own curriculum, which I often did, including getting a grant from the Amherst public school committee to develop an early example of the multicultural curriculum in my high school, I succeeded. And that has kind of been foreshadowing for the rest of my life. If I can get some resources, even meager ones, then I can really excel. But if I have to fit into a program, I'm not very good. I'm mediocre at best.

So imagination came from some interesting science classes where I made my own class. For example, one class was "How Life Would Be Like 100 Years from Now." A lot of it was like me drawing pictures of what I had envisioned being the technological utopia. I was really caught by the science-fiction bug in particular. So that's what I would do. Or if we were learning negative numbers . . . I wrote a play, a musical actually, about Negative Land—another universe that operated with negative numbers instead of positive numbers. So when I'm master of my house, even though it is a small house, it's the house I'm most satisfied with, and I think it's a better house then the bigger house that other people build that follow standard mainstream blueprints. So I've always been about constructing my own vehicles, my own instruments. And even the baritone saxophone, I've been on a quest to journey, to transform that instrument—not so much physiologically but much more, I guess, in my use of it as less a Western instrument and much more an "Eastern" instrument. To play it much more like a double-reed instrument than a single reed.

So I've been resistant, for example, to the domination of mainstream bebop. For the longest time I tried to learn and internalize the standards. And again it was really mechanical and rote for me. It wasn't my language, my sensibility. Of course the music of Coltrane in the '60s, what I call the vanguard music of the Black Arts

Movement, the so-called Free Music, spoke much more to me. I did better with that. I wasn't about trying to find validation—being a jazz player. That wasn't important to me. The jazz tradition is certainly glorious, but I only see part of it as my own tradition. You know I think the spirit of the '60s really ignited for me the sense that jazz should not be confined to being an American music even though that's its origin. But even that is only partially true, because its origins include many international influences. But really it is a planetary music, as I've said in many essays—a revolutionary music for the 20th century. Those components of that revolutionary music are what will help make a new world. I think the Americanization of jazz, whether it is the ideological pronouncements of jazz as America's classical music to the ossifying of tradition, is counterrevolutionary. In many ways counter . . . I would say anti-Black. I think the black "essence" of the music is a music that refuses to be Americanized: assimilated into the dominant class, racial, national hierarchy, refuses to be a puppet or tool, an apologia for imperialism. But rather is a music of oppressed people wanting liberation and wanting to change the world.

MIYOSHI: So how does this all fit into what you do?

FRED: I think that you know for me it's been both an aesthetic and an organizational struggle. Aesthetic to find what you want to do artistically, musically, organizationally in the sense of the direction you want to go in, how you want to do things. You know the vehicles you construct to get you to that point. So I've never been an insider in the jazz world, so to speak. There are very few magazine features about me in the mainstream jazz media and so forth, even though my accomplishments rate with those of anyone else. You know I was saying to someone, "when was the last time McCoy Tyner did a 33-city USA tour traveling with 23 people on the road?" It was barely mentioned in the jazz press that I did a major tour, but luckily by Bill Shoemaker in a feature on Asian American jazz. He wrote that at the last minute realizing that I was ending this tour right in his area—the D.C. area.[1] He came out to see our performance; that was on a Sunday matinee. We had already performed the night before to a sold-out audience of 2,000 people. And that Sunday matinee was almost all kids—800 kids. Then he compared what he had seen last night: another group led by an Asian American bandleader at the Smithsonian and only 30 people were in the audience. So these are the things that the jazz press is clueless about: the work that I've done in multimedia ballets, creative DVDs. In many ways I'm free of that because I've never looked for any kind of acceptance or legitimating from the jazz press, except for very early on in life. I've kind of since then left that completely. In fact I'm more than simply disinterested, I'm pretty much in opposition to where I think the "jazz" industry is headed, and that's into this reified, insular, narrow canonic, small scene.

I think that Frank Driggs, the historian-archivist who mostly focuses on pre-'40s jazz, came up to me after one of my shows at the Guggenheim and said that what I'm doing with martial arts and jazz is really what the tradition is about. And that's creating a dynamic, what Sun Ra referred to as a popular avant-garde. Something that the masses can enjoy, have a good time with it. At the same time it's challenging music, challenging thinking. And that was a heavy compliment coming from someone like him, whom I thought would have been, you know, an apologist for Wynton [Marsalis]. But he actually said what Wynton is doing is antijazz. And that's how things have become so flipped. The jazz mainstream is actually antijazz. The so-called jazz avant-garde is really the upholder of the tradition. And that's the paradoxical, contradictory essence of 21st century life in U.S. imperialism: when terrorists become heralded as bringers of freedom and true freedom fighters are labeled as terrorists.

MIYOSHI: It seems that you are more or less just intentionally edited from the mainstream press.

FRED: It's an edit . . . it's intentional . . . sure.

MIYOSHI: But I think it is important for work to entertain and not preach, which is nice about your work. It seems like people are more receptive to a message if they can be entertained.

FRED: Well, you know, *Voice of the Dragon* deals with themes such as betrayal, opportunism, the cooptation of the canon, but it is done through a fantasy action adventure story with spectacular martial-arts choreography. I think that it's fun for me to create and fun for audiences to experience and I wouldn't have it any other way. You know, I have to have fun myself. And I would hope that it has impact upon people.

MIYOSHI: Speaking of the martial arts, how has it allowed you to expand your art, your music, and change your way of thinking?

FRED: On many levels, I would say. 1. Philosophical, 2. Aesthetic. Philosophically, I am not a pacifist by any means; I am a militant because

I believe that if you don't hit it, it won't fall. And I'm not only talking about things physically, but incorrect ideas as well. If you don't attack them and dismantle them and bring them down, they're not going to come down on their own. So philosophically on many levels the journey to eliminate ego in this day and age would seem to be an oxymoron since so many of the "young lions" are such huge egomaniacs. Then the culture and music suffers, because what you have—you have huge technical abilities but very little political social consciousness. Therefore it is a waste. And it is somewhat a metaphor for society: amazing technology but very little in terms of values and progressive applications. I could go on and on and on.

However, I think what the martial arts philosophically offer . . . you know, "the point of technique," as Bruce Lee says, "is to have no technique." The martial artist never fights for self-gain, but only to spread truth and justice. I believe these precepts, if embodied by today's performing artists, we would have a lot more artists who are warriors, have backbone, who would challenge the malignancies so prevalent in our society where lies replace the truth. But we don't have that because most artists are little egos looking for career self-aggrandizement.

Aesthetically, that every movement, every breath, every note must have impact, must have devastating impact. It is not the quantity of notes, it is the right ones. Something I was telling someone recently, "it is not how hard you hit, it's how hard you get hit and keep moving forward." And it is not even about winning. It is really about integrity. It is how hard your integrity gets hit and you keep moving forward with it. To reach the people it is not about watering things down, fitting into a trend or fad, which so many people do, so many musicians do. They always think that that is the conundrum: being popular means playing down to the masses, rather than being really just the opposite and creating something that's so irresistible and overwhelming that the people will just have to respond to it.

And what is that? What is that? Can it happen when social conditions, social climates, social movements are very weak and fragmented? I don't have a clear-cut answer for that, but I think that the minute we stop pursuing, that is the moment we fail. That failure is irreparable. You can't regain that which you have severed. It doesn't come back. So you have to stay on that course.

So aesthetically, learning how to make my saxophone like Joshua's trumpet: a sound that will bring down the wall. Find that sound! Things that will illuminate the possibility of new ways of relating to one another. Music becomes an experiential template for a new kind of social existence. And that's what the revolutionary characteristics of the process of jazz making were like for the 20th century—the dialectical interplay between soloist and leader and side people. The transcendent characteristics that were so powerful in the music transcended this individual, that instrument, that role. For example, every single instrument transformed what it was in the Western-European concert situation—I've written a lot about that. But even more than that I would have to say the social process of how people interacted. There's a lot of talk about this. This comes from a bourgeois point of view about individualism in jazz, and I would say that that's not really the point. It's missing the key thing. I think the real thing is that the community from which it comes can only catalyze the ingeniousness of individualism. That no one is an isolated singular genius irrespective of all the players' community in which they journeyed through, *I think that's the key thing.* When people talk about, "oh your influences," that's just the beginning of a discussion about that kind of interactivity, of the community from which one comes out of as a player. The interactive nature of this music, what I call dialectical because it is this interactivity. But it is also as you interact, you change, it transforms and doesn't become too discrete. There are no discrete elements to it, is what I am saying. It becomes a real synthesis. It is that revolutionary synthesis and all features and applications and processes of the music that became a template in many ways for a new kind of social existence.

MIYOSHI: Are you referring to music as a component of creating human change or bettering social existence?

FRED: I'm trying to write an essay when I get better about the music as a template for political organizing. Without the occulted personality, without hierarchy, without authoritarianism, without overcentralization or commandism. All those things that make politics so detestable to people, where it is about the great leader, the great man, or now in this case perhaps the great woman. It becomes that focus rather than expanding the creativity and collectivity of the community.

MIYOSHI: I understand. I think a little ego is healthy in the community because ego gives one the confidence to create and want to challenge.

FRED: I don't even think about that because I think that, in some ways, was Bruce Lee's downfall. His early death comes from the fact that he himself could not embark upon a complete journey to eliminate ego. And that hemorrhage in his brain, if that's what it was, was self-induced. I don't think the Triads [Chinese organized crime] or anyone else assassinated him. I think that he imposed a tremendous amount of stress upon himself; he wanted success in mainstream terms and achieved it to a certain degree, and more so after his death. But that desire, that goal, was his killer.

I think that ego is a bourgeois Freudian concept. It develops with Freud and rises in the 20th century with the rise of bourgeois individualism. We are all unique, cellularly unique, but that uniqueness is oftentimes repressed. And it is really about unleashing the uniqueness that we all have. Now realizing just because someone may be technically virtuosic doesn't mean they have the most to offer. This worship of technique—things that are faster, bigger—doesn't mean that it is better. This fetishism with those measurements and calculations much more fixated on the quantitative rather than the qualitative will be the undoing of humanity. Humanity, even though we are given the capacity for technological development, we are also given the capacity for decision making and whether to use certain things. Just because you can make it does not mean it should be used or used in a way that is about quantitative accumulation.

So these are things that I am learning in my integration of some of the ancient martial arts philosophies. Some of it I don't agree with, I guess with my Marxism . . .

MIYOSHI: Such is life.

FRED: Yes. Because life is about a synthesis. It's not about worship, a fixed thing.

MIYOSHI: Practicality. How are we doing on time? You okay?

FRED: I'm okay.

MIYOSHI: Just curious about the types of projects that really interest you at this point in life, given your health situation. I know you have some projects that you are currently developing, but what is it that you really want to do at this point? Projects, trips?

FRED: Well the immediate thing on the agenda, if I don't accomplish this, because everything else won't happen, is to rid myself of cancer.

I thought I had achieved that, but I wasn't absolutely sure when I finished chemotherapy in March of 2007. But then two tumors were found by the fall of 2007. So I realize the war is going to be more protracted and harsher than I had anticipated. And I think that that . . . someone said to me very long ago that I have to get my ass kicked to really learn something. I guess that's really true. I have to have it really delivered to me *hard*. So this is the gauntlet now. As I am going through this gauntlet, I've been able to start some things. I am writing a lot more—not so much music, although I am writing music. But I am writing much more essays. My "Cancer War Diary," when it is completed, I'd like to publish and share with people. I have two books coming out. *Afro Asia*, which is an epic collection dealing with one of my major political cultural foci in life and that is African American, Asian American unity building.[2] I am coediting that with Bill Mullen. It is coming out on Duke University Press. Then my select writings, by University of Minnesota Press, for April 2009.[3] I began the Sun Ra opera *Mr. Mystery*, with Quincy Troupe; I intend to finish that, stage that. I want to do something called *Divas of the Deep*, an opera–underwater synchronized swimmer ballet.

I basically want to work with people that I am very interested in. I have no need for gigs. Of course if people call me to do performances, then I am more than happy. But I don't go out and solicit gigs anymore—that's not important to me. Financially, I am secure for the rest of my life as long as I stay on this minimal, guerilla lifestyle that I have. So I don't need more. Financially speaking, I have more reasons to put on these projects to pay my artists better, but not for myself personally. I continue to design clothing primarily for myself and I've embarked much more into footwear. Designing more kinds of moccasins and boots and shoes, which I'm very happy with how they are coming out. I also want to snorkel a lot more with large pelagics, particularly whale sharks, sperm whales, and orcas. So I am going to pursue that as soon as I can.

Teaching; that is, I teach in a noninstitutional mode. I teach best when people come to me. I've been leading Marxist studies groups for 30 years. I continue to do that, when people ask me to do that. I don't solicit. And also teaching creativity, the process of creativity. I had to postpone this artist-in-residency at the University of Wisconsin–Madison.[4] I was going to teach a workshop on Afro Asian spoken word and performance. But I have a fully nonfixed curriculum approach. It's kind of the way I taught myself, which is much more exploratory and investigative. It's not done by this week we finish this book and next week we go on to that. It is not that linear kind of way. I'll give you an example. Like with spoken-word artists, I teach them, I show them, I tell them every week discover five new words you didn't know and go back to your poems and put those words in your poems without changing the meaning of your poems. Or learn how to recite your poems accenting every other word so that the common spoken-word lilt that is so prevalent in all these Russell Simmons *Def Jam* rhythms can be altered.

So my whole thing is to be able to teach people how they can instill themselves the ability to stretch, constantly stretch. Rework their material to deepen their imagination with what they have. So when I audition, I'm never looking for what you can do, I'm looking for what the potential could be. So I am in the very beginning of figuring out a pedagogy that's very contrary to the institutionalization of schooling. I believe in resources, in great libraries, materials for people. I tell people the best places I go to are secondhand stores. I find old records, old books that will never be reissued as CDs, never republished, that are just actual gems. Some of them self-published. Those are my libraries, as well as institutional libraries. I believe more money for libraries and those things should happen. But also community resources, too.

I believe if you are going to be a performer you need to exercise. Because I am in very good shape, playing baritone saxophone for 30-plus years is not taking a physical toll. I don't have back problems like so many people do. They have to wear harnesses, they can't play standing up. I don't have any of those problems. I believe it is the holistic thing of mind, body, and spirit. You need to work on all three areas.

Like in this class I was going to teach, I was going to make everybody do certain exercises to build up their stamina, energy, flexibility. People would say, "well, what does that have to do with writing, what does that have to do with music?" My whole thing is if all you do is stand there and recite and perform in a dull, drab, monotone way, even though your ideas maybe scintillating, the overall impact won't be. You have done yourself a disservice and your audience. I'm not about flamboyancy or showmanship, but it's all about understanding that it's a total experience with performance. Even the consideration of your hair, the clothing you wear. What does that say about you? What's the experience you want to convey? What's the ideology you want to convey? And it's not a marketing thing. It's not about "how do I gimmick myself up?" It's really getting more deeply into what you really believe in and why you were put on the planet. And being about that 100-plus-percent. Living it. Embodying it fully. It's really about building a movement. All of the components of building a culture have to go into it. What is culture? It's a totality of a shared way of life. So that way of life includes clothing, appearance, food. Everything.

MIYOSHI: Absolutely. Just look back at very early history and notice the design and color among people when marketing did not exist.

FRED: Yeah. And you look at even the Black Arts Movement, and I take a lot from that. Events, the food they had there. The clothing. Decor of the place. Every thing was about communicating values of Black Liberation. I think that it was all for the better.

MIYOSHI: I have a few follow-up questions. Just curious about where you go to snorkel.

FRED: I go wherever I know there will be big pelagics.

MIYOSHI: I know some people have preferences for certain areas of the country.

FRED: Well, my best encounter in the water with whales has been this area called the Silver Banks, 90 miles north of the Dominican Republic, right in the middle of the Caribbean Sea. It is a 30-square-mile area where humpback whales migrate during the months of late February through mid-April to give birth. Dolphins all over the place: Hawai'i, Bahamas, Hilton Head Island [in South Carolina].

MIYOSHI: And the curriculum you are developing, is that an expansion of the multicultural curriculum you first started as a high school student?

FRED: You know what it is, Miyoshi? From an early age, I realized that it is not enough to critique and complain about something; it's about building something. So if I didn't like the education system, then what kind of education system would I create? So that's really what the journey has been about, is to figure out those things. If I don't like the jazz industry, what would I like it to be? So I've just been endeavoring to figure out and implement different things. One of the things I've always respected and taken as an influence from Amiri Baraka as a propagandist—even if they are outlandish—is the fact that he offered proposals. Even if I might not agree with him, there was an effort to try to figure out what needs to be done. And maybe that comes out of the strong Leninism, always asking that question, "What is to be done?" I've always believed in that. That's why I've always had to be at the frontlines, because I've always been trying to apply what I believe in and test things out and see how things work.

So I've always been about action—not blind action. I've always believed the need to develop theory—some strong comprehensive analysis and critique—but to couple that with active plans.

MIYOSHI: Are you looking at marketing or selling your clothing?

FRED: Not really. (*Laughter.*) It's like my music.

MIYOSHI: I know people see your clothing and obviously comment about how it looks or inquire about its origin. Is it in stores?

FRED: No. No.

MIYOSHI: Are you sewing for people?

FRED: I do. Like this great indigenous Alaskan woodcarver, who is out of the tradition of totem poles, but he's more innovative. Stephen Jackson. He's young. He's getting married next year in Alaska; he wants me to design a suit for him. So I'll do like that. But it's very selective; I don't do it from the point of view of any commercial interest. Why? There's nothing special to that. If someone else wanted to figure that out, then fine. But I don't want to figure that out.

And I also think that masculine identity in a patriarchal world has not opened itself up yet to deal with my concepts. I'm a cross-dresser. For example, my dusters, even though they are dusters, which are "masculine" types of wear, are taken from the very fabrics of women's wedding kimonos. Those are feminine fabrics, but it's different culturally in Japan. But there are no men who would wear that. I wear fuchsia, turquoise, really bright, different colors because they evoke the tropical rainforest for me. But men would not wear those colors. I'm designing cowboy boots now that have mostly feminine colors, but they are certainly rugged.

The specialness of my footwear is the elegance, but they can withstand any climate in the world, including volcano. That's the criteria. I should be able to walk across a bed of volcano lava that is still steaming with my footwear, along with going through snow, saltwater, along with everything else. But there are very few men who could accept that. It's not about gender identity for me. It's about planetary consciousness for me. What's most useful lasts forever—completely, imminently, practical to the max—yet evoke the love of life and the planet. Dullness, drabness, monotones do not do that. The Earth is not that way. The places I love the most are the rainforest and the ocean. So my colors are drawn from that. If you swim in tropical waters, all those colors you see on the fish—that's where I get my color combinations. So I see fish with those color combinations and then I look to make clothing that reflects that.

MIYOSHI: Sounds like your boots will destroy the product-life-cycle framework.

FRED: Yes. Yes. (*Laughter.*) My boots will be something that you'll hand down to the grandkids; they'll fight over them. My boots were inspired by my trip to Angkor Wat and Angkor Thom in Cambodia and the Karnak Temple in Luxor, Egypt. Those have been standing at least for millennia. Still vibrant forever. So I feel like anything that we create should be that.

See that's why the term *marketing* is so limited for me. It's about what's the latest fashion. What's the latest trend? I'm not interested in that. I don't look at magazines and see what other people are designing. I don't particularly care. In designing this suit for Stephen, we first had to find the right fabric; we talked about it. For example, like you don't want to wear this just once in your lifetime, you want to be able to use it in as many situations as you can, even as just something to kick around in, to going to a major opening for yourself. I said, you know that if you are stuck on mainstream [suit jacket] collars, you are going to be stuck to fashion. So let me come up with a creative lapel that does not exist, so your jacket will be immortal. (*Laughter.*)

I am looking at the immortality of the creation. And of course we look at high-quality fabrics, something that will not wear out. And like a good pair of boots, the more you wear it, the more dynamic it becomes.

MIYOSHI: It seems like it is more difficult to find quality fabrics in the States.

FRED: Well, no. That's why I live in New York City. Because if you were in Philadelphia or any other city, you would be tremendously limited. But New York City, even though the fabric industry has shrunk quite a bit, there is still a lot of importation. But then I travel. My last dozen or so creations I've used fabrics I found in Cambodia or ironically from my local thrift shop. A piece of fabric comes in and I'll love it. It speaks to me and I get the fabric. Later an idea comes.

MIYOSHI: Given your political interests, how are you viewed in Asian communities?

FRED: I've always been controversial because I've always been outspoken. A radical. I'm not concerned about superficial critiques or proposals. I want to get at stuff that's substantial.

I've been extremely contrary to the mainstream. I've created groups that have become mainstream: the Asian American Arts Alliance, here in New York, that I founded in the early 1980s. It's a very mainstream organization. I don't have a problem with that per se, but I believe that the mainstream stuff naturally is more acceptable and gets more of the attention. So I've always championed the avant-garde, so to speak, politically and culturally. I'm part of the Asian American Left. I'm not defensive about it. I don't aspire for anything mainstream; I don't seek it out. I would have to say that all change that is meaningful happens on the periphery. It is where there's more creative space—certainly a lot less resources, but more creative space.

I don't think anybody in the Asian American community that's entrenched in the mainstream necessarily champions me, per se. I think that some would rather see me swept under the table and kept hushed up. Out of sight. But I'm not concerned with them. I think that they contribute to the model minority myth; they contribute to assimilationism and they contribute to the glorification of whiteness. And I'm against that. So when they do that, I'm opposed to it. If a mainstream Asian American person or organization promotes white assimilation, model minority myth, genuflection to the altars of white supremacy, I'm their biggest enemy. If they contribute something to Asian American liberation, self-empowerment, self-reliance, I'm for that. So I go on a case-by-case basis.

MIYOSHI: How much do you think class factors into everything?

FRED: Very much so. It's all class related. See when you're dealing with whom you're seeking acceptance from, do you see power being conferred by white mainstream institutions or white individuals? Or do you see power coming from yourself, your community? Which may be a powerless community, but no community is really completely powerless. The dialectic political irony is that the powerless are exploited primarily because their labor is extremely productive and profitable. When you don't buy into this marginalization . . .

I have a statement: Chinese and other Asian Pacific Americans have not been marginal to American history; we've been marginalized by American history. There's a major distinction. We are made powerless because we are divested from and prevented from the fruits of our labor. But we do labor, and out of that labor has come tremendous productivity. So it is not that we are not productive. It's that the fruits of our productivity are not for our benefit. And oftentimes, we are told that we are not creating anything productive. With that is mental oppression. But it happens with all oppressed people. They are told they have no history, no contributions. Just the opposite is true.

MIYOSHI: Given the obstacles of racism, oppression, you've come out of this standing, and with a large body of work. What is it that you are ultimately looking to achieve with your work?

FRED: I'll put it in a way that Bruce Lee says it: "It's not what I want to achieve, it's what it wants to achieve." I think that my work is struggling to make a revolution—to end all of the manifestations of exploitation and oppression. To allow a new humanity that would be devoid of the pursuit of profit and the pillaging consequences of the planet. I think that that's why the work is what it is. The work may be temporarily limited if I die, but I think that I've generated enough out there, and enough people have actually come to understand my processes, that the work would continue. I'm not worried about that. That's why I want to actually try to collect things in these books and some of these courses I want to teach so that they are more systematized and perhaps more available.

I came to understand a few years ago the reason why I was put on the planet: to do the work that must be done that no one else wants to do. In the realm of popular culture, to work with martial artists, professional wrestlers, synchronized swimmers—all kinds of people that are not considered in the fine arts. To create vehicles, projects for them. To talk about subject matter no one else wants to talk about. For example, I did the *Black Panther Suite* because the African American artists were messing it all up. I'm talking about Spike Lee, Roger Guenveur Smith, the Van Peebles. None of them wanted to talk about revolution, socialism; they didn't want to talk about the revolutionary character of the Black Panthers; they didn't even want to talk about self-defense, much less anything else. Anti–Vietnam War stance. They didn't want to talk about Malcolm as a revolutionary. They gutted it. The party was originally the Black Panther Party for Self-Defense. They developed what I would consider counterrevolutionary portraits. So that's why I did the *Black Panther Suite*—no one else. I understood the subject well enough and particularly grasped the politics more accurately than these other folks. So that's why I did it. That's why I do all of my work: because no one else has done it or it is being done wrong and something better has to be done.

Better is not a quantitative measurement. Better because, no, I didn't sell as much, not as many people saw my work as they would see these other folks.' But that's not the point; it doesn't make it better. Because more people saw the wrong thing, that actually makes it worse! When more people see the wrong thing it actually makes it worse, because it's more stuff that you have to fix among more heads. More minds that have to be cleaned up and the truth be told. So it makes my job harder. But someone has to do it. And I work best when I take on those kinds of challenges. I'm only mediocre when I have to follow the mainstream. When I have to fit in, go along with the program, when I play jazz standards, I'm only mediocre at that. I recognize that. People say Fred Ho is not really a jazz artist. But what does that really mean. Is the essence of jazz being able to play a standard? Okay if that's what you consider that to be, then I'd have to say that most people are far inferior to Charlie Parker. But I would have to go along with what Mingus said, that if Charlie Parker were gun slinging, then there'd be a whole lot of dead copycats. I think the revolutionary era of jazz came to end with the death of Max Roach. He was the last one of that so-called bebop era that continued the bebop iconoclasm. But without having to just regurgitate.

When he died . . . I think that Max realized later in his years that all of his peers that came up during the '40s were not going to go beyond that. So he remained friendly with them and respected them, but that's not where he was going to go musically. To the end, he remained counter-regurgitative. *To the end.* It wasn't this later period of Max where he's playing back in the '40s again, playing those same tunes. No! Obviously as he got older and his illnesses got worse, his technical abilities diminished considerably. But he was still searching out new players, new settings, even with his limited physical abilities, at his age, and with his illness. So I really believe the revolutionary era of jazz died with Max Roach. Died August 16, 2007. And what's going to come after that, is not going to use the word *jazz*. What? We don't know. It will be something else. The word, phrase, concept of jazz died August 16, 2007. We are now in the reign of the regurgitators. That is it.

Now you would say, well though, there are these people who are avant-garde. Well some of them are avant-garde regurgitators. But the ones who I feel are still dynamic and fresh really do not land anywhere within the orbit of "jazz." Yes, influenced by. Yes, coming out of it. Yes, having a history. Yes, all of that. Yes! We have lineage. But where they are at now reflects the dominant discourse going on in so-called jazz.

Now, I've declared that jazz is over.

MIYOSHI: Being faced with an illness, what kinds of recommendations do you have for health care with regard to insurance?

FRED: People who do not have medical insurance, especially those facing grave and potential terminal illness, are essentially presented a death sentence. For many years, due to my constant condition of impecuniosity [poverty], I had no insurance. My basic general primary care physician was a revolutionary socialist doctor who agreed to treat me for no payment, only reciprocal contributions such as free tickets to my performances, complimentary CDs and books and Sheroes calendars I would periodically produce. He was astute enough to notify me as soon as "no questions asked" state Medicaid benefits were being granted immediately during the aftermath of 9/11 to urge me to access these benefits, which I promptly did. Prior to his care, when my sister, who is a doctor, lived in New York City, I would get medical care from her.

Out-of-pocket expenses for my cancer treatment probably have cost almost $1 million, which would have been impossible for me, or my friends and family, to have met. If I didn't have medical coverage, I probably would have had to probably accept an early death, which, if I didn't subscribe to euthanasia, would have been extremely painful and miserable.

This is why I cannot and will not support any electoral candidates that do not stand for universal, single-payer health insurance, with the fundamental premise that health care to all is a right of citizenship, and for that matter, a basic human right. Short of destroying the private profiteering of the insurance oligarchy, most uninsured Americans will continue to face the fear, stress, and misery of having to pay for their health care from their own pockets, or the collectively from the pockets of their friends and families.

I would say that on an individual and micro level, that forsaking income in order to qualify for state coverage thresholds would be preferable than the grind, fear, and debilitations of inadequate and minimal [catastrophic] coverage. While one is young, having only catastrophic coverage is a stopgap measure. But as one ages, small ailments can quickly magnify and intensify into much more serious problems. For example, the American Cancer Society and mainstream U.S. medicine says that males in the United States should have a colonoscopy starting at age 50. Well, I was 49 when the colorectal cancer tumor was found. I should have had that test when I was 40. But at age 40, I had no insurance. I paid the price for that by deferring testing until the tumor became huge.

My lessons, analyses, and transformations have been documented in my cancer war diaries, available at my Web site, www.bigredmedia inc.com under Writings.

MIYOSHI: What's your health regime like?

FRED: When I am able . . . now I'm going through this real severe combo of chemo and radiation . . . I swim, do hand-to-hand combat training regularly. I have an eclectic diet. Lots of hydration. Mineral water. All kinds of juices and teas. Primarily what they call Mediterranean and East Asian foods. Although I avoid MSG, so a lot of Filipino, a lot of Korean, Vietnamese foods are out for me. I walk a tremendous amount. I've never owned a car in my whole life. I walk from anywhere to a mile a day or much more. I've started bicycle riding again. When I can swim, I prefer to swim not in a chlorinated swimming pool, but the ocean. When the weather is warm enough, I go to the ocean quite a bit and I find a lot of marine life. The last time I was at the ocean I was surrounded by thousands of bluefish and striped bass. Thousands. Fishermen couldn't catch them, but they were all around me. (*Laughter.*) Just five feet of water. Close to the shore.

MIYOSHI: That's interesting. Are you doing five or six weeks of treatment?

FRED: It's six weeks. One down and five more to go. Then six weeks of recovery. Then after that, we don't know. I may have to go to surgery, which will then mean six weeks of recovery. Then start chemoradiation again. Which would mean another six weeks of recovery. So we're talking about half of a year. So I'm off right now. The only thing I'm really engaged in is dealing with the Cancer War.

Figure 14. Fred Ho, age four, with sister Florence, 1961. Credit: Iyanna Jones

I learned from Sun Tzu that you can't fight two wars. That's why the United States ain't gonna win. It's in Afghanistan and Iraq—it's impossible. During the Vietnam War, the United States was fighting in Vietnam, then moved into Cambodia and Laos, but was also fighting a war at home. [Not fighting two wars at once]—that's a 2,000-year-old principle of warfare.

So I'm fighting cancer. And that's the main war that I'm fighting right now.

MIYOSHI: Okay. Thank you, Fred. Get some rest.

FRED: Great.

Notes

1. The work presented was *Voice of the Dragon*, in April 2003, at George Mason University in Virginia.

2. Fred Ho and Bill V. Mullen, eds., *Afro Asia: Revolutionary Political and Cultural Connections between African Americans and Asian Americans* (Durham, N.C.: Duke University Press, 2008).

3. Published as Fred Ho, *Wicked Theory, Naked Practice: A Fred Ho Reader*, ed. Diane C. Fujino (Minneapolis: University of Minnesota Press, 2009).

4. Fred completed the residency in fall 2008.

10

Go On, Shoot

KALAMU YA SALAAM

In a few weeks—March 24, 2008—I'll be 61. Even though I've appreciably less energy than even six years ago, and though I accept that I have less control of my increasingly unreliable body and its functions, still I don't feel old. Sure, I've had to come to terms with how long it takes me to sit down on the floor to circle up and hold a conversation on the carpet with a group of youngsters, not to mention the slow roll to one knee and reaching out for something to steady myself on the long push up after the conclave is concluded, but that's just the reality of not being as agile as I used to be; that's not a case of feeling old.

What I do feel is weariness. I'm tired of friends dying. Close friends I've embraced for years. Many of them comrades. We've shared struggles, swam together against the mainstream, survived repression and internal conundrums but the challenge we haven't answered, the battle we can't win is how does our "we" survive funerals when one of our "we" dies?

Individuals continue but death permanently severs the friendship bond.

I know, I know. The death of fellow travelers goes with a long journey through life, but isn't mortality the ultimate irony? As we struggle through our senior years, increasingly, unceasingly, and irreversibly dealing with death becomes a major part of life as a person continues to live.

• • •

He had buzzed me in and was now standing, holding open his apartment's front door. Fred looked surprisingly fit. Not emaciated, nor tentative in manner or moving in halting steps like he was recuperating from a debilitating attack that had knocked him flat on his ass, nor quietly, slightly stooped over with the cautious air common to folk after a major operation and how they move about slowly and carefully less they rupture a suture or reinjure a wound.

In the familiar slits of Fred's eyes, in the vigorous way his tight grip shook my hand, heartily clasped my shoulder, in the way he moved about the kitchen finishing up the welcoming meal he had prepared, in all of that was a reassertion of the Fred I had always known.

Indeed, I had never seen him on his sickbed. Always it was the barrel-chested, bouncing on his toes as he walked, booming baritone as he talked, the (to quote our mutual friend Jayne Cortez) "cheerful and optimistic" warrior who was eager to go hand-to-hand with any and all foes, that was the Fred of my experience and the Fred before me was virtually a twin.

"No, well, I'm not out the woods yet. There's a ten-year window." That's what Fred said to me (I'm paraphrasing from memory but, if not his exact words, that was certainly the tenor of the sentiments) when I went to visit him. It was autumn in New York. No, actually, as I think on it clearly, it was summer. I was there for a Voices for Cultural Equity conference. This was my first post-cancer-operation opportunity to visit with Fred.

On the phone the day before, we had set a time to visit. He said he would fix dinner. I was to take a cab from the NYU area in lower Manhattan over to Brooklyn, where Fred now lived after selling his long-time apartment. The conference ran long and it took me a minute to get a cab but finally I arrived and I was really relieved when it appeared that Fred was the same Fred I had always known.

My relief was tempered by the realization that he was far from totally cured. Cancer is not easily licked. I knew that his struggle had been a major battle. I knew he had had operations, that at one point he had been near to death. I knew that the prognosis had been a long and slow recovery, if there was indeed to be a recovery.

I also knew that Fred was a fighter. That he attacked the cancer with the gusto of an experienced athlete working to get an underweight and flabby body back into shape after a long lay-off, and most importantly, I knew that Fred was mentally fit and up for the challenge. Characteristic of Fred he was never reticent about his condition, the bouts with nausea, the inability at some points to perform minor tasks.

But this was Fred. He laid out the battle plan, gave his supporters their marching orders, and was critical of any wavering in terms of keeping commitments. As much as cancer attacked Fred, Fred attacked back. Fred was firm in his resistance and resourceful in marshaling allies to provide both frontline and rearguard support. He kept all of us fully informed of his plans for dealing with the condition and up-to-date on his progress in battling cancer. Typical of Fred, his emails to us had been like Che Guevara–inspired field notes on the Congo campaign. He had been comprehensive in his overview on the conditions, brutally frank in his day-to-day assessments, unsentimental and clear-eyed in his views of the future. In a sense this was a war of national liberation; his body was a country invaded by the imperialism of cancer. No quarter was given nor expected. *¡Victoria o muerte!*

Yes, there had been losses. Serious losses, particularly in terms of playing the baritone saxophone. He had lost facility with his hands. His breath was short. But even with those limitations he never gave up. He continued to compose music. He may not win, but he was not going to lose.

As I enjoyed the meal he had prepared, Fred calmly told me that the cancer could return at any moment and that only after ten cancer-free years would he feel confident that he had licked it. As we talked about fighting back against cancer, we could have been discussing Angola, how with the critical help of the Cubans the Angolans licked the South Africans and were now engaged in the long and difficult postrevolutionary victory efforts to reconstruct their society. But then, Fred was always like that. Always ready for the revolution. Aware of the difficulties ahead and eager to engage the enemy at every turn.

• • •

I've been trying to write this essay for over a year. I've finally figured out the blockage. I was afraid to fail Fred. I knew I was physically weaker. I knew that I had not made the singular commitments he had. I remember Fred talking about why he, like another friend, Bill Strickland, had never married. I had not only chosen marriage but had a family of five children. And then again, had I really chosen marriage or was I just doing what I had been reared to do, just acting out of received cultural values and behavior that I never bothered to closely examine to determine whether I really believed?

Fred was a true believer in his philosophy. Fred willfully lived his life. Did what he espoused and in so doing set a high standard, a standard most of us seldom met. Even in his illness, Fred was putting a lot of pressure on us to keep up. Or was he? Actually, we were putting pressure on ourselves. We knew that we should be better about this. We knew that we all should be doing more than we are doing. We knew, but . . . coping with all of this was so hard. Damn, Fred. Dealing with you dealing with cancer is hard, but is us dealing with you harder than you dealing with cancer?

Some days I don't want to think about Fred.

Fred never has a day when he can afford not to think about the cancer. Never has a day off when he can just walk down the street in the sunshine and if he feels like popping into a store he is passing and grabbing an ice cream, he can just do it. Never a time when he can forget about routines and spend a whole day doing nothing—there's always medication to take, always situations to avoid, always therapy, always.

I get tired of always.

Does Fred get tired?

Yes, I'm sure he does. But when he gets tired, does he give up? I don't think he does. And even if he does pause for a minute, he probably spends the next hour catching up. Fred is relentless. Cancer doesn't know who it's messing with. Fred don't play.

• • •

How did I first meet Fred? Baraka Sele hooked us up in Houston, thought we would hit it off together. Baraka was running a festival and had separately invited both of us to participate. We had a small dinner and Baraka arranged for us to sit next to each other. She had not connived, in fact the brilliance of what she did was manifested in that she told both of us what she was doing and encouraged each of us to get to know the other. Fred and I left the meal mouthing that cliché that artists often say without really meaning it: we ought to get together sometime and collaborate on something.

I was a writer, Fred—a musician.

We actually did get together as a duo, The Afro-Asian Arts Dialogue. Even produced and printed promo pictures: he wailing on his horn, me with arm upraised my mouth wide open. We registered with Speak Out, a progressive, West Coast–based booking agency.

We did not perform often, but getting together was no problem. I believe that more than ideology or personal affinity, what we have in common is the music, particularly creative improvisation. The music allows us both to stretch out without stepping on each other's toes. If Fred starts a phrase, I can hear where it is going and can time my recitation to fit his phrasing and vice versa. Plus, we can talk about ideas for performing using the music as a reference point. One of my great joys in terms of working with Fred is the way his saxophone and my voice intertwine without our having to prearrange the performance.

I remember a gig at a college in Flint, Michigan. We were in an atrium in the student center (or maybe some other building). While we were setting up and doing the sound check, a young black guy stood to the side watching. After our performance that same guy came up to us, smiling. He said he liked what we did but at first couldn't figure out what in the world we were going to do together.

He was not alone. This was in the nineties. A number of people couldn't figure out what a former black nationalist and an unabashed Chinese American Marxist were going to do together. Ultimately, although ideology is extremely important, cultural affinity is also important. There are people who I agree with politically but don't particularly like in terms of their aesthetics. While some might argue that aesthetics are a political concern, I believe that cultural preferences and proclivities are not necessarily indicative of what we usually mean by progressive or conservative or whatever persuasion.

Fred's music is angular, heavy on tension, with a strong sense of rhythm. In New Orleans I used to perform with avant-garde saxophonist Kidd Jordan, so I was comfortable with that approach. Ultimately, we become friends with people with whom we are comfortable. There is a big difference between friendship and comradeship. I have had friends with whom I did not share politics, and political comrades with whom I did not share friendship. I genuinely enjoy Fred as both a comrade and a friend.

In 1974 I had stood on the Chinese-built Tan-Zam railroad in Tanzania and had seen Chinese workers at a cigarette factory in Zanzibar. I led a tour of educators from independent Black schools to China in 1977. By the end of the seventies I had already confronted biological essentialism and by the eighties was through with nationalism. Fred had briefly been a Black Muslim (had his "X" and everything) and continued to be a strong supporter of the Black Panthers.

I did not have much day-to-day contact with Asians. After Hurricane Katrina in 2005, I began working with Vietnamese American students at Eleanor McMain Secondary School in New Orleans. That was easy for me but it is qualitatively different from my work with Fred. Most of the ethnic-Vietnamese students are U.S. born, and many of them do not speak fluent Vietnamese—indeed, a significant number of them don't speak any Vietnamese. Moreover, most of them do not espouse radical ideas, although a few of them are involved in organizing in their community.

I think there is a danger in essentializing ethnicity and/or race. For me the real struggles are political and economic. Although we have differences, I believe Fred and I share that general orientation.

Philosophically, Fred and I were a good fit, not ideologically the same but nonetheless strong allies who formed a solid partnership. We shared a propensity toward frankness and an ability to listen closely to criticism without being defensive nor offended. We both valued improving ourselves and learning from each other.

I never told Fred how much I admired him. I enjoy solitary work and am not fond of just hanging out, but sometimes with Fred we'd roam through lower Manhattan checking out used bookstores or going to a nontouristy, non-Anglo-oriented Chinese restaurant. Even on a New York subway I'm sure we were a sight, taking great delight in analyzing and debating social events and finer points of political struggle. Fred with his big baritone saxophone case and me with a large black bag containing computer, books, papers, and electronic peripherals. Will we ever barrel beneath the streets of New York City again, delighting in each other's company like lovers savoring stolen moments?

New Orleans is a long way from New York, and even though I have a daughter living in Brooklyn, the distance between Fred and me stretches far into the distance, much further than either my eyesight or my reluctant expectations. There, more by inference than direct statement, I've admitted it: I may not see Fred again.

Fred's fight with cancer frightened me.

I don't want to face this inevitable loss. I mean, I know we all die, but do we have to go like this? A phone call early one morning letting me know a major part of me is diminished. Soon there will be nothing left of me but memories.

My mother died of cancer in 1975. I was much younger then, in my early twenties.

I've lost a number of others who were close to me. Some suddenly like David Sibeko, a member of South Africa's Pan African Congress. He had just been in New Orleans and we had had inspiring dialogue. This was in the seventies. Word wound its way back from Tanzania. David had been assassinated. Shot in the head.

Hoyt Fuller died of a massive heart attack at the side of a road in Atlanta (or at least that's the way I half-remember the circumstances).

My mentor Tom Dent slipped away while I was in Germany. I had visited Tom in the hospital a few days before he died and oh, the sadness settling inside me as I sat beside him in the hospital, aware that his time might be nigh—for some reason I cannot finger, I felt like both he and I knew that hour was approaching, and it was a bitter resignation. I left the hospital that day, left the country the next day carrying the horrible realization that he would not be . . . when I got back. I didn't want to say it even though I was thinking it.

For years now, I've been dealing with death but it seems like what was once a now-and-then occurrence is lately becoming an avalanche of sadness.

A number of these deaths are cutting deeper, approaching the depth of my father's sudden demise that sent me into a tailspin from which I am not sure I ever fully recovered.

He had been strong all my life. Until that Friday morning in 1987, when I brought him to a hospital just to be safe. He had not been slept well the night before. My brother, Dr. Keith C. Ferdinand, was at a medical conference in San Francisco and had left specific instructions of what to do should anything happen with Daddy. I had taken Daddy to Dr. Woods as per Keith's directions, and after an examination in his private office, Dr. Woods had sent Daddy to the hospital to run tests. After the funeral Dr. Woods said he ordered Daddy to the hospital simply as a precaution and because he was close friends with Keith and would have felt badly had something gone wrong, but his in-office examination of my father had not turned up anything serious. Friday afternoon Daddy told me to tell people who wanted to visit to come on Saturday, he wanted to rest and he was feeling a lot better. Later that night he slipped into a coma. Sunday morning he died.

I'm tired of telling this story about my father—for some reason it seems like I keep repeating it, keep finding reasons to share the tale of how my father died. Why? Why do I keep talking about it, writing about it, thinking about it?

What does Fred have to do with my father? My father is a memory. I don't want Fred to be a memory. But what does life care about what I want?

So I am facing a difficult truth: although I am not afraid of my own death, what disconcerts me is the deaths of those close to me, and right now I know even though I do not want to face this hard fact, life is forcing me to acknowledge that they are falling around me. They. The friends who give meaning and substance to my own life.

• • •

The food was so good; Fred is an excellent cook. The conversation was so good; I would have been satiated by just his words. The madness of a last meal—at the time I wasn't thinking of that dinner as an ending, indeed, I was relieved and believed that Fred's recovery was near certain.

Back home I was sitting with Doug, another close friend who also had cancer and was losing the yearlong battle. For 13 months or so I sat with him four, five, sometimes six nights a week. Toward the end physically lifting him from the bed, hugging his frailness to my chest as we changed sheets and changed his diaper. Doug was my age but weighed less than a healthy adolescent when he transitioned. I wrote a poem about his leave taking:

THE LAST REDD LIGHT!

(a eulogy of sorts for Douglass Redd, December 1947–July 2007)

1.
What would you do if you knew
You were going to die tomorrow, or maybe
Just had a vague feeling that the knocking
At the door was a death rattle, or maybe
You just ached real bad and instead of words,
Moans slobbered sideways out your mouth? What
Would you do if your hand wasn't working and
You couldn't control your bladder
And just had to lay in whatever . . ., you know
What I'm saying? . . .

Life sometimes asks us some tough unanswerable questions like
What would you do if you failed the ultimate survival test?

2.
His flesh was still soft.
I looked down on the calm of his face,
The peaceful repose was the . . . I can't make it pretty,
I mean I could describe it with pretty words but
It would still be fucked up.

A man with whom I have spent most midnights
Over the last three hundred and some days,
I was in his presence even when he was too sick
To appreciate that I was there, now, his corpse
Was laying there, unmoving, untwisted, unhacked
By coughs and phlegm. He looked better
Than I've seen him for weeks. You know
It's bad when a cadaver looks better
Than a fitfully breathing body.

3.
When you say someone you love is dead
What do you mean?

Outside the sun was shining, inside,
All inside of me the sky was crying. I was standing
At the last Redd light.

Following Doug there had been my other friend, visual artist John Scott. I visited him in a Houston hospital a week before he gave up the ghost. For Scott I wrote:

I STARE INTO THE AIR

I came to see you
Did you know I was there?

I don't think so. Your head was
Back, your mouth wide open,
Your eyes closed. The sound
Of the machines was louder
Than your labored breathing.

I thought of Picasso, how he painted
That horse, it pained me
That you looked like a wounded animal.
I know you were knocked out—morphine

Morphine is not medicine
That's what they give to you when
They don't know what else to do.

About three or four hours later
We returned and now you were awake,
Or at least your eyes were open

I held your hand, lightly, I did not want
To hurt you so I was careful
With my touch and my jokes

I knew you couldn't laugh. That hurt
Me too. I will never forget the deep
Rumble of your laughter, how your
Eyes would glow, how laugh lines
Were all over your expansive face

You would even reach out and slap
My shoulder but not that day. All
You did was blink to let me know
That you heard me, that you knew
I came to visit you the weekend
Before you died.

I went home glad to have seen you
Sad to have seen you like that

Almost exactly one week later
The call early in the morning did not
Surprise me. I did not cry. I wanted
To. I did not curse. I should
Have. I did not do anything except
Sit back in my chair and stare
Into the nothingness of the air
In front of me.

All of this was ensnaring me. I had seen how cancer wastes away the body, how particularly gruesome the last days can be. I had held a dying friend in my arms, had seen another shot up with morphine, laying grotesquely twisted in a dying bed. Psychologically, I was prepared by recent events to face death, and simultaneously, because I have already been so intimate with friends dying, I am loath to go through another downer.

But all of that is no excuse. The question is not how we feel or what we think but rather, given specific conditions and circumstances, what will we do?

• • •

Over six months later I received an email from Fred that the cancer had returned. He would have to have another operation.

I promised to write an essay for an anthology on Fred. I did not want to write an elegy and certainly not an obituary. I wanted to write something cheerful and optimistic. I wanted to share aspects of Fred that would encourage others to carry on.

Is this it? Are these words strong enough to carry the message, to transmit the meaning of Fred's existence? Che's last words in front of the execution squad are said to have been an order to the soldiers to shoot, not to hesitate. I wonder what my words will be when I face the final test. Will I order death to give me its best shot? I'm confident that Fred won't blink. Will I?

By taking so long to write these pitiful words, am I blinking?

I can (and have on a couple of occasions when survival was at risk) stared down the possibility of my own death. Why am I hesitating now?

My hesitation is the basic selfishness of social life. I want Fred to be with me as long as I am alive. In an indirect way I am saying I would prefer him to deal with my death than for me to deal with his death.

Figure 15. Fred Ho and the Afro Asian Music Ensemble. Credit: Ken Shung

When I heard about the second surgery and how necessary it was, I took the implications to a logical conclusion. Reason is a cold calculation. No body can stand repeated serious cancer operations. Not even Fred, who had kayaked through the Alaska wilderness. Fred is dying.

I was a writer and a friend. Shouldn't I be able to write something cheerful and optimistic, something uplifting? Why am I crying these words onto paper?

Go on, cancer, shoot!

EXCERPTS FROM "RE-ENGLISH, FOR FRED HO"

Northern abolitionist poems were so beautiful a slaveholder
reading them over breakfast wouldn't even lose his appetite.
"Quicker to a field of blood than to a wedding."
What can reliably be said: the Roman withdrawal from Britain
was complete in 407. 449 the Britons hire the Saxons as mercenaries
for protection against the Picts.
Among the soldiers on the three Angle, Saxon and Jute ships
a soothsayer foretold they would occupy the client-country
300 years, plundering it half three hundred.
Not only from the get-go—
forked before the fact.
Quicker to a wedding than a march against war.
In his original draft Eisenhower called it the "military industrial
congressional complex," but was persuaded to remove the
"congressional" attribute (though I'm not sure by whom).
Quicker to a car wash than count the notes of a black-capped
chickadee.
The sound's the same. Some hear "kindness," some hear "kill" "kill."
My holy mountain is a stack of dirty dishes, daffodils.
As you can see, the contrary to "peasant" is not "noble":
working poor bilker
wage slave snake-in-the-grass
the jobless the ignominious
bohunk hornswoggler
debt dupe picaroon
toiler flimflammer
hayseed hoodwink
simpleton diddler
vassal sleazebag
employee double-dealer
pauper swindler

peon   shyster
stagnated wage earner   confidence man
toiler   finagler
undocumented worker   chisler and scumpuff
Would that we were safe.
So that we keep going going.
So that mispronunciation is not sickness . . .
Had we instead put butter on the fire to make it rain . . .
Had we known. The point at which air's itself the sauce.

—Robert Kocik

Afterword

ARTHUR SONG

I am one of those anomalous friends of Fred Ho. I am not artistic, though I am a fan of "jazz" (especially Fred's music). Nor am I political. My lifestyle has been desultory, perhaps, in Fred's words "flakey." But since the time we met in the mid-1980s, during the days of my profligate life in New York City, and then from the early 1990s when I retired and moved to Bangkok (to admittedly continue my profligate and hedonist ways!), Fred and I have stayed in touch.

I suspect there are reasons on both sides for our ongoing friendship even though our respective interests and beings are so vastly different. For me, I have admired Fred as the baddest Asian American badass on the planet! I'm roughly a generation older than Fred, and during the early 1970s, when I lived on the West Coast, I thought the writer Frank Chin, who has fashioned and postured himself to be a "Chinatown cowboy," represented our avatar of Asian American manhood: tough-talking, defiant to racist whites, intimidating to wishy-washy yellows (his term for us Asians in the United States), emulative of militant blackness.

Fred, on the other hand, I think welcomed my adulation of him, not in a conceited sort of way, but because I think he recognized that I recognized something about him, his core being, that others couldn't see or were not willing to see: that Fred could walk his talk, and woe to those who either tried to obstruct or derail him! And over the years, I've come to see that there have been many, some having been former comrades and best friends to him, and others, perhaps of equal intensity or egotism, who have regarded him with jealousy or competitively. And there has been a wake of antagonism.

After I left the Big Apple, Fred and I would communicate occasionally by letter or phone, and then with more ease and facility once he bought a computer (in 2000) and joined the World Wide Web. He visited me in 2004 in Bangkok and we had a terrific time.

The essays in this magisterial Buckley-Roberts compendium tell of Fred Ho as warrior artist–revolutionary activist. Some essays also provide insight into the personal Fred Ho, but mostly in the context of collaborating with him in his art and activism. I write this afterword commenting on him strictly as Person and Friend.

At the time of Kalamu ya Salaam's writing (approximately 2008), all of us—while confident that Fred would fight the advanced colorectal cancer with all of his might and, some of us, reading carefully and regularly his Cancer War Diaries or speaking to him on the phone—knew that Fred's fight for his life had taken a toll and, more than literally, a pound of flesh from him. After a third tumor (what the doctors called a secondary primary, meaning that it was not a recurrence of the first tumor, which was the case for the second tumor, but a new tumor in the same region) and after he had transferred his care to the much-vaunted Memorial Sloan-Kettering Cancer Center, he was given 1 in 30,000 chances of living. After yet again another surgery, the searing pain Fred endured in which his massive scar tissue prevented the surgeon from sewing him back up (the needle wouldn't hold, just as shredded fabric doesn't allow a sewing needle to hold), for the first time in his life Fred admitted, both to his friends and later, via his blog, that he had considered suicide. Stephanie Athey, a good friend of Fred's, expressed that Fred's 12 days without sleep and constant pain from the slightest movement was indeed an experience of torture (Athey is a specialist on torture!).

Fred credits his Warriors for Fred (a circle of love that self-organized to care for and support Fred within a week of his initial diagnosis in August 2006) with saving him. While he was thinking of suicide, they wouldn't allow it and kept him with us on this planet.

I have seen remarkable changes, so much so that I am one of the few people who knows him to actually confirm that he is indeed the New Fred Ho. (What many would feel is Fred making humor—the old Fred Ho having died August 4, 2006, the day of his initial diagnosis of cancer, and now being the New Fred Ho, about four years old in age—I for one don't think he's joking, but is actually very, dead serious about this.)

What's the difference between the old Fred Ho and the New Fred Ho?

There are many, and the differences keep growing day by day, even minute by minute, second by second, as if his very cellular makeup is being transformed.

Some challenge this contention, questioning if he really has changed, and contend that he may be regressing and evincing the same characteristics as the old Fred Ho. He's still tough and a hard-ass, demanding, focused, determined, uncaring about what society thinks, still revolutionary. Some have commented that they really liked the old Fred Ho! But it is clear to me that the New Fred Ho wants nothing to do with the old Fred Ho and has moved on, accepted the death of the old and totally focused upon the experiences and experiments of the New.

For the naysayers, yes, all true, but there is no more carcinogenic content to the internal person of the New Fred Ho. Fred never accepted that he was simply collateral damage in the escalation of cancer rates throughout the toxic capitalist-industrial world. During the Cancer War, he believed, as any good warrior-strategist must, that he had to go down to the cellular level to both know *why* cancer attacked him, *what* is it about his own traits and way of life that made him vulnerable and susceptible, and *how* he had to fight it, at the cellular level, and fundamentally change the conditions of the enemy's aggression, because the warrior always fights to win!

Fred often quotes Chairman Mao's dictum that "External contradictions always operate through internal ones." And he mercilessly applies that analysis to himself. He is bold and quick to admit that he gave himself cancer, that it was his carcinogenic life, as he terms it, which explains why the disease happened for him.

I don't want to say too much on this, as he is preparing a new book, *Diary of a Radical Cancer Warrior: Fighting Cancer and Capitalism at the Cellular Level*, which will detail the war and his means and methods of strategy and tactics he developed (in real time) in fighting that brutal war.

As the New Fred Ho is four years old, he is a constant work-in-progress, a life experiment. Here are some principal aspects to the New Fred Ho: the New Fred Ho is on a journey to eliminate all ego from within himself, and that includes all anger. Profoundly opposed to all injustice and exploitation and oppression, Fred now won't allow himself to internalize any anger, from anything. He says that he is striving to be cool, calm, and collected, to be a truer warrior who must be dispassionate in a lifelong campaign to defeat the enemy and bring about something new and qualitatively better.

He is also solely focused on his mission, his understanding of why he was put upon this planet, for whatever days remain until his expiration date, and that is "to do the music/art and politics that no one else can or will do." I jokingly call this "Mission Impossible!" He is now fond of quoting Sun Ra's assertion that "Everything possible has been tried and nothing has changed. What we need is the Impossible."

Musically, he continues the great Sun Ra's quest, to advance into "beyond the beyond" regions, including musical telepathy, esoteric and extreme technical challenges, individualized and emotional expressivity in every breath and note played, ultimately all to make a music "that will bring down the walls of Jericho." Biblical-like goals, indeed!

Politically, convicted to creative Marxism, he is drafting his Manifesto against Manifest Destiny Marxism, tackling all the things that 20th century Marxism, especially as done in the United States, has either ignored, refused to deal with, or worst, written off. These include indigenous-centrism (Fred contends that Marx and Engels's communism was founded on Native American preinvasion society), matriarchy (the abolition of gender and the restoration of "mothering" as the rightful proletariat), and, perhaps the hardest for most Marxists, revolutionary Ludditism (to oppose all technology hurtful to the Commonality). Bill Mullen's essay in this book outlines the starting principles to his new movement and, as always with Fred and all experimental and innovative activity, one that begins with a small number of committed people but with profound vision and huge hearts.

Many of us have been impressed by the accomplishments of the old Fred Ho, which is what most of this book is about. From all allopathic accounts, Fred is in remission ("no medical evidence for carcinoma"). The New Fred Ho is a part-time farmer (Farmer Fred is his nickname). The New Fred Ho no longer calls his music "new American multicultural music" but Revolutionary Earth Music. The New Fred Ho politically calls himself a "revolutionary Matriarchal Luddite creative Socialist." The New Fred Ho rejects the patriarchal, technocentric socialist past and is building at the cellular level a future movement that carries no baggage of the past, and is traveling very light (in terms of ecological impact and doesn't cling to past truisms, but affirms both individual and systemic revolution). And the New Fred Ho has no anxiety about his own pain, suffering, or death.

Everyone should hear his new compositions, listen to how the new Fred Ho plays that badass baritone sax, check out, and if you can, join his new activist projects. Watch out World, the New Fred Ho is comin'!

Appendixes

Discography

Note: Year of release is first, followed by recording dates

1985 *Tomorrow Is Now!*, Fred Houn and the Afro Asian Music Ensemble, Soul Note Records, Milan, Italy, recorded and mixed at Nola Studios, New York City, on April 5, 8, and 9, 1985, featuring Fred Houn (leader and baritone sax); Sam Furnace (alto sax); Al Givens (tenor and soprano saxes); Richard Clements (piano); Kiyoto Fujiwara (bass); Taru Alexander (drums); Carleen Robinson (vocals); and special guests Jon Jang (piano) and Sayyd Abdul Al-Khabyyr (tenor sax and flute). Liner notes by Amiri Baraka. Chicago Observer Best Album of the Year; Village Voice Choice Albums of the Decade.

1986 *Bamboo That Snaps Back*, Fred Houn and the Asian American Art Ensemble, Finnadar (Warner/Elecktra/Atlantic), recorded and mixed at the Music Annex, Menlo Park, Calif. on September 14 and 15, 1985, featuring Fred Wei-han Houn (baritone and soprano saxes, flute, leader, poetry, vocals); Taru Alexander (drums); Kiyoto Fujiwara (bass); Jon Jang (piano); Jodi Long (vocals); Allen Won (alto sax, flute, alto flute, background vocals); Francis Wong (tenor sax, flute, background vocals). Cover art by Yong Soon Min, liner notes by Genny Lim. Coda Magazine Critics Choice Album of the Year.

1988 *We Refuse to Be Used and Abused*, Fred Houn and the Afro Asian Music Ensemble, Soul Note Records, Milan, Italy, recorded and mixed at Baragozzi Studio, Milan, on November 26 and 27, 1987, featuring Fred Wei-han Houn (baritone and soprano saxes, flute), Sam Furnace (alto and soprano saxes, flute); Hafez Modir (tenor sax and flute); Jon Jang (piano); Kiyoto Fujiwara (bass); royal hartigan (multiple percussion, Chinese opera percussion, African donno drum). Liner notes by Brian Auerbach. Village Voice Choice Albums of the Decade.

1988 *A Song for Manong*, Fred Houn and the Asian American Art Ensemble, AsianImprov Records, recorded at the Music Annex, Menlo Park, Calif., on February 28, 1988, at the Music Annex, Menlo Park, featuring Fred Houn (baritone and soprano saxes, flute, artistic director); Sam Furnace (alto and soprano saxes, flute); Doug Harris (tenor sax, flute and alto flute); royal hartigan (multiple percussion); Mark Izu (bass); Jon Jang (piano); Fe Bongolan (vocals) and Kulintang Arts: Danongan Kalanduyan (master traditional kulintang artist); Robert Henry; James "Frank" Holder; Joey Maliga; Dana Nunez. Liner notes by Fred Houn.

1994 *The Underground Railroad to My Heart*, Fred Ho and the Afro Asian Music Ensemble, multiple recording dates: February 7 and 8, 1990, and February 4 and 5, 1991, at the Music Annex, Menlo Park, Calif.; December 9, 1991, at the Platinum Factory, Brooklyn; February 11 and 12, 1993, at Baby Monster Studio, New York City; featuring Sam Furnace (alto and soprano saxes); Allen Won (tenor sax); David Bindman (tenor sax); Peter Madsen (piano); Kiyoto Fujiwara (bass); royal hartigan (drums and percussion); also features the Journey beyond the West Orchestra (later renamed the Monkey Orchestra): Pei Sheng Shen (sona and oboe); You Qun Fu (erhu); Pauline Hong (san shuen); James Norton (alto and soprano saxes); Francis Wong (tenor sax, flute, and piccolo); Martin Wehner (trombone); John Shifflett (bass); Fred Ho (baritone sax and flute); royal hartigan (Chinese percussion and drum kit); Hafez Modirzadeh (special tenor sax); Cindy Zuoxin Wang (Chinese soprano vocals). Liner notes by Fred Ho. Village Voice Best Albums of 1994.

1994 "Song of the Mountain Stream" and "On the Golden Mountain of Beijing" on the Chen Hongyu recording *Contemporary Compositions Recital by Soprano Chen Hongyu*, China Record Corp., Peoples Republic of China, recorded on the China Record label, featuring soprano Chen Hongyu, Allen Wong (tenor sax), royal hartigan (percussion), and Fred Ho.

1995 "Contradiction, Please! The Revenge of Charlie Chan," Relâche Ensemble recording *Outcome Inevitable*, O.O. Discs 17, recorded at Acoustical Concepts Inc., Eddystone, Pa., 1994, featuring Relâche: Laurel Wyckoff (flute, piccolo); Lloyd Shorter (oboe, English horn); Ken Ulansey (alto sax); Chuck Holdeman (bassoon); Doublas Mapp (electric bass and contrabass); John Dulik (piano); Helen Carnevale (percussion); guest artist Fred Ho (baritone saxophone).

1996 *Monkey: Part One*, Fred Ho and the Monkey Orchestra, Koch Jazz, recorded at the Music Annex, Menlo Park, Calif., on February 7 and 8, 1990, featuring Pei Sheng Shen (sona and oboe); You Qun Fu (erhu); Pauline Hong (san shuen); James Norton (alto and soprano saxes); Francis Wong (tenor sax, flute and piccolo); Martin Wehner (trombone); John Shifflett (bass); Fred Ho (baritone sax and flute); royal hartigan (Chinese percussion and drum kit); Hafez Modirzadeh (special tenor sax); Cindy Zuoxin Wang (Chinese soprano vocals).

1997 *Monkey: Part Two*, Fred Ho and the Monkey Orchestra, Koch Jazz, recorded at Avatar Studios, New York City, on October 31, 1996, mixed at Studio Masuo (aka Current Sounds), New York City, on November 8, 1996; featuring Fred Ho (baritone sax); Sam Furnace (alto sax); David Bindman (tenor sax); Hafez Modirzadeh (chromodal phone, Persian karna); Marty Wehner (tenor and bass trombone); Wu Man (pipa); Tang Liangxing (erhu); Pei Sheng Shen (sona, oboe and vocals); Cindy Zuoxin Wang (vocals); conducted by Jerome Korman.

1997 *Turn Pain into Power!*, Fred Ho and the Afro Asian Music Ensemble, O.O. Discs, Black Rock, Conn., portions of this recording are reissues of some material from *Bamboo That Snaps Back* (tracks 9–10), while tracks 1–7 were recorded December 9, 1991, at the Platinum Factory in Brooklyn, and track 8 was recorded February 4–5, 1991, at the Music Annex in Menlo Park.

1997 "Beyond Columbus and Capitalism," on the Rova Saxophone Quartet recording *New Works: Volume 2*, Black Saint Records, Milan, Italy, recorded at Bay Studios, Berkeley, Calif., in August 1995.

1998 *Yes Means Yes, No Means No, Whatever She Wears, Wherever She Goes!*, Fred Ho and the Afro Asian Music Ensemble, Koch Jazz, Port Washington, N.Y., recorded at Harmolodic Studios, New York City, on December 12, 1996, at Harmolodic Studio, and mixed December 27–28, 1996, at Kampo Cultural Center, New York City, featuring Fred Ho (leader and baritone sax); Sam Furnace (alto sax); David Bindman (tenor sax and African percussion); Kiyoto Fujiwara (bass); royal hartigan (drum set and African percussion); Diana Herold (marimba, vibraphone and African percussion) with special guess Robert Levin (trombone and African percussion); Peter Madsen (keyboard); Valecia Phillips (vocals).

1999 *Warrior Sisters: The New Adventures of African and Asian Womyn Warriors (A New American Opera)*, Fred Ho and the Afro Asian Music Ensemble, Koch Jazz, Port Washington, N.Y., recorded at Avatar Studios, New York City, on January 13, 1998, and mixed January 26–27, 1998, at Studio Masuo, New York City, featuring Sam Furnace (alto sax, flute); David Bindman (tenor sax, flute); Andy Laster (baritone sax); royal hartigan (drum set, Chinese percussion); Santi DiBriano (bass); Richard Harper (piano); Diana Herold (marimba, percussion) and Fred Ho conducting. Singers: Ann McPhail, Alison Easter, Shan Min Yu, Liza Lapira, Kenneth Williams, Lynn

Randolph, Greg Purnhagen, Anthony Alioto, Peter Stewart, Anna DeVera, Shirley Barnes, Phenisher Harris, and Dong Lin.

1999 "Absolute Solo: Farewell to the New World Order," on the *China Exchange* recording, Composers Recordings Inc., New York City (this track was previously released on the *Yes Means Yes . . .* recording).

2000 *Night Vision: A New Third to First World Vampyre Opera*, Fred Ho opera soundtrack, libretto by Ruth Margraff, Autonomedia/Big Red Media, Brooklyn, recorded at Avatar Studios, New York City, on October 3, 1999, and mixed October 12, 1999. Featuring: Fred Ho, conductor; Peter Madsen (electric keyboard); Mikele Navazio (electric guitar); royal hartigan (drum set); Gene Torres (electric bass); Sweet Sue Terry (alto and soprano saxes); Michael Weisberger (tenor sax); Ray Franks (baritone sax); Joshua Fried (electronic processing). Singers: Daphne Gaines, Dr. Sa'di Al-Hadithi, Craig Wedren, Kaipo Schwab, Keith Adkins, Gregory Purnhagen, Asa Somers, Culver Casson, Funda Duyal, Kim Gambino.

2001 *Once upon a Time in Chinese America . . . The Martial Arts Epic*, Fred Ho and the Afro Asian Music Ensemble, Innova Recordings, St. Paul, Minn., recorded at Current Sounds, New York City, on December 14, 1999, featuring Shyaporn Therrakulstit (Narrator); Fred Ho (baritone sax/leader); Sam Furnace (alto sax); David Bindman (tenor sax); Diana Herold (marimba, vibraphone, percussion); Ayodele Maakheru (electric bass); royal hartigan (drum set, Chinese percussion). After this recording sold out, a second release was done in 2003.

2001 *The Way of the Saxophone*, Fred Ho with the Brooklyn Sax Quartet [features one Fred Ho composition, "Hipster Harvey (for Harvey Lichtenstein)"], on Innova Records, recorded July 29, 2000, at Current Sounds Studio, New York City.

2002 *All Power to the People!: The Black Panther Suite* (DVD), Fred Ho and the Afro Asian Music Ensemble, music recorded at Avatar Studios, New York City, on March 3, and mixed May 11, 1998, at Current Sounds Studio (formerly Studio Masuo), New York City, and edited May 12, 1998, at Jon Rosenberg's apartment, featuring Fred Ho (baritone sax/leader); Sam Furnace (alto sax); David Bindman (tenor sax), Diana Herold (marimba, vibes and African percussion); Wes Brown (bass); Robert Levin (African percussion); royal hartigan (drum set and African percussion); Mikele Navazio (electric guitar). Video production by Paul Chan in 2002.

2003 *All Power to the People! The Black Panther Ballet Suite* (DVD), Innova and Big Red Media Inc.

2004 *Stranger than Fiction* (Undone/Arabesque) with the Strange Attractors Band (Fred Ho, baritone sax; Steve Goldstein, lap top electronics; David Means, electric guitar and electronics with guest artist Carei Thomas, keyboards), recorded live at Metro State College, St. Paul, Minn., in 2002. This recording has never been released due to a legal suit against the record company.

2005 "Fishing Song of the East China Sea," "The Black Nation Suite," and a Fred Ho–arranged version of Billy Strayhorn's "Lush Life" featured on *The Far Side of Here* (Omnitone), Brooklyn Sax Quartet, "Fishing Song" and "Lush Life" recorded May 8, 2004, and "The Black Nation Suite" recorded October 26, 2003.

2005 *Red Arc: A Call for Liberación* (Wings Press) Fred Ho, baritone sax with poet Raul Salinas, recorded at Edit Point Studios in San Antonio, Tex., in September 24, 2004. Liner notes by Alejandro Murguia.

2010 *Celestial Green Monster* (Mutable Music/Big Red Media) Fred Ho and the Green Monster Big Band, recorded at Systems Two in Brooklyn, N.Y., on December 17, 2008, and released January 2010.

2010 "I Wor Kuen" and "No Home to Return To" featured on *The NYFA Collection: 25 Years of New York New Music* (Innova Recordings 223), compilation.

2011 *Year of the Tiger* (Innova) Fred Ho and the Celestial Green Monster Big Band, recorded at Systems Two, Brooklyn, N.Y. in January 2010, though two selections were previously recorded.

2011 *Deadly She-Wolf Assassin at Armageddon!/Momma's Song* (Innova and Big Red Media), Fred Ho and the Afro Asian Music Ensemble with special guest artists; recorded at Systems Two, Brooklyn, N.Y., and Studio Masuo, Manhattan, N.Y. ("Momma's Song"), 2006. Combination Manga-CD-Book.

2011 *Big Red!*, Fred Ho and the Afro Asian Music Ensemble, recorded at Systems Two, Brooklyn, N.Y., October 24, 2004.

2011 *The Sweet Science Suite: A Scientific Soul Music Honoring of Muhammad Ali,* Fred Ho and the Green Monster Big Band, recorded at Systems Two in Brooklyn, N.Y., January 16, 2011.

2011 *The Music of Cal Massey: A Tribute,* special chamber orchestra featuring the compositions of Cal Massey, recorded at Systems Two, Brooklyn, N.Y., April 25, 2011.

2012 *Snake-Eaters,* Fred Ho's Saxophone Liberation Front, recorded at Lofish Productions, Manhattan, N.Y., July 24, 2010, except "Beyond Columbus and Capitalism" (recorded July 29, 2000).

Production History

Bound Feet

October 1986, 2nd annual Asian American Interdisciplinary Arts Festival, presented and produced by the Alliance for Asian American Arts and Culture (now called the Asian American Arts Alliance), Henry Street Settlement, New York City.

Bamboo That Snaps Back!

World premiere fall 1986, the Whitney Museum at Phillip Morris, New York City; earlier and subsequent performances were part of performance repertoire of the Asian American Art Ensemble.

A Chinaman's Chance (opera)

Early concert versions of work-in-progress of the score were done in 1986 at Pace University with Music from China, New York City; November 1987 at the New Performance Gallery presented by the Pear Garden in the West, San Francisco, Calif.; April 1, 1989 (world premiere), Majestic Theater, Brooklyn Academy of Music, Brooklyn, presented by Dance Giant Steps Inc.

"A Song for Manong" (Part 3 of *Bamboo That Snaps Back!*)

World premiere February 22, 1988, at the Herbst Theater, San Francisco, with a subsequent run February 24–27, 1988, at Life on the Water Theater, San Francisco.

Turn Pain into Power!

Excerpts of this multimedia (music, poetry performance, and slides) work have been performed often as part of the concert repertoire of the Afro Asian Music Ensemble; major multimedia performances took place in fall 1992 in Boston, Brooklyn, Philadelphia, and at the Smithsonian Institution, Washington, D.C., as part of Fred Ho's role in the worldwide antiquincentennial campaign to oppose the celebration of the Christopher Columbus "discovery" of the Americas.

Chickens Come Home to Roost

1996, the Kitchen, New York City.

Journey beyond the West: The New Adventures of Monkey

January 1990, staged production of "Monkey Meets the Spider-Spirit Vampires," Julia Morgan Theater, presented by the Pear Garden in the West, Berkeley, Calif.

January 1991, concert version of "Uproar in Heaven," presented by the Pear Garden in the West at San Francisco City College and the Julia Morgan Theater, Berkeley, Calif.

February 10–11, 2005, concert of acts 1 to 4, the Public Theater, New York City.

October 29 and 30, 1996, work-in-progress semistaged excerpts of "Act 2: The Journey Begins," the Guggenheim Museum, New York City.

November 26, 28, and 29, 1997, full stage production of "Act 2: The Journey Begins" and "Act 3: Monkey Meets the Spider-Vampire Demons," and concert of "Act 1: Uproar in Heaven," Brooklyn Academy of Music Next Wave Festival, Brooklyn.

November 1998, concert of "Act 2: The Journey Begins," Herbst Theater, San Francisco Jazz Festival, San Francisco.

February 26, 2000, concert of "Act 2: The Journey Begins," the Flynn Theater, Burlington, Vt.

March 7, 2002, concert of "Act 4: The Journey Home," the Great Hall at the Cooper Union, New York City.

December 14–15, 2003, work-in-progress of staged excerpts from "Act 1: Uproar in Heaven" and "Act 2: The Journey Begins," Guggenheim Museum, New York City.

Warrior Sisters: The New Adventures of African and Asian Womyn Warriors

November 28 to December 2, 1999, the Kitchen, New York City.

September 29, 2001. Gammage Auditorium, Arizona State University, Tempe, Ariz.

Night Vision: A New Third to First World Vampyre Opera

Concert version presented October 1 and 2, 1999, at the Cooper Union Great Hall, New York City.

Full stage production world premiere January 26 to February 19, 2000, at Here, New York City.

All Power to the People! The Black Panther Music/Video/Martial Arts Ballet Suite

February 12 and 13, 1999, work-in-progress video and music presentation, the Kitchen, New York City.

August 27 and 28, 1999, video and music world premiere, Walker Arts Center, Minneapolis, Minn.

Full stage production world premiere with music, video, and martial arts, October 3, 2003, Northeastern University, Boston.

Music and video concert March 17–18, 2007, the New Freedom Theater (copresented by Peregrine Arts Inc. and the New Freedom Theater), Philadelphia.

Voice of the Dragon: Once upon a Time in Chinese America . . . The Martial Arts Epic

February 1997, Mutable Music and the World Music Institute Interpretation Series Merkin Recital Hall, New York City, work-in-progress showing.

June 1999, John Harms Center for the Arts, JVC Jazz Festival (New Jersey).

Fall 1999, the Guggenheim Museum, Peter B. Lewis Theater, Works and Process series production. Mary Sharp Cronson and PBS's *Eye on Dance,* Celia Ipiotis, New York City.

September 2000, Solomon R. Guggenheim Museum, Peter B. Lewis Theater, New York City.

August 18, 2000, Northeastern University Center for the Arts, Boston.

May 12 to 19, 2001, Seattle International Children's Festival, Seattle Repertory Bagley Wright Theater, Seattle.

November 7 to 11, 2001, Brooklyn Academy of Music Next Wave Festival, Brooklyn.

2002–2003 Columbia Arts Management Inc./Big Red Media Inc. North American tour to performing arts centers in 33+ cities: Hancher Auditorium, Iowa City, Iowa; New Jersey PAC, Newport PAC, Newport, Oreg.; Arlene Schnitzer Concert Hall, Portland, Oreg.; Silva Concert Hall, Hult Center for the Arts, Eugene, Oreg.; Mondavi Center for the Performing Arts, UC Davis, Davis, Calif.; Van Duzer Theater, Humboldt State University, Arcata, Calif.; Center Theater, California Center for the Arts, Escondido; Riverside Municipal Auditorium, Univ. of California, Riverside McCallum Theater for the Performing Arts, Palm Desert, Calif.; Smothers Theater, Seaver College of Pepperdine University, Malibu, Calif.; Scottsdale Center for the Arts, Scottsdale, Ariz.; Beckman Auditorium, California Institute of Technology, Pasadena; Carver Community Cultural Center, Lila Cockrell Theater, San Antonio, Tex.; Fox Cities PAC, Appleton, Wisc.; Pabst Center, Milwaukee, Wisc.; Power Center, Ann Arbor, Mich.; Southern Theater, Columbus, Ohio; Vern Riffe Center, Portsmouth, Ohio; Chicago Theater, Chicago, Ill.; Ford Theater, Honeywell Center, Wabash, Ind.; Zellerbach Theater, Annenberg Center, University of Pennsylvania, Philadelphia; Palace Theatre, Stamford Center for the Arts, Stamford, Conn.; Tilles Center for the Arts, Brookville, N.Y.; John Harms Center for the Arts, Englewood, N.J.; Colonial Theater, Keene, N.H.; Cubb Theater, Capitol Center for the Arts, Concord, N.H.; Garde Arts Center, New London, Conn.; Jorgensen Auditorium, University of Connecticut, Storrs; Community Theater, Morristown, N.J.; Center for the Arts Concert Hall, George Mason University, Fairfax, Va.; Carpenter Center for the Performing Arts, Richmond, Va.; Shubert Theater, New Haven, Conn.; and other smaller, more informal venues.

VOD 2: Shaolin Secret Stories

January 8 to 10, 2004, the Apollo Theater, New York City.

Deadly She-Wolf Assassin at Armageddon!

April 29 and 30, 2005 (excerpt of work-in-progress), Japan Society, New York City.

June 24 and 25, 2006 (full stage production, world premiere), Drexel University, presented by Peregrine Arts Inc., Philadelphia, Pa.

VOD 3: Dragon vs. Eagle: Enter the White Barbarians!
January 2007, work-in-progress reading of book only, the Apollo Theater, New York City.
June 15 to 16, 2007, concert reading of full score and book, the Apollo Theater.

Mr. Mystery: The Return of Sun Ra to Save Planet Earth!
Libretto by Quincy Troupe. July 2007, excerpt of libretto, semistaged reading, directed by Walter Dallas, Whitney Museum of American Art, New York City.

The Sweet Science Suite: A Scientific Soul Music Honoring of Muhammad Ali
Composed by Fred Ho for the Green Monster Big Band, choreography by Christal Brown, world premiere at the Guggenheim Museum Works and Process series, November 2011, subsequently booked for Middlebury College, Vermont, and the 2013 Brooklyn Academy of Music Next Wave Festival, New York City.

Deadly She-Wolf Assassin at Armageddon!
Music and Concept by Fred Ho, book by Ruth Margraff and Fred Ho, May 2–19, 2013, off-Broadway run at La Mama E.T.C., New York City.

Curriculum Vitae

Big Red Media, New York City
bigredmedia@hotmail.com
http://www.bigredmediainc.com

Management: Joseph Yoon, Spectrum Music
joseph@spectrummusic.net
718.383.2313
www.spectrummusic.net

Bandleader

Afro Asian Scientific Soul Duo with Salim Washington, founded 2009
Afro Asian Music Ensemble, founded 1982
Green Monster Big Band, founded 2008
Monkey Orchestra, founded 1990
Afro Asian Arts Dialogue with poet Kalamu Yu Salaam, founded 1991
Asian American Art Ensemble, 1981–88
Brooklyn Sax Quartet, cofounded with David Bindman, 1997–2006
Caliente! Circle around the Sun, with poets Magdalena Gómez and Raul Salinas, 2005
Fred Ho's Saxophone Liberation Front, founded 2010

Sideman

Julius Hemphill Sextet, 1993
Change of the Century Orchestra, 1987
Gil Evans Orchestra, 1987
Charlie Persip Superband, 1982–87
Archie Shepp Attica Blues Big Band, 1985–86

Composer (Commissions)

"The Soul Science Stomp," Harvard University Jazz Big Band, Cambridge, Mass., 2011.

Sweet Science Suite: A Scientific Soul Honoring of Muhammad Ali, Guggenheim Museum Works and Process series and the Brooklyn Center for the Performing Arts, 2011.

Fanfare to Stop the Creeping Meatball, Boston Symphony Orchestra for the Tanglewood Festival, 2011.

"Take the Zen Train," Harvard University, Cambridge, Mass., 2009.

Every Time I Open My Mouth to Sing, Thomas Buckner/Mutable Music Inc., New York, 2008.

When the Real Dragons Fly, American Composers Orchestra, Zankel Hall/Carnegie Hall, New York City, 2008.

The Struggle for a New World Suite, Temple University, Peregrine Arts and the Pew Charitable Trust, Temple University, Philadelphia, 2007.

Two Poems by James Tate set to Music ("Teaching the Ape to Write Poems" and "Dear Reader"), Mrs. Mary Sharp Cronson and the Works and Process series at the Guggenheim Museum, 2006.

Dragon vs. Eagle! (Enter the White Barbarians; Voice of the Dragon 3), the Apollo Theater Foundation, Peregrine Arts, New York City and Philadelphia, 2005, Rockefeller Foundation Multi-Arts Program.

Suite for Matriarchal Shaman Warriors, IIIZ+ ("three zee plus": Japanese *koto*, Korean kayagum, Chinese zheng plus percussion) and Meet the Composer Commissioning Program, Juneau, Alaska, and New York City, 2005.

The Raven Suite, CrossSound and the National Endowment for the Arts, Anchorage, Juneau, Ketchikan, and Sitka, Alaska, 2005.

Deadly She-Wolf Assassin at Armageddon!, Big Red Media Inc. and the New York State Council on the Arts (for cowriter Ruth Margraff), the Japan Society, New York City, 2005.

Suite Sam Furnace (dedicated to the alto saxophonist who worked 20 years with Fred Ho and passed away January 27, 2004), Chamber Music America Jazz Commissioning Award and Fred Ho and the Afro Asian Music Ensemble, New York City, 2004–5.

Josephine Baker's Angels from the Rainbow, Imani Winds and Meet the Composer Commissioning Program, New York City,2003.

Voice of the Dragon 2: Shaolin Secret Stories (sequel to *Voice of the Dragon: Once upon a Time in Chinese America . . . The Martial Arts Epic*), Caribbean Cultural Center, the Apollo Theater Foundation Inc., the New York State Council on the Arts and the Mary Flagler Cary Charitable Trust, New York City, 2002

All Power to the People! The Black Panther Suite (with Live Digital Interact Video Mixing and Martial Arts Ballet), the Walker Art Center, Minneapolis, Minn.,

1999; Northeastern University Center for the Arts, Boston, and the Rockefeller Foundation, 2002.

"Hipster Harvey" (saxophone quartet), Brooklyn Academy of Music in celebration of the retirement of Harvey Lichtenstein, Brooklyn, 1999.

"From the First Pop! . . .," commissioned by Harvard-Radcliffe Office of the Arts to celebrate the retirement of Myra Mayman (founder-director), Cambridge, Mass., 1999.

Night Vision: A New Third to First World Vampyre Opera, Ruth E. Margraff, librettist, Here Arts Center and the Rockefeller Foundation, New York City, 1998, 1999.

Warrior Sisters: The New Adventures of African and Asian Womyn Warriors (opera), Ann T. Greene, librettist, the Mary Flagler Cary Trust and Aaron Davis Hall/City College of New York, New York City, 1998; commissioned in part by Arizona State University–Tempe Public Events, 2000.

Once upon a Time in Chinese America . . . The Martial Arts Epic, World Music Institute, New York State Council on the Arts and the Mary Flagler Cary Trust, New York City, 1995.

The Journey beyond the West: The New Adventures of Monkey!, Monkey Orchestra, Meet the Composer, Brooklyn Academy of Music Next Wave Festival and the Joseph Papp Public Theater, New York City, 1997 and 1995.

"The White Peril: Too Wrong for Too Long!," Music in Motion and Zeitgeist Ensemble, Fleischer Art Museum, Philadelphia, and Walker Art Center, Minneapolis, Minn. 1994.

Yes Means Yes, No Means No, Whatever She Wears, Wherever She Goes!, Afro Asian Music Ensemble, Brooklyn Women's Anti-Rape Exchange and WHAM! National Endowment for the Arts, New York City, 1993.

Contradiction, Please! The Revenge of Charlie Chan, Relâche Contemporary Music Ensemble and Meet the Composer, Philadelphia, Pa., 1992–93.

Beyond Columbus and Capitalism, Rova Saxophone Quartet, Meet the Composer, San Francisco, Calif., 1992.

Havoc in Gold Mountain, music theater, Association of Performing Arts Presenters/Lila Wallace Readers Digest, Boro of Manhattan Community College, New York City, 1992

Turn Pain into Power!, bilingual multimedia oratorio, Brooklyn Art and Culture Association, New York City, 1991.

A Chinaman's Chance, Afro Asian opera, American Music Center and New York State Council for the Arts, Brooklyn Academy of Music, New York City, 1989.

"A Song for Manong," music theater score, Life on the Water, San Francisco, Calif., 1988.

XX, solo baritone sax musical theater score for a Genny Lim play, San Francisco, Calif., 1986.

Recordings

(See discography above in appendix.)

Books

Raw Extreme Manifesto: Change Your Mind, Change Your Body and Change the World by Spending Almost Nothing! With Peter Lew. New York: Sky Horse Publishing, 2012.

Diary of a Radical Cancer Warrior: Fighting Cancer and Capitalism at the Cellular Level. New York: Sky Horse Publishing, 2011. (This book grew out of a series of group emails informally referred to as "The Cancer Diaries.")

Wicked Theory, Naked Practice: A Fred Ho Reader. Edited by Diane C. Fujino. Minneapolis: University of Minnesota Press, 2009.

Afro Asia: Revolutionary Political and Cultural Connections between African and Asian Americans. Coedited with Bill V. Mullen. Durham, N.C.: Duke University Press, 2009.

Legacy to Liberation: Politics and Culture of Revolutionary Asian Pacific America. Coedited with Carolyn Antonio, Diane Fujino, and Steve Yip. San Francisco: Big Red Media and AK Press, 2000.

The Sheroes Womyn Warriors Calendar. Autonomedia/Semiotext, published annually since 1998.

Sounding Off! Music as Subversion/Resistance/Revolution. Coedited with Ron Sakolsky. Brooklyn, N.Y.: Autonomedia, 1995. Winner, American Book Award, 1996.

Articles

This list does not include articles and essays collected in Fred Ho's books.

"How Does Music Free Us? 'Jazz' as Resistance to Commodification and the Embrace of the Eco-Logic Aesthetic." *Capitalism Nature Socialism* 22, no. 2 (June 2011): 52–61.

"Beyond Bandung: From the Third World to the New World, a Tribute to Amiri Baraka." In *Let Loose on the World: Celebrating Amiri Baraka at 75*, 190–92. N.p.: Amiri Baraka Commemoration Committee, 2009.

"Diary of a Radical Cancer Warrior: Fighting Cancer and Capitalism at the Cellular Level" (excerpts). *Black Renaissance Noire* 8, no. 2 (spring 2008): 128–43; 9, no. 1 (winter 2009): 92–113; 9, no. 2–3 (fall–winter 2010): 228–37, New York University Department of African-American Studies.

"A Tribute to Max Roach." *Black Renaissance Noire* 8, no. 1 (winter/spring 2008): 12–15, New York University Department of African-American Affairs.

"A Request from Ishmael Reed: Highlights in the History of 'Jazz' *Not* Covered by Ken Burns." *Shuffle Boil* 6, no. 5 (2006): 63–66.

"Kickin' the White Man's Ass: Black Power and Aesthetics and the Asian Martial Arts." In *AfroAsian Encounters: Culture, History, Politics*, edited by Heike Raphael-Hernandez and Shannon Steen. New York and London: New York University Press, 2006.

"Fred Ho's Tribute to the Black Arts Movement." *Critical Studies in Improvisation* (Canadian music journal on improvisation) 1, no. 3 (2006), www.criticalimprov.com.

"Fred Ho's Tribute to the Black Arts Movement." *Centennial Review* 6, no. 2 (2006): 141–89.

"Bamboo That Snaps Back! Resistance and Revolution in Asian Pacific American Working-Class and Left-Wing Expressive Culture." In *Left of the Color Line: Race, Radicalism, and Twentieth-Century Literature of the United States*, 239–58, edited by Bill V. Mullen and James Smethurst. Chapel Hill: University of North Carolina Press, 2003.

"New and Experimental Genres." In *The United States and Canada*, edited by Ellen Koskoff. Vol. 3 of *The Garland Encyclopedia of World Music*. New York: Routledge, 2001, 334–37.

"The History of the Harvard-Radcliffe Asian American Association." In *H-R AAA Handbook*. Cambridge, Mass.: Harvard University, 2001.

"Doing It Yourself: Big Red Media, a Composer/Musician-Driven Production Company." *American Composers Forum Newsletter* (summer 1998): 1.

"Beyond Asian American Jazz: My Musical and Political Changes in the Asian American Movement." *Leonardo Music Journal* 9 (1999): 45–51.

"Fred Ho, Musician and Composer: A Response." In *Yellow Light: The Flowering of Asian American Arts*, edited by Amy Ling, 347–54. Philadelphia: Temple University Press, 1999.

"Doing It Yourself: Big Red Media, a Composer/Musician-Driven Production Company." *American Composers Forum Newsletter* (summer 1998): 1.

"How to Sell But Not Sell Out: Some Personal Lessons from Making a Career as a Subversive and Radical Performing Artist." *Movement Research Journal* 12 (1996): 18.

"What Makes 'Jazz' the Revolutionary Music of the 20th Century, and Will It Be Revolutionary for the 21st Century?" *African American Review* 29, no. 2 (1995): 283–90.

"From Banana to Third World Marxist." In *Boyhood, Growing Up Male: A Multicultural Anthology*, edited by Franklin Abbott. Freedom, Calif.: Crossing Press, 1993; republished, Madison: University of Wisconsin Press, 1998.

"Asian Americans Are Not Exotic!" *Asian American Arts Dialogue* (winter 1993): 5, 11; reprinted in *Movement Research: Performance Journal* 8 (1994): 7.

"Marxism and Asian Americans: The Struggle Continues!" In "Asian Pacific American Special Issue," edited by Fred Ho, Meizhu Liu, Ellen Somekawa, and Dang Tran, *Forward Motion* 11, no. 3 (1992).

"A Call for Cultural Guerillas: U.S. Imperialism in Its Monopoly Stage and Its Effects on Where American Culture Is Going." *Movement Research: Performance Journal* 4 (winter/spring 1992).

"Nobody Knows the Trouble I've Seen: Political Détente through the Medium of Jazz, Notes from a Work in Progress." *(Brooklyn, N.Y.) City Sun*, June 19–25, 1991, 27, 31, 35.

"The Real Next Wave: Multicultural Artists and Empowerment as Sources for New American Art." In *Reimaging America: The Arts and Social Change*, edited by Craig Little and Mark O'Brien, 124–27. Philadelphia: New Society Publishers, 1990.

"Asian American Music and Empowerment: Is There Such a Thing as 'Asian American Jazz'?" In *Views on Black American Music*, 27–31. 17th Annual Black Musicians Conference, University of Massachusetts–Amherst, 1989.

"Tomoe Tana: Keeping Alive Japanese American Tanka." *Asian Week*, June 17, 1988, 18.

"Introduction: The Cutting Edge—Asian American Creativity and Change"; "Revolutionary Asian American Art: Tradition and Change, Inheritance and Innovation, Not Imitation!"; "An ABC from NYC: 'Charlie' Chin, Asian American Singer and Songwriter"; "The Brown Power Poet: Serafin Malay Syquia (1943–1973)"; and "Best of the Best: Recent Book and Record Releases." All in a special issue of *East Wind: Politics and Culture of Asians in America* 5, no. 1 (spring/summer 1986), guest-edited by Fred Ho.

Reviews

Review of *Insights on Jazz: A Musician's Guide to Making a Recording, Arts Midwest* newsletter.

Awards

2011 John P. Simon Guggenheim Foundation Music Composition Fellow
2010 Letter of Distinction, American Music Center
Harvard Arts Medal, 2009–10
Citation, Brooklyn Borough President's Office, 2009
Chamber Music-America/ASCAP Special Award for Adventurous Programming, 2008
Museum of the Moving Image Ultimate Urban Warrior award for leadership in promoting Blacks and Latinos in Chinese Martial Arts, 2008
McKnight Fellowship and the American Composers Forum, 2000
Rockefeller Foundation, Multi-Arts Projects, 2005, 2002, 2000, 1999, 1998, 1991
Julius Hemphill Jazz Composers Awards, Boston Jazz Composers Alliance, 1998
National Endowment for the Arts, Opera-Musical Theater Fellowship, 1994
National Endowment for the Arts, Music Composition Fellowship, 1993

Honoree, Chinese for Affirmative Action (San Francisco), 1991
American Music Center Copying Assistance Grant, 1989, 1991, 1993, 1994, 1996
New York Foundation for the Arts Music Composition Fellowship, 1989, 1994, 2004
Duke Ellington Distinguished Artist Lifetime Achievement Award, 17th Annual Black Musicians Conference, University of Massachusetts, 1988
Peter Ivers Fellowship, Harvard University, 1987
ASCAP Composers Award, 1986–present
Meet the Composer, 1982–present

Residencies

University of Massachusetts-Dartmouth, 2010
University of Hawai'i–Manoa, 2010
Fundación Valaparaíso, Mojácar, Spain, 2010
University of Wisconsin–Madison Arts Institute, fall 2008
Ucross Foundation Residency, Clearmount, Wyo., 2005
David and Julia White Artist Colony, Ciudad Colón, Costa Rica, 2004, 2006
Civitella Ranieri Center, Umbria, Italy, 2001
Walker Art Center, Minneapolis, Minn., 1999
Djerassi Resident Artists Program, Woodside, Calif., 1999, 2004
Rockefeller Foundation Bellagio Study and Conference Center, Italy, 1998
Northeastern University, Boston, Mass., 1996
Music in Motion, Fleischer Art Museum, Philadelphia, Pa., 1993–94
Atlantic Center for the Arts, New Smyrna Beach, Fla., 1993
University of Illinois, Urbana, Ill., 1992
Composer-to-Composer, Telluride, Colo., 1991
New College of California Arts and Social Change Program, San Francisco, Calif., 1990
Painted Bride Arts Center, Philadelphia, Pa., 1989
Stanford University, Palo Alto, Calif., 1988
Harvard University, Cambridge, Mass., 1987, 2009

Community Activities

Scientific Soul Sessions, Harlem, New York, www.scientificsoulsessions.com
Community and Immigrant Labor, Here Local 17, et al. McKnight Residency, Minneapolis–St. Paul, Minn., 2000–2001
Coalition to Free Mumia Abu-Jamal
John Brown Anti-Racism Conference, Hunter College, 2000
Asian Pacific American Ad-Hoc Committee
Critical Resistance: Beyond the Prison Industrial Complex
Jericho Movement for Amnesty for U.S. Political Prisoners

Eastwind Magazine, Contributing Editor/Writer, 1983–89
Co-Founder, AsianImprov Records, Oakland, Calif., 1988
Founding Artist, Asian American Jazz Festival, Jazz Center of New York, 1985
Project Director, First Annual Asian American Interdisciplinary Arts Festival: Roots to Reality: Asian America in Transition, 1985
Owner/Founder, Transformation Art Publisher, New York, 1984
Member, Asian Americans for Jesse Jackson, 1984
Executive Committee, Alliance for Asian American Arts and Culture, New York, 1981
Member, Chinese Progressive Association, New York, 1981
Founder, Asian American Resource Workshop, Boston, 1979
Founder, East Coast Asian Student Union, 1978
Founder, Harvard-Radcliffe Asian American Association, 1976
Founder, New England Pacific/Asian Coalition, National Institute of Mental Health, Boston, 1975
Founder, Harvard-Radcliffe Task Force on Affirmation Action, 1975
Founder, Amherst Asian American Education Committee, 1974
Numerous benefits for anti-Asian violence, Asian women's shelters, Asian cultural organizations, community groups, political campaigns, workers strike committees, prisoners, etc., throughout the United States

Professional Activities

BOARD OF DIRECTORS

Meet the Composer, 1993–96

CURATOR

Music Committee, Dance Theater Workshop

PANELIST

National Endowment for the Arts, Music Panel/Access to Artistic Excellence, 2010
American Music Center, numerous times during the 1989–94, 2010
Massachusetts Council on the Arts Composers Fellowships, 2001, 2007
Music Series Curatorial Committee, Dance Theater Workshop, 1993–96
Arts Midwest Jazz Masters Award, 1992
Meet the Composer, 1992 (twice), Van Lier Fellowship (2010)
New England Foundation for the Arts, 1991
New York Foundation for the Arts, 1994
Mid-Atlantic Interdisciplinary Arts Re-grant Program, 1989
Ohio Arts Council (2009)
New York State Council on the Arts, 1982–85, 2010–13

FEATURED SPEAKER

National Jazz Service Organization, 1992
Keynote address: "Imagine the Impossible: Perpetuating the Avant Garde in African American Music," "What's Avant-garde About the Avant-garde?" Fourth Annual Interdisciplinary Jazz Studies Colloquium, University of Kansas, March 30–31, 2007

SPEAKER

National Asian American Studies Association, 2007
University Jazz Studies: "What's Avant-Garde About the Avant-Garde?"
MELUS (Society for the Study of the Multi-Ethnic Literature of the United States), 2004
American Studies Association, 2004
National Asian American Studies Association, 2004, 1992, 1993
National Association of Latino Arts and Culture (NALAC), 2003
College Art Association, 1994
Cultural Diversity Based on Cultural Grounding Conference, Network of Cultural Centers of Color, 1993
National Asian American Studies Conference, 1990, 1991, 1993
Business Volunteers for the Arts, San Francisco, 1988
Jazz and World Music, Wesleyan University, 1986

NOTEWORTHY

National advisor, Plymouth Music Series, Minneapolis, Minn. (ongoing)
Featured artist, A Great Day in New York Festival, Chamber Music Society of Lincoln Center, 2001
Featured Artist, Brooklyn Academy of Music Next Wave Festival 1997, 2001
Signed to Columbia Artists Management Inc. (CAMI) for 2002–3 North American Tour of *Voice of the Dragon: Once upon a Time in Chinese America . . . The Martial Arts Epic* (33 U.S. cities and major concert/performance venues).

Guest Lectures, 1986–2008

Arizona State University
Aucksburg Community College
Bard College
Baruch College
Bates College
Berkshire Community College
Borders Bookstores, Honolulu and Kauai
Boro of Manhattan Community College
Boston College

Brandeis University
Brown University
Bryn Mawr College
Bunker Hill Community College
California State University, Sacramento
Caribbean Cultural Center, New York City
Claremont and Pomona College
Columbia University
Connecticut College
Cooper Union
Cornell University
Emory and Henry Flagler College
Hamilton College
Hampshire College
Harvard University
Haverford College
Holyoke Community College
Hunter College
Jamaica Arts Center, New York City
Kapiolani Community College (Hawai'i)
Lasell College
MacAlester College
Metro State University
MELUS (Multi-Ethnic Literatures of the United States)
National Asian American Studies Association
National Association of Latino Arts and Culture (NALAC)
New College of California
New School for Social Research
New York City Public Schools
New York University
Northeastern University
Notre Dame University
Oberlin College
Princeton University
Purdue University
Rhode Island College
Sacramento City College
Saint Mary College
San Francisco City College
San Francisco State University
San José State University
Sarah Lawrence College

Scripps College
Smithsonian Institution
Stanford University
SUNY–New Paltz
Swarthmore College
Syracuse University
Temple University
Trinity College
Tufts College
University of California—Berkeley, Davis, Los Angeles, Santa Barbara, and Santa Cruz
University of Colorado—Boulder and Denver
University of Connecticut, Storrs
University of Delaware
University of Hawai'i, Manoa
University of Illinois, Urbana
University of Missouri, Kansas City
University of Maryland, College Park
University of Massachusetts—Amherst and Dartmouth
University of Michigan—Ann Arbor and Flint
University of Minnesota
University of Southern Florida, Tampa
University of Texas—Austin and San Antonio
University of Vermont
University of Virginia
University of Washington—Seattle and Tacoma
University of Wisconsin—Madison and Whitewater
Vassar College
Williams College
Yale University
Yavapai Community College, Prescott, Ariz.

Education

B.A., Sociology, Harvard University, 1979

Representation

AsiaNetwork (European representation)
Big Red Media Inc., founder and president, a multimedia production company
Francis Goldin Literary Agency (for print publishing)
Columbia Artists Management Inc. (CAMI) for 2002–3 U.S. National Tour of Voice of the Dragon

Membership

ASCAP

Scholarly Publications Featuring Fred Ho

Asai, Susan M. "Cultural Politics: The African American Connection in Asian American Jazz-based Music." *Asian Music* 36, no. 1 (winter/spring 2005), published by the University of Texas Press for the Society for Asian Music, 87–108.

Chan, Sucheng. *Asian Americans: An Interpretative History.* New York: Twayne, 1991.

Kastin, David. "Fred Ho and the Evolution of Afro-Asian New American Multicultural Music." *Popular Music and Society* 33, no. 1 (February 2010): 1–8.

Kingman, Daniel, and Candelaria, Lorenzo. *American Music: A Panorama.* Belmont, Calif.: Schirmer/Thompson, 2006.

Mullen, Bill. *Afro-Orientalism.* Minneapolis: University of Minnesota Press, 2005.

Wong, Deborah. *Speak It Louder: Asian Americans Making Music.* New York: Routledge Press, 2005.

Zhang, Wei-hua. "Fred Wei-han Ho: Case Study of a Chinese-American Creative Musician." *Asian Music* 25, nos. 1–2 (1993–94): 81–114.

Zheng, Su. *Claiming Diaspora: Music, Transnationalism, and Cultural Politics in Asian/Chinese America.* London: Oxford University Press, 2006.

Film Featuring Fred Ho

Diary of the Dragon: The (R)Evolution of Fred Ho. Dir. Tylon Washington; prod. Iyanna Jones. Black Waxx Moving Images, forthcoming.

Contributors

ROGER N. BUCKLEY is a professor of history and the founding director of the Asian American Studies Institute at the University of Connecticut at Storrs. He is the recipient of numerous research awards and fellowships, among them the National Endowment for the Humanities, the American Council of Learned Societies, the Social Sciences and Humanities Research Council of Canada, the Sir William Osler Medical Library Fellowship at McGill University, the Provost Fellowship at the University of Connecticut, and the John Carter Brown Library Fellowship at Brown University. His numerous books and journal articles, which include works of historical and popular fiction, have been published in the United States, the United Kingdom, India, the Netherlands, Jamaica, Puerto Rico, and St. Kitts. His scholarly books include *Slaves in Red Coats*, *The Haitian Journal of Lieutenant Howard*, *The Napoleonic War Journal of Captain Thomas Henry Browne*, and *The British Army in the West Indies: Society and the Military in the Revolutionary Age*. His fiction includes *Congo Jack*, *The Death and Life of An Irish Soldier*, and *I, Hanuman*. *Singh's Choice*, his latest novel, is currently under review. He is currently writing a history of the Japanese community of Montreal. For more information, visit www.rogerbuckley.com.

PEGGY MYO-YOUNG CHOY is a choreographer-dancer-educator and warrior woman for social transformation. She is founder and director of the Ki Project Inc., an organization dedicated to creative thinking and intercultural performance for future generations. Her dance-theater works are informed by her childhood in Hawai'i, Javanese and Korean dance and martial-arts training, and long-term artistic interchanges with Sasminta Mardawa, Sun Ock Lee, and Fred Ho. Choy teaches in the University of Wisconsin–Madison Dance Department and the Asian American Studies Program.

JAYNE CORTEZ is the author of eleven books of poetry and performer of her poems with music on nine recordings. Her voice is celebrated for its political, surrealistic, dynamic innovations in lyricism, and visceral sound. Cortez has presented her work and ideas at universities, museums, and festivals around the world. Her poems have been translated into many languages and widely published in anthologies, journals, and magazines. She is the recipient of several awards, including Arts International, the National Endowment for the Arts, the international African Festival Award, the Langston Hughes Medal, the American Book Award, and the Thelma McAndless Distinguished Professorship Award. Her most recent books are *The Beautiful Book* (Bola Press) and *Jazz Fan Looks Back* (Hanging Loose Press). Her latest CDs with the Firespitter Band are *Find Your Own Voice, Borders of Disorderly Time* (Bola Press), and *Taking the Blues Back Home*, produced by Harmalodic and by Verve Records. Cortez was organizer of the international symposium "Slave Routes: Resistance, Abolition and Creative Progress" (New York University, 2008), and director of the film *Yari Yari Pamberi: Black Women Writers Dissecting Globalization*. She is cofounder and president of the Organization of Women Writers of Africa Inc. and appears in the films *Women in Jazz* and *Poetry in Motion*.

KEVIN FELLEZS, is assistant professor of music at Columbia University, where he shares a joint appointment in the Institute for Research in African-American Studies. His *Birds of Fire: Jazz, Rock, Funk and the Creation of Fusion* (Duke University Press) is a study of fusion (jazz-rock-funk) music of the 1970s framed by insights drawn from ethnic studies, jazz studies, and popular music studies. Fellezs has published articles in *Jazz Perspectives, Journal of Popular Music Studies, Popular Music History*, and the *Institute for Studies in American Music Newsletter*. He is also a pianist, keyboardist, and composer. His compositions have appeared on a variety of recordings, including a waltz, "C. Howsheruns," on Gerald Beckett's recording *Black Eyes* (2002, Wolfetones). Fellezs holds a PhD in the history of consciousness (American Studies) from the University of California, Santa Cruz.

DIANE C. FUJINO is professor and chair of Asian American Studies at the University of California, Santa Barbara. Her teaching and scholarship center on the Asian American movement, Japanese American history, and Afro-Asian radicalism. She is the author of *Heartbeat of Struggle: The Revolutionary Life of Yuri Kochiyama*; and *Samurai among Panthers: Richard Aoki on Race, Resistance, and a Paradoxical Life*; and editor of *Wicked Theory, Naked*

Practice: A Fred Ho Reader, all with the University of Minnesota Press. Her current research focuses on Japanese American activism in the early Cold War, the contested nature of citizenship, and radical democracy.

MAGDALENA GÓMEZ, a Bronx native and Springfield, Massachusetts, resident, is an award-winning poet, playwright, performer, and arts educator. Gómez is the cofounder and artistic director of the first Latino theater in Springfield, Massachusetts, Teatro V!da. Gómez was named an Unsung Heroine of 2007 by the Massachusetts Commission on the Status of Women. Gómez has received awards from the Augusta Savage Gallery at the University of Massachusetts and from the National Association of Latino Arts and Culture in support of her creative work. Other awards include the Master Artist Award from the National Endowment for the Arts presenters, Pregones Theater in New York City; the Massachusetts Cultural Council Playwriting award; and the 2008 Black Women Playwrights Group Whisper Laugh Shout Award, among others. Gómez is a columnist for *An African American Point of View* newspaper and a regular commentator for New England Public Radio. Her work has been widely published, in the *Berkshire Review*, *Tea Party Magazine*, *Latino Boom*, *Massachusetts Review*, and the *Ollantay Theater Journal*, among many others. Gómez has been a regular collaborator with Fred Ho on music and poetry performances throughout the United States and is a member of Sleeping Weazel, the vision of playwright and scholar, Charlotte Mehan. Gómez is the coeditor, along with poet María Luisa Arroyo, of the first-ever intergenerational, multicultural, and multigenre book on bullying: *Bullying: Relies, Rebuttals, Confessions, and Catharsis* (Skyhorse Publishing, 2012). Gómez is currently on the roster of www.bestkeynotes.com.

RICHARD HAMASAKI recently coedited with Mei-Li Siy Westlake, *Poems by Wayne Kaumualii Westlake (1947–1984)*, published in 2009 by the University of Hawai'i Press. In 2001, the University of Hawai'i Press published Hamasaki's collection of poetry, *From the Spider Bone Diaries: Poems and Songs*. Since 1974, he has been active in Hawai'i's literary arts, collaborating with poets, musicians, artists, photographers, filmmakers, writers, scholars, and teachers locally, regionally, and internationally.

ESTHER IVEREM is a journalist, poet, and visual artist whose most recent book is *We Gotta Have It: Twenty Years of Seeing Black at the Movies, 1986–2006* (De Capo Press). She is also the author of two books of poems, *The Time: Portrait of a Journey Home* and *Living in Babylon* (Africa Word Press). A former staff writer for several newspapers, including the *Washington Post* and *New York Newsday*, she is founder of SeeingBlack.com, a Web site for Black critical voices on arts, media, and politics. She is also a producer and host on WPFW Pacifica Radio, a member of the Washington Area Film Critics Association, and a member of the Alliance of Women Film Journalists. She is the recipient of numerous honors, including a University of Southern California Annenberg/Getty Arts Journalism Fellowship, a National Arts Journalism Fellowship and an artist's fellowship from the D.C. Commission on the Arts and Humanities. After meeting Fred Ho when she interviewed him for *New York Newsday*, she wrote and performed libretti for two of Fred Ho's works, *Turn Pain into Power* and *Yes Means Yes, No Means No, Whatever She Wears, Wherever She Goes!* The pair have also teamed up for poetry-saxophone duets, including an April 2012 performance at Busboys and Poets in Washington, D.C.

ROBERT KOCIK, poet, essayist, and activist architect, lives in Brooklyn. He has recently completed the Enfranchisement Ranch—a rural doctors' office correlating the built environment with medicinal benefit. For the Environmental Art Department at the University of Art and Design in Helsinki he has recently proposed a climate crisis center that causally links our stress with environmental stress. He is currently working on plans for the Prosody Building and developing a new field of research called the Prosodic Body. His publications include *Overcoming Fitness* (Autonomedia, 2001) and *Rhrurbarb* (Field Books, 2007).

GENNY LIM's live and recorded poetry-music collaborations have included jazz greats, Max Roach, Herbie Lewis, and John Santos as well as Fred Ho. Fred Ho was the musical director and composer of Genny's performance theater piece, *XX*, in 1987. She's performed at jazz festivals from San Francisco, San Jose, and San Diego to Houston and Chicago and has been a featured poet at World Poetry Festivals in Venezuela (2005), Sarajevo, Bosnia-Hercegovina (2007), and Naples, Italy (2009). Her play *Paper Angels*, directed by Victoria Linchong, was performed at Settlement House in New York City in 2009, and at San Francisco Chinatown's Portsmouth Square in 2010, winning a Top Ten SF Fringe Festival Award. Her performance piece *Where Is Tibet?* premiered at CounterPULSE, San Francisco, in December 2009. She is author of two poetry collections, *Winter Place* and *Child of War*, and coauthor of *Island: Poetry and History of Chinese Immigrants on Angel Island*.

RUTH MARGRAFF has cowritten six martial-arts operas with Fred Ho for BAM's Next Wave Festival, Guggenheim Museum, the Apollo Theater, and Performing Art Centers nationwide. She tours regularly with her Café Antarsia Ensemble and other working-class operas throughout the United Kingdom, Canada, Western and Eastern Europe, Russia, India, Japan, Azerbaijan, and Egypt. Her writing has been developed and produced at numerous New York City venues, including Ice Factory Festival, Hourglass/Century Ballroom/PS122, HERE Arts Center, the Cooper Union, Lincoln Center, the Kitchen; nationally her work has been produced at Actors Theatre of Louisville; Cincinnati Playhouse in the Park; Red Eye, Frank/Walker Art Center (Minn.); Rude Mechanicals, Salvage Vanguard, CentralTrak Gallery/Project X, Granada, Club Dada (Tex.); Iowa Playwrights' Workshop; Theater of Note, Bottom's Dream, Overtone Industries (Calif.); Chicago Cultural Institute/ Music Without Borders, Viaduct Theater with Ruth's new play *Anger/Fly* opening at Trap Door Theater in 2012 to critical acclaim and her play *Stadium Devildare* at the Red Tape Theater in January 2013 (Chicago). Ruth has received awards from the Rockefeller, McKnight, Jerome, Fulbright foundations, Arts International, TMUNY, NEA/TCG, NYSCA, Illinois Arts Council, among others, and her work is published by Dramatists Play Service, Kendall/ Hunt, Backstage Books, TDR, *Performing Arts Journal*, *American Theatre*, *Theater Forum*, Playscripts Inc., Applause Books, NuMuse Anthology/Brown, Conjunctions/Bard, Autonomedia, Innova Records, No Passport Press, Skyhorse, and others. She has taught playwriting at the Yale School of Drama, Brown University, the University of Texas/Michener Center for Writers, and is currently on sabbatical from the Art Institute of Chicago writing two new operas at residencies in France, Serbia, Greece, Turkey, and Austria. Ruth is an alumna of New Dramatists, core member of Theater Without Borders and League of Professional Theater Women, in residence at Chicago Dramatists, and represented by Susan Schulman. www.RuthMargraff.com.

BILL V. MULLEN is professor of English and the director of American Studies at Purdue University. He is the author of *Afro-Orientalism* (University of Minnesota Press, 2004) and *Popular Fronts: Chicago and African American Cultural Politics, 1935–1946* (University of Illinois, 1999). He is also coeditor with Cathryn Watson of *W. E. B. Du Bois on Asia: Crossing the World Color Line* (University of Mississippi Press, 2005). He is at work on a political biography of W. E. B. Du Bois and the nation.

TAMARA ROBERTS is a scholar and artist devoted to exploring the aesthetic, political, and spiritual potential of imaginative performance. Her current research investigates the forgotten interracial and intercultural histories of popular music in the Americas, most recently the collaborations between black and Asian American artists. Tamara received a PhD in performance studies from Northwestern University and is on the faculty of the University of California, Berkeley Music Department. Tamara also works as a composer, sound designer, and performer in music, theater, dance, and film.

ARTHUR J. SABATINI is an associate professor of performance studies in the Interdisciplinary Arts and Performance Department at Arizona State University. Sabatini holds a PhD from the Department of Performance Studies, New York University. He has been involved in new music and performance, with the Philadelphia-based Rêlache, the Ensemble for Contemporary Music. As a performer, he has worked with William Duckworth Nora Farrell on the Cathedral Project and Iorpheus. Sabatini has published extensively on new music, performance, and theater and is currently investigating artists' research and interdisciplinary performance.

New Orleans writer, filmmaker, and educator **KALAMU YA SALAAM** is co-director of Students at the Center, a writing program in the New Orleans public schools (http://sacnola.com). He is also moderator of Breath of Life, a Black music Web site (http://www.kalamu.com/bol). Kalamu blogs at http://kalamu.posterous.com. He can be reached at kalamu@mac.com or on twitter at http://twitter.com/neogriot.

MIYOSHI SMITH is a writer, media artist, health practitioner . . . Miyoshi's credits cover various disciplines and include the following, to name a few: writer-producer, *Even the Sounds Are Blue*; producer-writer, *First and Last Words*; editor-writer of the original video, *Hair Stories*; camera, *Les Flots de Libreville*; contributing writer to *Coda* magazine, *Acme Newspapers*, and *Sounding Off!* Awards include National Endowment for the Arts fellowships and Pennsylvania Council on the Arts fellowships.

ARTHUR SONG was born in 1937 in Fusan, China. His mother was a legendary martial-arts nun, excommunicated from her martial-arts order for bearing a child. As a single parent, she raised Arthur, her only son, after illegally immigrating to the United States in the late 1950s, during the height of the U.S.

exclusion against mainland China. Arthur Song was one of the first Asian American students to matriculate at Harvard University. He moved to New York City and became the first Asian American producer in network television. He met Fred Ho at the Jazz Center of New York in the mid-1980s at Fred's first tribute concert to Cal Massey, and they have been friends ever since.

A South African–based tenor saxophonist, **SALIM WASHINGTON** also plays the flute and the oboe and is an avid composer-arranger. He has performed in festivals throughout the United States, Canada, Europe, and Latin America, and now in southern Africa. His writing and playing are featured in his Harlem Arts Ensemble and in performances and recordings with many of New York's finest musicians. Salim is currently a member in the Donald Smith Quintet, Kuumba Frank Lacy's Vibe Tribe, James "Jabbo" Ware's Me We and Them Orchestra, and Ahmed Abdullah's Diaspora. He can also be heard as a leader on *Love in Exile* (Accurate Records) and *Harlem Homecoming* (Ujam Records), among others, including his upcoming Dogon Revisited (Passin Thru Records). He is a senior fellow at the Institute for Studies in American Music and Professor of Music at the University of KwaZulu-Natal in Durban, South Africa. He is coauthor with Farah Jasmine Griffin of *Clawing at the Limits of Cool: Miles Davis, John Coltrane, and the Greatest Jazz Collaboration Ever* (St. Martin's Press).

Index

Note:Page numbers in italics denote illustrations. There is also a list of illustrations in the "I" section of the index.

THE ASIAN AMERICAN EXPERIENCE

The Hood River Issei: An Oral History of Japanese Settlers in Oregon's Hood River Valley *Linda Tamura*
Americanization, Acculturation, and Ethnic Identity: The Nisei Generation in Hawaii *Eileen H. Tamura*
Sui Sin Far/Edith Maude Eaton: A Literary Biography *Annette White-Parks*
Mrs. Spring Fragrance and Other Writings *Sui Sin Far; edited by Amy Ling and Annette White-Parks*
The Golden Mountain: The Autobiography of a Korean Immigrant, 1895–1960 *Easurk Emsen Charr; edited and with an introduction by Wayne Patterson*
Race and Politics: Asian Americans, Latinos, and Whites in a Los Angeles Suburb *Leland T. Saito*
Achieving the Impossible Dream: How Japanese Americans Obtained Redress *Mitchell T. Maki, Harry H. L. Kitano, and S. Megan Berthold*
If They Don't Bring Their Women Here: Chinese Female Immigration before Exclusion *George Anthony Peffer*
Growing Up Nisei: Race, Generation, and Culture among Japanese Americans of California, 1924–49 *David K. Yoo*
Chinese American Literature since the 1850s *Xiao-huang Yin*
Pacific Pioneers: Japanese Journeys to America and Hawaii, 1850–80 *John E. Van Sant*
Holding Up More Than Half the Sky: Chinese Women Garment Workers in New York City, 1948–92 *Xiaolan Bao*
Onoto Watanna: The Story of Winnifred Eaton *Diana Birchall*
Edith and Winnifred Eaton: Chinatown Missions and Japanese Romances *Dominika Ferens*
Being Chinese, Becoming Chinese American *Shehong Chen*
"A Half Caste" and Other Writings *Onoto Watanna; edited by Linda Trinh Moser and Elizabeth Rooney*
Chinese Immigrants, African Americans, and Racial Anxiety in the United States, 1848–82 *Najia Aarim-Heriot*
Not Just Victims: Conversations with Cambodian Community Leaders in the United States *Edited and with an introduction by Sucheng Chan; interviews conducted by Audrey U. Kim*
The Japanese in Latin America *Daniel M. Masterson with Sayaka Funada-Classen*
Survivors: Cambodian Refugees in the United States *Sucheng Chan*
From Concentration Camp to Campus: Japanese American Students and World War II *Allan W. Austin*
Japanese American Midwives: Culture, Community, and Health Politics *Susan L. Smith*

In Defense of Asian American Studies: The Politics of Teaching and Program Building *Sucheng Chan*

Lost and Found: Reclaiming the Japanese American Incarceration *Karen L. Ishizuka*

Religion and Spirituality in Korean America *Edited by David Yoo and Ruth H. Chung*

Moving Images: Photography and the Japanese American Incarceration *Jasmine Alinder*

Camp Harmony: Seattle's Japanese Americans and the Puyallup Assembly Center *Louis Fiset*

Chinese American Transnational Politics *Him Mark Lai, edited and with an introduction by Madeline Y. Hsu*

Issei Buddhism in the Americas *Edited by Duncan Ryûken Williams and Tomoe Moriya*

Hmong America: Reconstructing Community in Diaspora *Chia Youyee Vang*

Pacific Citizens: Larry and Guyo Tajiri and Japanese American Journalism in the World War II Era *Edited by Greg Robinson*

Indian Accents: Brown Voice and Racial Performance in American Television and Film *Shilpa S. Davé*

Yellow Power, Yellow Soul: The Radical Art of Fred Ho *Edited by Roger N. Buckley and Tamara Roberts*

The University of Illinois Press
is a founding member of the
Association of American University Presses.

Composed in 10.5/13 Adobe Minion Pro
with ITC Officina Sans display
by Jim Proefrock
at the University of Illinois Press
Manufactured by Thomson-Shore, Inc.

University of Illinois Press
1325 South Oak Street
Champaign, IL 61820-6903
www.press.uillinois.edu